WINNING
a Billion
CONSUMERS

WINNING
a Billion
CONSUMERS

A Disruptive Approach for
Success in India

Atul Joshi

www.sagepublications.com
Los Angeles • London • New Delhi • Singapore • Washington DC

First published in 2016 by

SAGE Publication India Pvt Ltd
B1/I-1 Mohan Cooperative Industrial Area
Mathura Road, New Delhi 110 044, India
www.sagepub.in

SAGE Publications Inc
2455 Teller Road
Thousand Oaks, California 91320, USA

SAGE Publications Ltd
1 Oliver's Yard, 55 City Road
London EC1Y 1SP, United Kingdom

SAGE Publications Asia-Pacific Pte Ltd
3 Church Street
#10-04 Samsung Hub
Singapore 049483

Published by Vivek Mehra for SAGE Publications India Pvt Ltd, typeset in 11/13 pt Adobe Caslon Pro by Zaza Eunice, Hosur, India and printed at Sai Print-o-Pack, New Delhi.

Library of Congress Cataloging-in-Publication Data Available

ISBN: 978-93-515-0557-0 (PB)

The SAGE Team: Sachin Sharma, Saima Ghaffar and Ritu Chopra

To My Father

Bulk Sales

SAGE India offers special discounts
for purchase of books in bulk.
We also make available special imprints
and excerpts from our books on demand.

For orders and enquiries, write to us at

Marketing Department
SAGE Publications India Pvt Ltd
B1/I-1, Mohan Cooperative Industrial Area
Mathura Road, Post Bag 7
New Delhi 110044, India

E-mail us at **marketing@sagepub.in**

Get to know more about SAGE

Be invited to SAGE events, get on our mailing list.
Write today to **marketing@sagepub.in**

This book is also available as an e-book.

Contents

Foreword

The opportunity in the Indian market is one of the biggest global prospects for the business. The challenges in emerging markets like India are, however, extraordinary and mammoth. Most buyers are new to the shopping class; compared to the global benchmarks, they consume infrequently and inadequately. I have had many decades of rich and varied experience working with human capital. I have seen the markets in India transform, but we all know that much of the potential of the billion consumers is yet to be optimally realized. This book shows how companies can best actualize this potential in an enormously heterogeneous nation like India by leveraging their people and distribution assets at the last mile.

This book is structured around the research that shows that the companies that have deployed thoughtfulness, customer centricity, entrepreneurship, and a strategic rather than an operational lens in their last mile constructs have walked away with a disproportionate market share in the Indian market in the last two decades. Atul brings the important, critical subject of the last mile to a strategic level, questions historical models, and suggests a way forward that can substantially enhance the go to market capability of the companies.

Revenue Turbine, Zero Calories Value Chains, and Swarm Intelligence, amongst others in the book, are interesting concepts and frameworks to develop the business.

A business has to be a force of mutual good; it must contribute to the transformation of the society as it charts its own growth agendas. Atul's work is biased toward extraordinary success by creating meaningful enterprises. Atul has, over the years of his experience, viewed the business from the trenches, has societal goals in mind, yet retains the strategic and aspirational imperatives of the companies. I am confident that the book will succeed in opening up a new page in the theory and practice of business in India.

P. Dwarkanath
Independent Director,
GlaxoSmithKline Consumer Healthcare

Preface

"The Last Mile is the longest mile home," so says an American proverb.

My years of working in leadership roles across diverse sectors in the Corporate India, and an extensive research and consultancy thereafter across industries confirmed the idea of this book; the success in a multifarious, briskly growing nation like India is determined substantively at the last mile. Most competing products are generally a me-too, there is little difference in the technology deployed by rival brands, and largely all pertinent competitors have equal resourcefulness to access capital. The distinction lies at the point where forces external to the company, the likes of customers, clients, influencers, retailers, and distribution converge with forces internal to the company, equivalently your people, processes, and products, predominantly the arena of the last mile.

For long companies in India have strived for relevance in customers' life, they have tried to cope with our tenacious ecosystem, they have been repeatedly compelled to value size in a quintessentially thrifty market, and at one point of time or another, they have engaged in head-on battles for market superiority over their rivals. Yet in most categories, leave aside a few, inevitably, there is an enormous market that still remains unconnected to the products we make, and only a handful of businesses intimately understand consumers and consumption. A disruptive approach is needed to make us relevant to a larger populace, to unlock aspirations of a billion consumers, and to make success broad-based, in a market that perhaps is the largest global opportunity for the businesses.

Often, over the years, one has been puzzled about many existential questions on India. We want to know why our infrastructure is measly, even primitive. Why is it that our roads are so unkempt, and hostile to non-motorized transport? How do billions of dollars of electricity get lost in pilferage while many parts of the country go without power? Why do we have more private security guards than the police and armed forces combined? Why are fundamental institutions like public hospitals and state-run primary schools at best mediocre? And why are we a "forever-developing" nation?

You talk to people about this; the range of answers is beguiling. "We in India are like that only." "That's because we are a democracy and China isn't." "It's because we are a poor country." "India is not poor, but a few people are very rich." "India is too big, too populated, too diverse." Admittedly, all of these, and many more, are collectively, in varying intensity, the right answers. But let me add one more determining dimension to it. It is not only the quantum of resources that yield the outcome; the true value is decisively clinched toward the end of the road, the last mile as the product or service is finally delivered to the end user. Many products or services in its pristine form have a limited use, more often than not they have a human interface in its consumption, at times these have to be aggregated with another product, or their bona fide value comes out when the dimension of an experience and convenience is added to it. Additionally, in many instances, larger populace in emerging nations stands disenfranchised from what the companies and the government seek to put across; their produce are simply inaccessible, or iniquitous, unaffordable, or difficult to do business with. It is the aspects of efficiency, integrity, accountability, and the ones that establish customer empowerment in design and delivery, which nail down the eventual value to the user.

Consider this. On a range of healthcare parameters, we trail behind sub-Saharan Africa, Bangladesh, and Nepal, whose per capita incomes are lower. The issues that impact health of the nation include the dismal medical infrastructure, both in quantity and quality, making India one of the largest global markets for private out-of-pocket expenditure on health. We are the 150th country on life expectancy out of a total of 193 countries. Poor sanitation, at the heart of our medical woes, accounts for 80 percent of all illnesses and pulls down the country's GDP by 6.4 percent as per an exhaustive study by the Water and Sanitation Program of the World Bank. A similar infirmity stares at us in the field of education. The government has set up more than a million elementary schools. Yet the only time India agreed to test for Program for International Student Assessment (PISA), we were 73 of 74 nations, only beating Kyrgyzstan on math, science, and reading abilities for the 15-year olds. We aren't talking about a handful of gifted brains of a billion people who are exceptional, but the general populace that goes to regular primary schools to study.

Such endemic failures of the last mile build up wastefulness and spiral costs of ownership for the customers. Often because of infirm value chains, people are compelled to confront difficult choices; either low-priced outcomes but poor quality, or to obtain better quality, but exorbitant, even exclusive products and services.

The research for this book took me across to sparse villages where I saw amazing astute technologies at work for the cause of inclusive consumption, the likes of *Gram Power* and *Sarvajal*, and to the corporate corridors of the finest companies across categories as diverse as *Steel, Pharmaceuticals, Personal computers, Media, Consumer goods, Appliances, and many others.* I worked with companies that sell electricity, the state-run enterprises, a company that procures the produce in the hinterlands and the new generation digital businesses. The canvas for this work is comprehensive.

On the basis of this research, my firm belief is that the successful companies are not necessarily selling a different product or service in comparison to their competitors; they are simply selling it strategically.

A trifle over two decades ago, India dispensed with Fabian socialist delusions of the state enterprises to control the "commanding heights" of the economy, and embraced the path of market reforms, choosing to put faith in private enterprise. This unleashed market opportunities at one end, and unprecedented competitive fury simultaneously at the other end. The research has validated the much expected deep churn after the protective arm of the state was lifted; and the rapidly widening divide between the incumbent companies that were together in 1991, but now miles apart on revenues, profits, and cash. Despite starting with no disadvantage, one set of companies across industries in India, which had a market position, capital abundance, and brand power at the time of liberalization in 1991, have 20 years hence lost out. Amid all this combative turmoil post-market reforms, a few companies demonstrated their efficiency, customer understanding, and supremacy in the more competitive, aggressive, brave new India; these companies I call as *Turbonators* because like a hundred years old scientific invention by the name of "turbine," these companies have profitably channeled the colossal potential of a billion consumers for mutual good.

This book challenges the companies to see a strategic purpose at the interface points, the markets, the customers, and the society. The companies that treat the last mile as a transformative asset, like the Turbonator companies, continue to prosper. The last mile is always the hardest, but it is also the most important.

II

This book is about solutions; it seeks to learn from the winners and strives to get the future right.

The book is organized thematically into three parts.

Part One contains the case for seeing the last mile as a cardinal and decisive asset, and the impact it has on the fortunes of the company.

Part Two demonstrates the tools and frameworks used in revitalizing our existing last mile constructs. This part of the book distils a range of strategies pursued in the emerging markets and fosters an understanding of the task of demand procreation in markets where both consumers and consumption are heterogeneous, young, and inexperienced. Companies must make the job of formulating and executing last miles systematic to bring in consistency and order, market mindfulness, and a strategic sense of purpose. The proprietary tools in the book help unlock the key to the market opportunity by systematically creating a framework that addresses the last mile imperatives.

In *Part Three*, we get to the must-have mandate in the India market. Some competencies are non-negotiable; these are the starting blocks for a company that aspires to create a market position. Zero calorie value chains, a connect with the quintessential millennial population of India, the right blend of men and man-made technology, in nations with abundant manpower, and the ability to build an execution supremacy, this work corroborates, hold the key to success.

III

My father is a distinguished academician. As a child, I would sneak into his study and leaf through pages after pages written in his neat handwriting. A cognitive educationist, a mathematician by training, a Professor Emeritus, and an administrator, he wrote at a time when computers weren't invented and ink-stained, squeeze-filler fountain pens did the work. Not that I understood it, but perhaps the love for writing material took its roots in those days. Today this book is a humble tribute to the man, my father, who started it all by inculcating the spirit to question and examine, learn and unlearn, and perhaps find a few answers.

Mark Twain, known for pithy observations and witticism, is one of the most frequently quoted author, and there are many quotes that he never said, but get attributed to him. It is believed that one such misattributed quote actually should be credited to H. Jackson Brown Jr, who had said, "Twenty years from now you will be more disappointed by the things you didn't do than the ones you did do. So throw off the bowlines. Sail away from the safe harbor. Explore. Dream. Discover." In the story of the winning a billion consumers, determined substantively at the last mile, perhaps lie some answers to the future of business. I invite you to the same fascinating journey that I am on.

Acknowledgments

This book is about success. The purpose of this work is to challenge companies and managers to get right the most important and strategic mile on the journey of their wares to the customers, the last mile.

I have had significant help in actualizing this book working with many companies and the talented people there. It is their insights and teaching of their strategies that resonate in this work. During the course of this research, many managers have helped shape the original ideas. Many of my friends and colleagues have helped me in the process of reaching out to such companies, among many, Ripudaman Kaur, K.V. Ramachandra, Ajay Kapila, Rajender Sud, Divij Jain, Gagan Preet Uppal, Samit Saxena, and Malini Gupta deserve special mention.

An idea that one intensely believes in can never reach the summit of its culmination without untiring and unquestioning support of the family. Asavari for being the eternal motivator, Jayanti Pandey, for seeing me through this long and difficult journey, for your support, critiques, comments, edits, thank you, Geetanjali Shree, my brothers, and large, immensely supportive families around me deserve a special mention for encouraging me.

I have had the privilege of insightful suggestions from some of the brightest minds. Sudhir Chandra did the most unexpected favor by going through the manuscript word-by-word, and helped me broaden my research with his insightful comments. Gyan Pandey guided me to the right path early on by his critique of the first chapter. Shashank Sinha went out of the way for me to traverse the hitherto unknown world of publishing. My gratitude to Sunanda Ghosh for being supportive of my work. Sachin Sharma from SAGE Publications has been a thorough professional, and this work does owe a gratitude for his untiring support, feedback, and guidance. Saima Ghaffar, the Production Editor of SAGE Publications has been a pleasure to work with in the process of this work being published. Dr Nilanjana Bhatacharya voluntarily became an engaging sounding board for many of the ideas. Farida Kaliyadan's imprint on the book is visible. Her insights, and beliefs, have enriched this work far beyond what was otherwise possible.

PART I

THE LAST MILE
A STRATEGIC DIFFERENTIATOR

1 Winning in a Billion Consumer Market

I

THE IMPERATIVE

I am in Railwaypura, a small village in the Mehsana district of Gujarat. Off the main highway, a couple of thousand people live here. Belying its name, no trains pass through this village. Once inside, roads are unmetalled, a small market sells items of daily needs, some thatched roofs, a few concrete houses, narrow lanes, haphazard development, soil drenched with fresh rain, children playing cricket on a makeshift ground, cows moving around as aimlessly as the many men of the village. Dudhsagar dairy, which is one of the biggest producers for *Amul*, India's largest milk brand, sources produce from this village. As twilight sets in, I watch villagers, mostly women, carry milk to the dairy collection center.

Today, Amul is a $2.5 billion enterprise, growing at a healthy double digit, late teens' rate of growth. This inspiring story has been told many times before. What makes the Amul narrative uncommon to me is how all that is still proclaimed as amiss with India, and wrong with us, was secured as an opportunity decades ago.

Imagine you are the charismatic Verghese Kurien, tasked to start this business in 1949. A young man with a degree in mechanical engineering, you land up in a small town called Anand, far detached from your ancestral roots, knowing neither the local language nor the culture of the place. In those times, there was a near monopoly market leader in Polson's, a giant brand setup in 1915. Middlemen had a stranglehold on the business, and exploited the suppliers. The raw material, milk in this case, is perishable, and has to be sourced twice a day from thousands of farmers in the hinterlands. At ground level too, the concept of a confederation itself was fraught with risk in a land where education and infrastructure is a challenge, and people were sharply disunited along caste and communal divides, even more around the time of Partition and Independence, when this company was born. The tiny and courageous idea of cooperatives, at the heart of milk revolution, built on the edifice of first doing what is right for the society, has contributed to transform India from a milk deficient nation of those times to the world's largest milk producer today, accounting for "17 percent of the global milk output."[1]

The story of Amul is the key to understanding brawn of a billion consumers that India holds the promise for, thus far unrealized for most categories. Unlike companies that singularly manufacture a product and then push it to buyers, Amul has focused on concurrent development, and demonstrated that business can be a force of mutual good. For them it is supply and demand, farmers and the customers, and society and the market. It is not either or, it is both. The essential idea behind the organization of marginal and disenfranchised farmers into a cooperative was to prevent market failures endemic to small producers. A sense of trust and fair play pervades their entire value chain. Purposive enhancement of the product mix, starting with liquid milk, and going up the hierarchy of value pyramid has enabled Amul to grow at a rate better than the rate of growth in the availability of milk. Quintessentially a farmer's organization, with a farmer as the Chairman of the company, they have had the marketing suaveness to grasp momentum for the category of milk to grow in the country, when worldwide drinking milk confronts headwinds, and has even yielded share in the shopping basket to other beverages like colas and beers. To now win, a new entrant has to create a brand as strong as Amul, have thousands of milk producers committed to be their dedicated suppliers, and access a million shops that have the capability to stock and sell a perishable product. The difference between the selling price of milk in the market and the sourcing price of milk from farmers is a reasonable

---

[1] K.R. Balasubramanyam, "No Water, So They Make Milk," *Business Today*, Cover Story, Edition (January 6, 2013).

number. Amul has not left inefficiencies in the value chain on the table either for a competitor to exploit it by way of superior operational efficiencies, and gain market. Six decades later, Amul continues to grow in this market, largely uncontested thus far.

It will be unfair to credit Amul entirely, since it is one of the many producers and a substantive part of milk business is still disorganized, but milk is one of the rarest of rare categories I find in India wherein we are on par or better than global averages in per capita availability. A quote from Amrita Patel, Chairperson, National Dairy Development Board, substantiates the perspective:

> Over the last five years, India's milk production has increased by about 25 million tonnes compared to an increase of about 6.6 million tonnes in the United States, 5.4 million tonnes in China, 2.7 million tonnes in New Zealand and 1.6 million tonnes in the European Union.[2]

At the other end of the spectrum, just to drive the distinctive Amul story home, is a glaring example of a hugely inefficient last mile value chain. This product too, like milk, is sourced from rural markets. It is a product where we are the world's second largest producer.

I visited the wholesale market for fruits and vegetables in Delhi. Such markets are similar in all Indian cities, but Azadpur seemed a world of its own, completely untouched by advances in technology and management. I made my way through ramshackle large trucks, often decorated like a new bride with labels and garlands. The sight was perplexing: Never-ending mountains of sacks of produce, most crated, a few box tops partially opened for inspection by brokers and wholesale buyers; old-style metal weighing scales; women and children precariously balanced on the floor sorting out chilies and ginger; an unbearable stench of rotting farm produce; cows merrily munching on the waste; a flurry of activity, trading and auction of whatever had landed in the morning in this Mandi. The last mile

---

[2] Quote of Amrita Patel at the 42nd Dairy Industry Conference, India's per capita milk availability above world average, reported by *The Times of India*, December 13, 2013.

has indeed changed hands innumerable times, often as many as seven times, by way of intermediaries, and piles up costs and inefficiencies, before reaching the end consumer.

The scenario does not come as a total surprise. It is, however, debilitating to find that farmers get no more than a fraction of the inordinate price consumers pay for the crop, and that most of the profit ends up in the pockets of a small multi-layered group of middlemen. A large multiple of price, in an essentially poor and developing country, and in a category wherein we are self-sufficient, is simply lost in the movement of goods. The value gets destroyed, or pocketed, depending on whose side you are, for something as simple as a crop, that unlike milk needs no processing before it is made available to consumers.

A nation of a billion people, desperately trying to secure to its people a decent standard of living, can ill afford to lose any value in transmission, yet the same inefficiency stares at us as we look at the delivery of the last mile in a range of other public services from water distribution to power to health and education. Sixteen major rivers, 55 minor ones, an ocean on both sides, and adequate rainfall, yet no potable water! There is no sanitation for reportedly 840 million people. We are self-sufficient in food grains; purportedly $14 billion is spent in its procurement, yet half of the country's children below 5 years are malnourished. Of the electricity we generate, a good quarter is estimated to be lost in transmission, distribution, and commercial losses alone. Two out of five people have no access to grid power, which means no electricity, no refrigerator, no fan, and no water. This and much more evidence points, for some parts, to scarcity of resources certainly, but much more disturbingly to a deeply fractured last mile.

This *last mile* crisis around us is pervasive, urgent, and debilitating. In all cases of endemic failures cited above, and many more, alternative industries proliferate to fill the vacuum, but these are hardly a solution to the real issues at hand. In the case of potable water, or the lack of it, for instance, an estimated one-fifth of communicable diseases are related to unsafe water. It has sired a multi-billion dollar industry for pharmaceuticals. As desperate sections of the public seek clean water, we now have a $1.5 billion packaged bottled water industry growing in excess of 20 percent every year, an equal sized water pump industry that aids the cause of water mining, a half billion dollar industry in water purifiers and filters, and many others. Just sheets of mild steel plate rolled into a drum and fixed on top of a truck, called a tanker, collecting, transporting, and selling water are an ugly symbol of perfidious water commerce that runs in India. And as water pumps increasingly spurt rampantly, the groundwater table in India has depleted, forcing people to dig deeper and deeper, where the water is more liable to have carcinogenic content. A single failure mode cascades in many other spiraling consequences.

The corporate world is better managed in its last mile, but not very markedly, as our cross industry research reveals, and has stunning differentials in the quality of execution. An iconic brand, deep financial muscle, global credentials are also not enough to win this market of a billion consumers. Often when a company says that there is not enough demand for their kind of products, the probability is that they haven't quite got the last mile equation right. Either the prices carry inefficiencies, or the product is positioned poorly or the consumer's lack of knowledge has not been addressed. More simply put, they haven't figured out how to navigate the prevailing complexity and chaos. It's not enough in India if you have a great product, or even a great brand. It needs to be supplemented with a great last mile.

The structure of distribution does look daunting to the uninitiated. Reportedly, 14 million mom and pop stores traverse the length and breadth of the country, and form the backbone of how goods reach a billion people. Forty-five million small and medium enterprises, modern trade stores, online sales that currently cover one-tenth postal codes in India, and innumerable mono brand shops complete the landscape. The largest tobacco company, the most distributed product, has to directly or otherwise reach a good 6 million mom and pop stores, spread over differing ethnicity, languages, and culture, before the customer gets to experience their brand.

HUBRIS OF SUCCESS

Every business has a strategy. It stands refreshed every year. Most of the strategy exercise that I see across companies has been focused on finding points of difference versus the competition.

Rightfully, an approach like this offers a company a good shot at making money. Most of such strategy models, however, have originated in the West, and often do not relate to the crying needs of billions who aspire for but are far removed from even being in a consuming class. Worse, convinced that people who do not use our products must necessarily be the ones who can't afford to pay for what we make, companies do not unlock full potential even of customers who are aware of the category, and consume currently. They predominantly feel that the current business model, profit expectations, and consumption are reasonably well balanced, and any attempt to enhance consumption from existing consumers of theirs will come necessarily with dilution in margins. A handful of business understands both consumers and consumption deeply, and would constitute our success stories in the book. The natural last mile roadmap in India has to be one that unlocks the full potential of a large nation and its people.

This book does not seek to change the world entirely. It singularly, in a small way, focuses on the capabilities of the last mile to amplify our value propositions and lead companies to success. The central thesis is that we must not accept that being poor and developing is an explanation, even resignation to our helplessness. Just as we all feel so strongly about day-to-day struggle with organizing basics in life like water and electricity, healthcare and education, we must feel as strongly when our customers do not consume our products, or consume these indifferently. We can at the least dilute if not entirely eliminate losses in value transmission as our goods and services reach customers. And we can also use the last mile to educate and value add for all classes of customers so that many of them who currently feel disenfranchised with what we produce, are reinstated as our customers.

Hubris of success is a term coined by Jim Collins referring to a stage in the life of a company when past accomplishment creates a false sense of invulnerability and a guarantee of future success. In almost all companies, last mile models are historical and have existed for generations. The entire sales machinery runs on folklore, on how market wars were won in the past and on a set of practices that is steeped in history. It is not to say that nothing new has been tried, but the center of gravity of efforts has been more in regenerating the old rather than inventing a new model that can take and keep companies firmly in the future. Evidence of this is the fact that as the scale increased exponentially post-liberalization more than two decades ago, costs of reaching a customer of innumerable corporates did not decrease in percentage terms. More scale has rather meant more of the same: extra distributors, enhanced reach into low-profit geographies, product extensions that are not necessarily distribution friendly and need high stock turns, more manpower, new channels like organized retail that are expensive, and so on, keeping distribution costs exactly where they were. We are doing more of the same. It is like a government attempting to build more schools and hospitals without resolving issues that currently impact its quality and acceptance with the people for whom these are being built. Disproportionate resources, meager as these are, needlessly get wasted. They do create some impact, but it is too little and too expensive. What we need is an urgent resolution of a simple question: Why do countless people not consume what we produce, and what will it take to unlock that huge minefield of opportunities?

"YOUR TIME IS LIMITED; DON'T WASTE IT LIVING SOMEONE ELSE'S LIFE"

The spirit of the above quote from Steve Jobs hasn't had many converts in India. As I worked through market models from categories as diverse as media to automobiles to telecom, one thing struck me. Within the industry, the last mile models across competitors are identical. Everyone has a last mile, but step back, chances are that it is an exact replica of their competition. It's neither disruptive nor innovative in most instances. It appears as if it is a mere mule carrying goods to its destination and not a competitive differentiator capable of enacting the script of unlocking demand. Most competitors, even marginal market players, tend to replicate the leader without really having the strength of leader's balance sheet. All they end up doing is replicating the costs and the impact on revenues is marginal.

However, firms that instead chose to question the industry structure and create their own model have made an impact even in an adverse market.

A fortune in the personal computers (PCs) space is like a relay with the baton of leadership getting passed on every few years. In India, the industry is about $7 billion. It has traditionally operated a three-layered distribution to reach 25,000 retail outlets, insignificant compared to millions of outlets being serviced by the other consumer goods companies. It is not the complexity of reach that needs this heavy-duty distribution. Indeed PC penetrations are low. Barely 10 percent of households are equipped with a PC and in any town, a handful of markets and shops tend to specialize in computer business. It was the historical need to grease retail with adequate credit in a high-cost product that led to a distribution that starts from master distributor to state distributor to actual distributors.

Personal computer companies spend more than half of their gross margin by way of trade commissions. Because their product is spread across innumerable distribution points, and for other operational reasons, the industry generally has low-inventory turns. A $7 billion industry, thus, is likely to have operating margins that run into fractions in the trade channels of distribution. It takes their business in enterprise and peripherals to tilt the color of the bottom line to a somewhat respectable green.

In 2007, *Dell* in India had sold just 80,000 laptops, for almost a million of Hewlett Packard. They realized that direct-to-consumer model that has been a trendsetter in the US would be difficult to replicate given the abysmally poor understanding of the category in India. The biggest change they brought about when they started their journey toward market leadership was in editing the industry distribution structure. Until then structures were multi-layered, high on costs and credit. Small shops, manned by poorly informed sellers for a category like technology, would indifferently sell computers. Dell refused to run expensive multi-layered distribution, as was the industry norm. Instead it created master sales affiliates under whom thousands of individual sales affiliates would reach out to individual customers and demonstrate the product. The touch, feel, and information dissemination was a critical element in the acceptance of their brand, in a category historically plagued with low diffusion. They ventured first time into retail à la *Apple* by establishing mono brand stores where consumers could again touch and see the product. In the process, they came close to the actual point of sale, and the real customer. Simultaneously, they began manufacturing in India and leveraged their service capabilities to reach smaller towns and smaller enterprises.

Dell achieved the leadership position with 15.20 percent share in Q2 of the year 2010 as per IDC PC market tracker data and was leader again in Q3 with 16.70 percent share and sales of 1.1 million personal computers over the first 3 quarters of 2010, an astounding journey from mere 80,000 sold just 3 years ago.

SMALL IS NOT BEAUTIFUL IN INDIA

We are a country whose GDP is ranked number 3 on a Purchasing Power Parity (PPP) basis, after the US and China, and number 133 on a per capita basis. As individuals, we may not be very profitable to a company; collectively we are a fortune. Ask any telecom company, and they will tell us that minutes sold in India are the cheapest in the world. Yet put together by millions of subscribers, it has created a multi-billion dollar profitable industry. A last mile model that any company deploys in India must create scale and size to best realize the potential of a billion consumer market. Economies that a large scale alone can give, represents the classic source of cost advantage, which enables pricing that propels enhanced penetration of goods and services.

Industries that consciously control the price and effectiveness of their last mile deliver value to their consumers and are also able to better permeate the market. Their channel costs are reasonably low and stock turns high, enabling them to optimally balance consumer price and profit model of the company.

Generally in categories wherein the value chain is tight, no more than five, sometimes just three competitors, make up three-fourths of revenue. There is not enough value by way of operational inefficiencies for a new competitor to easily come and create a market position. The reverse also holds true. Categories that simply accept and pass on inefficiencies as a cost have to contend with three issues. *One* is poor diffusion of their products, *second* is a slower replacement cycle, and *third*, more competition by challengers who are lured by easy money left on the table.

Consumer durables and appliances, for instance, sell products that every household requires. Indeed in many parts of the world, your new house will come pre-fitted with most of these. In India only 3 percent households own an air conditioner, 21 percent own a refrigerator, 55 percent own a fan, 8 percent own a washing machine, and 2 percent households are equipped with a microwave. Worse, even if a customer owns it, the urgency to replace as the product lives its life, is feeble.

Part of the reason is our evolution from a supply deprived mindset that makes junking things as an avoidable luxury, but it is also because these very brands, let's say in comparison to mobile devices, do not work that hard at getting a customer excited to a new lineup of offers. Now, as you look deeper into their cost construct, a substantive part of their price is made of trade spends and profit margins. This cost overlay impacts category infiltration and industry growth. Growths will transpire, but the path to experience the full market potential in such industries gets long and arduous.

FIRST MOVER ADVANTAGE COMES WITH AN EXPIRY DATE

A substantive part of success for many a leader company of today can be attributed to first mover advantage, akin to occupation of high ground in a warfare. These companies happened to be at the right place at the right time, and did not throw away their legacy. Given the size of India, many managers truly and befittingly want to first get availability right. However, in categories that are maturing and with serious competition, it was found that top players now have identical meaningful reach, irrespective of their legacy. It, therefore, ceases to be the differentiator it was. What propelled their business in the past, and gave them their market position, does not create a competitive advantage any more. A lot of advertising in telecom, from the adorable dog in a *Hutch* advertisement to many memorable jingles, was around network reach. Today it is irrelevant, as most consumers believe that the top three players are pretty much everywhere. Indeed the market shares of these three top players now increasingly look like siblings separated at birth. Banks have ATMs, which dispensed cash only for their own customers. It was used as a sales tool to induce potential customers. Today these are universal ATMs.

Reach of distribution, while always vital in a country of a billion consumers, needs to be supplemented with new advantages as we go around harnessing the potential of a large consuming class. New points of differentiation, savvier, contemporary, and consumer-centric in the last mile en route the road to success can help create new market capabilities. And for many new entrants, currently overawed by India's size and complexity, all this offers a possible way to wrangle business away from lazy competition.

MARKET BOUNDARIES ARE LIKE CHECKPOINT CHARLIE, GETTING SMASHED

Checkpoint Charlie was the best-known border crossing in the era when the Berlin wall divided East and West Germany. It signified the border as also the division between communism and capitalism. Often business erects its own industry boundary, which like Checkpoint Charlie, is historical, inefficient, and restrictive.

The answers to this quest for last mile competitive differentiation, for managers are unlikely to be found within the contours of the industry they are in. Almost all competitors appear to be having an identical lens, and primarily benchmark their distribution prowess within their category. But as you step out and look from the lens of a customer, across industries, some answers may be found. A direct-to-home media company for instance has 200,000 outlets that sell their recharges. There is no one in the industry that has substantively larger numerical reach in a category like this wherein their product has ubiquitous reach. A telecom company is also in the business of selling recharges and top ups, just like direct-to-home media companies. It typically sells from 1.5 million points of sale. Similarly, mobile devices are available in 200,000 outlets, laptops at best in about 25,000 outlets. There perhaps is a case here to add substantive market strength by benchmarking beyond the industry. It can also be a case for non-competing categories to partner and leverage strengths of each other. *Max Life Insurance Company* for instance and *Axis Bank* have had a relationship underpinned by an equity arrangement. It is not a mere distribution point for their Bancassurance product. By picking up equity, the two entities shared common goals and deeper partnership.

THE IMPENDING COLLAPSE OF FEUDAL MINDSETS

Let us face it. The market process by definition has so far been feudal. The seller sells and holds more power. What price to sell at, how to sell, how much information to pass on, it has all been controlled by the seller and shared in a manner and at time that serves their purpose much more than influencing the buyer to make informed choices. Many government-controlled companies have in the past best symbolized this mindset. They could neither find a widespread proliferation for their products, nor were their own customers happy with the service. Consumers have wasted no time in dispensing with such unequal relationship as soon as alternatives became available.

> Consider an entirely different example, focused on empowerment, the case of sanitary napkins in India. As per a Neilson study, only 12 percent of India's 355 million menstruating women use sanitary napkins. Over 88 percent of women resort to shocking alternatives like unsanitized cloth, ashes, and husk sand. Incidents of reproductive tract infection are 70 percent more common among these women.[3]

A school dropout from an underprivileged family in South India, Arunachalam Muruganantham, has created an innovation that has cut costs of sanitary napkins dramatically. But that is half the

---

[3] Kounteya Sinha, "Sanitary Protection: Every Woman's Health Right," *Times of India*, January 23 (2011).

solution. By itself, it cannot lead to the acceptance of the product. The mindsets are so steeped in history that in many parts of India, even today, women are prohibited from entering kitchen on days they menstruate. Then, such products are uniformly sold from shops run by men, making it markedly uncomfortable for women. Arunachalam Muruganantham's last mile model is unique. It is not sold indifferently at a cheaper price from regular retail shops. Manufacturing is outsourced to local women entrepreneurs. They take help of other women in stitching sanitary napkins on machines. The woman entrepreneur thereafter goes from village to village, educating girls and their family, and yes they sell the product too in the process.

Companies that help shed a feudal ethos and demolish the boundaries that separate producer and consumer, are best placed to co-create value with consumers. Companies may be global, but the consumer is always local.

II

THE FINANCIAL IMPACT

It's hard. It's complex. It's unique. And yes, *the last mile* is expensive too

Across a range of categories/industries, it was found that the cost of intermediation dilutes gross OIBDA margin of India Inc. by a good 50 percent to 55 percent. This money was spent on trade margins, cost of unpaid inventories and debts, warehousing, transportation, front end manpower, below the line activations, and deferred incentives or payouts using ways like service revenues and free product samples as in the case of pharmaceuticals. The impact is more severe in categories where either the costs are high, and/or gross margins poorer. In either case, dilution will be high, and the substantive part of what is earned from customers is simply spent on just making the product available. Telecom, which relies largely on revenues from subscribers already acquired, does provide a cover to everyone else and makes the average look better than it is.

There obviously are many caveats to this data. Businesses within industry perform at differing efficiency levels. Accounting standards are not uniform across companies. Every industry has a unique commercial structure. Some industries are fundamentally profitable (appliances), in a few you need to dig profits out by being more efficient (paints), in industries like cement the cost of logistics is value destructive, and in still other the headroom by way of relative intrinsic profitability is low (tyres). The formula to earn money varies therefore depending on the architecture of the industry. The idea, however, is not to arrive at a precise number, it is rather to learn from the spirit these sets of data point to. The Last Mile cost to gross OIBDA across some of the sample companies is as exhibited in Figure 1.1.

THE IMPACT OF TURBONATION

We set out to quantify impact of *the last mile* capability on companies. This work has been spread across categories and presents a fair picture of the industry. Such things are tough to measure, as business success is made up of innumerable factors, often unique to each industry. Yet some conclusions are still possible. It is also time to take stock of what really transpired since liberalization was introduced, that event being critical in having created for once a market that is real and competitive. What we find is that since the market reforms of 1991, over 20 years hence, many a company has added years to its life, only a few have added life to their years.

"No power on earth can stop an idea whose time has come. I suggest that the emergence of India, as a major economic power in the world happens to be one such idea. Let the whole world hear it loud and clear. India is now wide-awake. We shall prevail. We shall overcome."

On July 24, 1991, Manmohan Singh, hardly known to be an orator, made what perhaps was the second most stirring speech in India after Jawaharlal Nehru's "tryst with destiny" on the eve of our independence in 1947. In one stroke, India in 1991 bid farewell to the socialist pattern of many decades and chose to embrace market-led development. Dismantling of government controls and

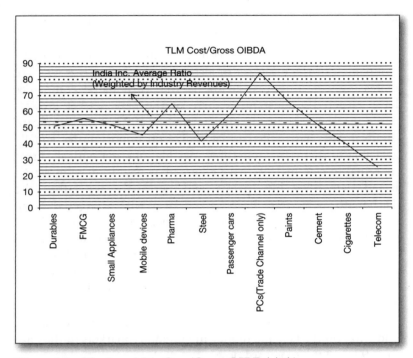

Figure 1.1   The Last Mile Cost/Gross OIBDA(%)*
Source: Author's own.

*Numbers may not be entirely exact, and will vary between compaines in an industry, for illustration purposes only.

in a way laying faith on individual enterprise as opposed to the government to propel the economy was the centerpiece of this revolution. It was an acid test for India Inc. to rise up and be counted.

While opportunity in India is real and substantive, everyone has not equally seized it. The competition and market force of two decades has separated men from the boys.

At the cusp of market reforms in 1992, competing firms were relatively competitive, their market size and share was not entirely dissimilar. The situation began to change when market forces were unleashed. The impact, however, was still not deep and stark till almost 1998. The balance of power was hardly disturbed. But subsequently, we see the polarization of performance across industries. There are either winners, whom we call *Turbonator* companies, or the other set of also-rans, the *Incumbents* who are increasingly getting marginalized. The Turbonator companies have garnered a substantive share of the new market growth, while the Incumbents, despite starting in 1992 at no significant disadvantage, have failed to capitalize on opportunities equally available to them. In some categories like pharmaceuticals, firms marginal in size in 1992 have emerged as new leaders; in established categories like paints and personal care either the Turbonator companies have walked away with a larger share of market revenues or substantively enhanced profit share, or both. Commodity categories have seen additions to manufacturing capacity and distribution play. Many government controlled companies from categories as diverse as telecom to hotels, which had a significant market position in 1992, have seen dilution to the point of oblivion.

A simple litmus test will validate this. Look at what markets and what products made money in our equity markets in the past, in 1992, and the scorecard now.

> In the last twenty years, the Sensex witnessed nearly an eight-fold increase, delivering annualized gains of 11.4 per cent. The index rose from 2,534 in January 1993 to 19,895 by end of January 2013. But only 14 per cent of the 1,108 companies that were listed in 1993 succeeded in beating Sensex returns during this period; 319 companies, constituting 29 per cent of the universe, managed to deliver gains, albeit lower than the Sensex. But 631 stocks, which account for 57 per cent of the universe, declined in the last two decades. Further, trading was suspended in over a fourth of the universe, putting investors' money in a virtual death trap.[4]

---

[4] V. Nalinakanthy, "Is it riches-to rags in the long run," *Hindu Business Line*, February 9 (2013), Chennai.

Post-1998, in the open economy era, it's almost a hockey stick swing at play, with less nimble players now increasingly in shadows. This increasing divergence in the performance between the two sets of companies is exhibited in Figure 1.2.

The impact is not only on the top line. Cash and profits from operations constitute the fuel for the business. It is a lead indicator of what will come down the chute unless serious recalibration of business model is undertaken. Not only is the revenue performance gap widening between the winner set of companies and the incumbents, as we have seen in the chart above, the differential is more acute if one looks at profits and cash, the fuel to future growths, as shown in Figure 1.3.

Since all players in the industry seem to have an identical last mile business model, it is no surprise that the industry leader does walk away with significant cost advantages. We did discover in many categories that financial superiority of the leading brand does not necessarily emanate only from lower cost to manufacture. It is their prowess in distribution that generates the financial advantage. The industry leaders have a clear cost advantage of 5 percent to 8 percent

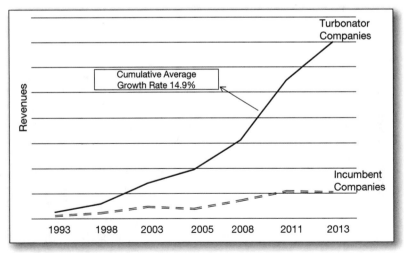

Figure 1.2   Gross Revenues: 1993–2013: (₹ Crores)
Source: Author's own.

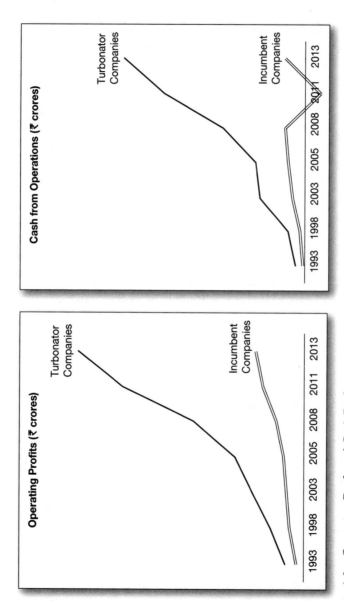

Figure 1.3 Operating Profit and Cash Performance
Source: Author's own.

of their fully loaded go-to-market costs. They are, in addition, able to recover money fast; indeed many get paid in advance. This better cash velocity generates a huge advantage in their return on capital employed (ROCE).

THE ANATOMY OF SUCCESS

While it is clear that a group of companies in each category continue to round up more revenues, profits, and cash than their peers, the real issue is why some of them are exponentially more successful than others.

Many factors contribute to define success and explain why some firms do better than their peers. Each industry has a story unique to itself. There are, however, some common legacy and behavioral traits. Almost all of these triumphant firms always had or developed a winner product that appealed to a mass segment. They have, over the years, worked in deepening their own success formulae, doing better on what they do best. They also had the wisdom to invest in nascent markets and geographies ahead of their peers; inevitably they have taken on the onus of market creation. The Turbonator companies are deeply aware of the profit architecture of their industry and have used their strengths in the mass market to now sell premium products. They have had the courage to attack adjacent markets, and have got into newer categories or segments, in the process liberating themselves from a strict definition of the industry they were in.

We find another common trait, integral to their success. This is their capacity to generate business, what we will throughout this book call the *Revenue Turbine*. Derived from a Greek word, the turbine is a mechanical device that extracts energy from a fluid force and converts it into useful work. It has revolutionized industries from air travel to gas to even solar energy. Just as in machines used, the revenue turbine in a company context is the umbilical cord between the firm's capabilities and its translation into profits. Definitely, none of the firms in the list of winners have a weak last mile competence. Companies may or may not differ in the technology they use, the products they make, or the cash they pump in to build a business. But they do differ in the capability to generate sustainable pools of customers and profits. Some are simply better than others, strategically differentiated; they have business capabilities that are scalable in size of the opportunity. The reverse does hold true. The incumbents who are less competitive today than they were at the starting point of 1992, do have a relatively underdeveloped Revenue Turbine.

WHAT WORKS TODAY, WILL IT WORK TOMORROW?

Amanda Palmer, singer lyricist, known for pushing boundaries both in her art and lifestyle, made headlines when she raised nearly $1.2 million via the website *kickstarter* from her fans. She went directly to her fans, and made the traditional distribution channels in music industry redundant. A whole lot of people get books published directly. When consumers buy on the Internet, they make a point that the existing facilitation does not add value, and they would rather do it themselves than enrich intermediaries whose contribution does not merit the costs. The growth of ATMs meant that for activities as basic as cash withdrawal and deposits, consumers do not fancy standing in a queue to be serviced. Many bank branches are forced to redefine their role and purpose in a customer's life. *Angry Birds* is a video game franchise created by Rovio entertainment. Inspired by a sketch of wingless birds, the game has seen over 2 billion downloads, and millions of users, all without touching any physical distribution infrastructure. The message is loud and clear. Either the last mile adds value or has no real reason to stand between the brand and the consumer. It's endangered species, unless the reasons for its existence, and delivery thereof, add value to the consumer.

Imagine a world where the manufacturer can dispatch goods directly to customers. There is nothing unusual or preposterous about it. e-tailers do the same with millions of products and customers. There is no reason why companies can't logistically do the same. Direct transfer of subsidies and benefits by the government to millions of beneficiaries is as well in response to the inevitable dilution such schemes have faced in the past in intermediation. The last mile will sooner or later meet the fate of intermediaries in many categories which have simply ceased to interfere in the relationship of manufacturers with their customers in case these have no value to add beyond mere availability.

III

THE AGENDA FOR RECONSTRUCTION

We have thus far talked of an imperative to see the last mile as a capability that goes beyond its lowest common denominator "functionality" of ensuring availability. We have also familiarized ourselves with the impact it has on the financial fortunes of a company in a heterogeneous nation like India. All this calls for an agenda for reconstruction. Let's look at five big, bold implications for our last miles in quest for success in a billion consumer market.

FROM POINTS OF SALE TO POINTS OF VALUE

We always equate ATMs with cash dispensing machines. Not too far from Mundka metro station, Savda Ghevra is one of the slum resettlement colonies in Delhi. It has a pay-and-use water ATM, a machine that dispenses clean drinking water at a per liter price of just one-third of a rupee. *Sarvajal,* a for-profit social enterprise of Piramal foundation, has completely disaggregated traditional ways of go-to-market. Instead of shipping clean water from factories all over the country, and indeed destroying huge value in the cost of logistics itself, Sarvajal provides a state-of-the-art purification machine at site. Their franchisees not only sell, but they also manage this water plant. Sarvajal uses state of art cloud technology to monitor the quality of the water being dispensed . The water is finally distributed using an ATM-like machine, and customers can buy prepaid water cards. It is cashless vending, a solar powered, and cloud-managed ecosystem; the three ingredients that seem to be a common theme in resolution of grave issues facing a vast majority of our populace.

Indeed as we will see in some more instances, the conventional way of operating whereby companies manufacture and trade partners only distribute has built-in prohibitive costs in the value chain. High costs have impacted the availability and denied true penetration of products. The same intermediary has the potential to also become a focal point for the delivery of more value to the customers by their ability to resolve current deterrents to consume.

Let us consider another illustration. Color choice for a customer is perhaps the only invigorating part of the process of getting home painted. The paint companies used to manufacture each individual color, in different pack sizes, and across a large range of interior and exterior products. A shade card was used by consumers to get a feel of what they intended to buy. Even then the customer was never satisfied. Skilled contractors and painters would then mix and match and create a color that didn't exist on the shade card. The frustration of the customer in the entire process is obvious. But from a business perspective, it made supply chain impossible to manage. Ability to forecast each SKU, and to correctly supply over thousands of shops, was a task fraught with errors and cash bottlenecks. Paint companies then broke up the process of manufacturing into components and found a solution by enlisting points of sale in their manufacturing chain. Today, only a base product is what gets manufactured in the factory. Retailers, depending on what shade and pack the consumer wants, mix tinters that give color to the product at the last mile. It has cut the cash dramatically that earlier was blocked in the supply chain, ensured reliable availability, and by giving consumers the choice of innumerable colors it enables them to have a home that's quintessentially theirs.

FROM CONSUMERS TO CONSUMPTION

India market is minting new customers as people move out of poverty. This is what has kept the center of gravity of efforts focused singularly on getting more customers for brands and enhancing product penetration. But the existing customers are also getting richer, a fact often ignored. Chances are that their consumption is disaggregated; a fair possibility in India. Many of us may have multiple bank accounts, a different partner for insurance, and someone else for our portfolio of loans, thereby splitting profits for financial companies. Within a category, enhanced segmentation of brand has been the preferred route for companies to build sales volume. Innovation funnels have proliferated and sired many extensions of the core product. Only a handful of companies have realized that while there is value in creating new customers and categories, there is value additionally in inducing the existing customers to consume more.

Tata Steel long products division used to sell only retro bars like any other steel company. Intrigued as to how a commodity product like steel is sold, how differentiation is created, and has the nature of purchase matured to a level that leads to choice beyond realms of pure play price, I went around with their distributors and saw what they do now. Their customers are either retail or projects. After the steel is bought, the customer has to cut and bend the product because every structure has different specifications. It costs them money and the pain of finding space and skilled labor. Today, distributors of Tata Steel have set up upstream cut and bend workshops. The customers do not get retro bars. Instead, they get the product in the shape they want, and at the time it is needed. It is not surprising that even in a commodity category like steel, as I looked at an array of colored charts that display an enormous range of market metrics, Tata steel commands a price premium.

Very few products and services are used in a vacuum. These may be defined as a finished good in the company vocabulary, but consumers spend a disproportionate value in consuming the product as designed by the manufacturer not necessarily in buying it. In this product-obsessed approach that historically exists across a vast spectrum of industries, they miss out completely on the opportunity to realize far higher value and create customer delight. The time has come to see distribution as sales to the customer.

FROM HOMOGENOUS CONSTRUCTS TO CLASPING HETEROGENEITY OF CUSTOMERS

India is not only large in scale; it is also enormous in heterogeneity. Building a unique product for each customer has been on the horizon for some time. But companies deep in mass manufacturing have struggled to deliver it profitably at scale. When people are on Facebook or Twitter, not only do they enjoy consumption, but they also fashion the manner in which this consumption happens.

There is profit in harnessing heterogeneity in customers. The current business models of companies are, however, built for similitude. A one-size-fits-all obviously leaves most customers either overserved or underserved, and abandons the value on the table.

However, some firms have realized that individual customer needs are impossible to be met within the strict boundaries of a company. The process of value creation must continue all the way to consumer and consumption, and not stop at the shores of a company.

Sephora, owned by Louis Vuitton Moet Hennessy (LVMH), the world's leading luxury goods group, has begun to demonstrate how digital proliferation can shape access and flatten the playing field. I saw the salesman there hold a device in hand the size of a mobile phone, scan a client's face, and arrive at an exact skin tone and shade. Then using an iPAD the store associate pulled up thousands of foundation products to get the perfect match, thereby putting to an end countless futile hours spent by women trying to get foundation that truly blends with their skin tone.

Paris Miki, the largest Eyewear retailer in the world, has similarly made use of technology at the last mile to transform the process of buying from pure play trial and error into a science. The system first takes a digital picture of each face, analyzes it along with the customer-stated preference, recommends a distinctive lens, and shows customers a picture of what they will finally look like in their new eye frames. In an hour, a customer can walk away with a new frame.

The issue with such examples is that while designed to deliver unique value to customers, they are unlikely to have an impact on a large scale. It is still a privileged service, and even in the West impacts a small population. To unlock the value of a billion consumers, we need innovations that bring people back into the equation. We need technology, but it must harness the value of human capital, which is in abundance in India.

Let us consider an example closer home wherein technology has been deployed to help incumbent jobholders to be more effective and useful. Forest fires are a key reason for degradation of forests in India. Humans initiate most of these fires. Historically, the guard in whose jurisdiction it happens, reports the event of a fire. The reports are always after the fire has ravaged the forest, often these do not get reported either. If we were to think of many a company, there is a parallel. Visibility and transparency of actual market place dynamics are low beyond high-level metrics that get reported. But to return to the issue of forest fires, Madhya Pradesh Government has developed Fire Alert Messaging System that reports real time, via a satellite, the exact location of the fire, and also sends out SMS alerts. The paradigm shift enables faster response time and forces accountability in the system. The role of guard stands transformed from someone who reports the incident to one who actively works at speedy control of potential collateral damage. It also helps the government in proper deployment of resources and long-term solutions to the root cause of these fires because now they can analyze information and decipher meaning-ful trends.

THE SEISMIC SHIFT—THE REDEFINITION OF A SALESMAN AS WE KNEW IT

Sales and service jobs run a serious risk of extinction if the core is manual labor and not value addition.

The other day when I flew *KLM*, I realized that short of flying the aircraft and serving food, I, as a passenger and their customer, did everything else—from search for the tickets, to paying online, choice of seat, and check in, to physically lifting my luggage and generating baggage tags at Amsterdam. I interfaced with KLM only at the time of boarding the aircraft. *McDonalds* in the Seville railway station has a touch screen where I punched in my order, paid cash, and picked up food. Innumerable retail stores have now a self-checkout. Dell has a 24×7 call center. Of all service queries they receive, a high number pertains to software glitches and are resolved over the phone, thus eliminating the need and cost of physical visit by a technician. The quality of manpower at a call center is of an expert, capable of resolving technical problems, and not someone acquainted with only telephone etiquette.

Not everyone finds this to be a sensible outcome. There is a contrarian view on what technology has been used to unleash thus far.

> We cannot stop tech, and there's no reason why we should. It's useful. But we need to change the innovation agenda in such a way that people come before tech. It will be an ongoing struggle, of course. From nineteenth-century mill owners to twentieth-century dot-commers, businesspeople have looked for ways to remove people from production, using technology and automation to do so.[5]

This contrarian but valuable advice of John Thackara, Founder of *The Doors of Perception*, an organization that is concerned with a sustainable future, alludes to the fact that all that technology has done over the years is to do the same work with lesser people. Today, it looks like sooner or later technology will take over many jobs. If all you do is book an order or read stocks at the point of sales for orders to be automatically generated or handle simple customer interface or sell uninvolved products, machines can provide superior cost advantage and consistency of customer experience.

The net result of all these forces is a redefinition of what skill-sets do people need in today's environment.

There is enough research on profiling sales people who are successful. The premise on profiling is simple: if we can identify what sales profile leads to success, we must logically hire to that specification so that we have a team of performers. Contrary to a lot of international research that I have read which unanimously concludes that relationships are dead, and the world of today is driven by commercial considerations alone, I find no such evidence across categories in India's billion consumer markets. Business is a team sport. You are dependent on others to succeed. Yes, just relationships may be a concept on deathbed, but it is not dead.

---

[5] John Thackara, "In The Bubble-Designing," in *A Complex World* (Massachusetts: The MIT Press, 2005), 4.

I find a combination of three skill sets at work. Successful sales people build relationships at the core; they deliver insights and value to their buyers, and consciously create newer markets for their products and services. Put together these three constitute just the right ammunition for winning in the Indian market. This is no longer a game of *what* you sell. It truly has become a game of *how* you sell and the insight delivered in that sales experience.

CROSS-POLLINATION IS NATURE'S KEY TO SURVIVAL; THERE IS LEARNING FOR ALL OF US

It is almost 3.8 billion years since life originated on earth. It is believed 99 percent of species are now extinct. The end game plays out over time, sometimes millions of years, but in a blink of a geological eye. Some species have survived without changes, some with increasing complexity, and many species that failed to respond to environmental are today extinct. Cross-pollination gives plants the genetic variety they desperately need to survive over time. It helps produce stronger and more vigorous plants than by way of self-pollination. In the absence of it, innumerable plant variants would have been extinct by now. In the same way when companies cross-pollinate ideas, business becomes stronger.

As I worked the roadmap for success, I realized that differentials are not so much between companies, as between industries. After all, everyone in a category has an identical last mile approach; of course, some are executing it better, but beyond that there is a limited strategic difference. Often a company is not experimenting enough. It does not necessarily get cross-pollinated by managers from diverse industries and backgrounds, for instance. The industry is, thus, ingrained in making better what they do best, than in trying to acquire incremental new competencies, unlike nature. But when the industry boundary was crossed, it was refreshing to see new perspectives. Cross-pollination has worked perfectly well with birds and bees, and in many product inventions, I believe it has a substantive value to add in the roadmap to success constructs as well.

IV

EXECUTING THE LAST MILE STRATEGY

Winning a billion consumers study has a fair mix of industries from consumer facing to B2B, new generation digital businesses to traditional, from new entrants to established players, from Indian companies to multinationals. The attempt has been to see the canvas in its entirety, respect industry dynamics and specifics, but also to discover practices that have the ability to cut industry lines.

We fully know that consumers reward companies that have the optimal balance of innumerable determinants like product quality, the brand, the service, and the distribution. While failure in distribution and supply chain will certainly knock out companies that did not get their model right in India, success is an interplay of multiple variables.

This work is split into three parts—the agenda for the last mile, the means and tools to engineer the last mile, and the must-have competence to compete in the emerging markets like India that form the backbone for the reconstruction of the business.

The next chapter fundamentally answers three questions. What makes Indian consumer and consumption so unique? What different ways do companies currently employ to reach their goods and services to a large, heterogeneous mass? And what last mile transformation is needed to make an impact in the Indian market? In doing that, the chapter essentially defines the context of India, current landscape, and the change agenda.

Chapters 3 and 4 introduce the frameworks for demand proliferation and the expanse of strategic paths available in emerging nations that help design, develop, and deploy the company agendas. Chapter 5 has the tool to create the last mile capability. Our last mile tool has dimensions of time (the construct of the last mile today and at the end point in the future), multiple options to compete (several market impacting metrics that enable a company to be unique and differentiated), it has a heart (the reason why customers choose us over our rivals), it marginalizes inhibitors to consumption akin to removing blockages in a heart bypass surgery, it endeavors to revamp processes (costs and efficiency), brings razor-sharp focus onto what we seek to accomplish (markets, segments, and geographies), and builds an assembly line capability to empower a company to scale up predictably to the enormous size of the India opportunity.

There are four critical competencies at work in transition of points of sales to points of value. These are non-negotiable in an emerging economy. Chapter 6 is about making sure that our value chains exude value and efficiency and not costs. Chapter 7 challenges disproportionate effort and time spent in seducing new consumers, rather than harvesting the wealth of existing customers. More importantly, by 2020, India will be the "youngest country" in the world, with three-fourths of the population belonging to the millennial generation. This chapter sets out to define the customer agendas relevant to the next generation of our customers. Chapter 8 explores the power of technology to transform markets and society. The path of progress is linear, not exponential, unless a disruptive technology is unleashed. A business has to answer three questions: Where are you right now? Where do you want to go? And how do you get there? Chapter 9 addresses the last of these questions, how to make things happen? The final chapter is on sustainability and renewal of the last mile.

Let us begin by looking at the singularity of the Indian context, the various last mile constructs as they exist today, and the transformation needed to be an engine that unlocks the potential of a billion consumers.

2 Cracking the Da Vinci Code

Searching for what can work in India is both exciting and elusive. Ask innumerable companies in India, they are still trying to unknot the might of opportunities that India presents for them. The plot that unearths what works in a nation of a billion consumers is as evasive as that mysterious and a controversial work by Dan Brown, *The Da Vinci Code*. On the right bank of the river Seine in Paris, spread over more than half a million square feet, inside the Louvre Museum, originally a royal palace, under the occult scrutiny of the Mona Lisa, a museum curator is gunned down. Just before death, he leaves behind a puzzling trail of clues. The gunman is an albino monk. A Harvard professor of religious symbols and art is, however, suspected by the police for murder. The professor races off into the dark night to prove his innocence. In the novel, Leonardo Da Vinci is said to have planted different codes and symbols in his work, in particular in painting, "The Last Supper." A large number of companies, despite years of incubation in India, are still searching for protocols and motifs required to maximally utilize India's vast business potential.

This chapter will try to answer three questions. What makes the Indian consumer and consumption so unique? What different ways do successful companies currently employ to reach their goods and services in a large, heterogeneous mass? And what last mile transformation is needed to make an impact in the Indian market?

I

WHAT MAKES INDIAN CONSUMERS AND CONSUMPTION UNIQUE?

How big and attractive is an India opportunity is the first, and often a perpetual debate across boardrooms in the world. There are unending arguments on whether 1.2 billion people would consume or not, with an air of distrust, even cynicism. This argument is uncalled for. Of course they will. At $4.6 billion, Hindustan Unilever Limited (HUL), the foremost company in the fast moving consumer goods space, and hence a good indicator of our consumption, was just one-eleventh its current size in 1993. The Indian software industry has grown at an average of 25 percent per annum over the last two decades to be worth $100 billion. We now have more than 800 million mobile subscribers. Stock market capitalization in India was $98 billion in 1993. Today, it's almost $1,200 billion.

Pioneered by *ACNielsen*, Living Standard Measure (LSM) has become a widely used marketing research tool. It seeks to replace traditional demographic segmentation. It divides the population into LSM groups, 10 being the highest, grouping people according to their living standards. Fifteen million households were in the middle belly (LSM 5 to 7) in 2004. One hundred and twenty-five million is the expected number in 2015. Population growth is slowing, and literacy levels are on the rise. This is symptomatic of a deep metamorphosis under way. Across product categories, there is low penetration and low per capita consumption, again suggestive of headroom for companies to grow and prosper. Urbanization rate in India, rapidly increasing, will have a profound impact on buying behavior as more consumers get exposed to next generation products. The rural story is intact too, while the urban India takes off. Diversification in sources of livelihood and a major diversion of funds by the government to rural sector will continue

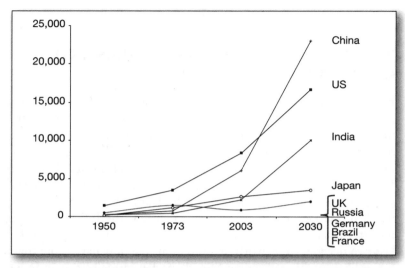

Visual representation (partial) basis Wikipedia; Angus Madison Statistics of the Ten Largest Economies by GDP (2007 Monograph, Contours of the World Economy.

Figure 2.1   Largest World Economies by GDP: 1950–2030: (PPP, 1990 International Million $)

Source: Author's own.

to propel demand. The faith in India story despite hiccups is indeed the point to begin with. A nation of a billion people cannot be ignored without consequences and eventual regrets.

The secular tend in India is growth. The India story has gravitas and substance. Often topical events divert our focus on the big picture. It will be good to step back and look at the growth of the economy over a longer time horizon so as to be dispassionate about events of here and now. The faith in India potential should be clear as we look at Figure 2.1 on top global economies over an estimated horizon of eight decades.

Every country brings its own challenges. With India, these are more than a handful. Chinese consumers are more than four times rich than Indians. The Chinese market for many sophisticated consumer goods is 10 times larger than that of India's. In case of luxury goods, their $25 billion market dwarfs India's. South Korea is similarly a sterling success story, with dramatic increase in GDP in recent years, and an even more dramatic reduction of poverty. Part of the consumer boom was financed by creation of global brands, and part by banks swashed with household savings. Protracted low interest rates have taken away their passion for savings. Korea's rate of household savings as a percentage of disposable income that used to be as high as 25 percent some years ago has slipped below 3 percent. Korea has binged on fancy cars, apartments, luxury goods, and education like no other society.

> An OECD report said that an average South Korean works more, sleeps less and kill themselves at a higher rate than citizens of any other developed country. They rank first in time spent online and second to last in spending on recreation, and the per capita birth rate scrapes the bottom of the world rankings. By 2050, South Korea will be the most aged society in the world, narrowly edging out Japan.[1]

India is neither China nor South Korea, or for that matter, most emerging economies that have taken the flight to development. In contrast, India has household savings that remain rock solid into the mid-20s. A high savings rate is a cultural issue, symbolic of an aspiration in every Indian to leave a legacy for their offspring, but it is also a reflection of poor safety nets in a society, compelling its people to provide for rainy days like a medical emergency or retirement. The learning is that the Indian consumer will splurge, but a lot more meditatively. Yet in 20 years, India's economy could be as big as China's economy today. Unlike other Asian populations, Indians will stay young and energetic for years to come. The average age of the Indian in 2020 will be 29, while the average age in both China and the US will be 37, and in Europe and Japan 45 and 48, respectively.[2]

---

[1] Blaine Harden, "Opening their wallets, Emptying their savings," *Washington Post Foreign Service* (July 30, 2009).
[2] Chitra Narayanan, "The Indian Consumer, 10 years on," *The Hindu Business Line*, November 25 (2010), Chennai.

DEALING WITH THE SMART INDIAN CONSUMER

A competitive quality, at more affordable prices, is enough to lure an Indian consumer away from what you confidently presumed is your revenue pool. For every Goliath like *Samsung* and *Apple*, a substantive market lies outside with David's despite iconic brands. It's a mirror image across categories whose value chains leave room for a nimble player to enter. Almost two-thirds of the watch market is made up of cheaper imports, half of the batteries sold are from the unorganized sector, private label brands make up 30 percent of the huge pharmaceutical industry, of the 2 million annual car sales, luxury car makers account for 30,000. The India opportunity is not one of uniform growth. The enormous challenge in India is in unlocking demand that has diversity within the opportunity that the country offers.

A new entrant can more easily play with a new set of rules. The primary reason why fringe players become mainstream competitors is not because they necessarily discover an entirely new phenomenon, it is because the entrenched market leaders don't always find a cause to change or even respond to the refreshed value curve of a new entrant.

UNLOCKING VALUE OF COMMERCE IN INDIA

India has in history a long-standing suspicion with the business. The British East India Company was originally a trader, as were many other invaders that finally kept the land and its people subjugated for centuries. Trust is the first vital ingredient to success in India.

Joyce Meyer is a charismatic speaker and author. She has penned an inspiring piece called "I am in a hurry and God's not." To quote her,

> We all want good things to happen in our lives, but too often we want it now…not later. When it doesn't happen that way, we are tempted to ask, 'When, God, when?' Most of us need to grow in the area of trusting God instead of focusing on the 'when' question.[3]

---

[3] Joyce Meyer, "When God's timing is taking too long," http://www.joycemeyer.org/articles/ea.aspx?article=when_gods_timing_is_taking_too_long. Accessed on August 04, 2015.

The long-time cycles in India frustrate many companies, but unlocking value will necessitate capability to wait with patience and understand that timelines here from seedtime to harvesting is rather complex. What works all over the world, works here, but not entirely. New, frugal, adaptive ways are a necessity. This doesn't mean cutting corners and circumventing processes. It simply means an ability to discriminate between value-adding and cost-adding activities of the organization, and the will to eliminate the latter.

In large parts of the world, for instance, small retail has yielded to large format supermarkets. This process of aggregation of demand into fewer but bulkier buyers has shifted the balance of power between manufacturers and sellers, and as a consequence got private label products jostling for the very same shelf space that big brands had assiduously monopolized for decades. In India, however, still most consumers buy small, but often. Even the retail works with limited working capital. The entire velocity is different. The high cost of retail space and high cost of credit keeps this vehicle always overheated and cramped in dimensions. To compound issues, India has 18 million credit card users versus 160 million in the US. It's a clear indication of the currency of use, and a poor appetite for living on borrowed money. All these are an impediment to unlocking the value of commerce in India. These are also opportunities, if you have the mindset to remodel, innovate, and engage consumers on their turf.

II

THE SEVEN LAST MILE MODELS IN INDIA

For now, let's turn our attention to the seven last mile models of distribution that emerged as we revisited the India of today. These are:

- *True billion consumer model*, focused on mass distribution of products.
- *Inclusive distribution model*, one that touches rural and disenfranchised hinterlands effectively.
- *Advocacy model*, one that sells essentially to influencers and intermediaries rather than final points of sales.

- *Direct to consumer*, a model that leverages personal relationships rather than commercial establishments in the task of distribution.
- *Value creation model*, one that fuses buyer and seller as one entity with common objectives to create a new value curve.
- *Sapience sales model*, one wherein the seller has deep subject matter expertise, the buyer is savvy too, and strategic commercial transaction is executed by the seller on the basis of their deep insights on the clients business.
- *New Age model* that uses the vast power of digital and media capabilities of today to sell goods and services.

TRUE BILLION CONSUMER MODEL: MASS MARKET ACCESS

If denominated in $100 bills, a $1 trillion would be enough to fill 4.5 Olympic-sized swimming pools, with a total volume of 398,000 cubic feet.[4] US economy is $16 trillion and serviced by 3 million retail outlets. China has estimated 16 million outlets for a $10 trillion economy. India has reported 14 million shops for a $2 trillion economy.

Imagine you buy something that is consumed frequently, often in small quantities, the need for such products is universal, and there aren't many large format hypermarkets where all this demand gets aggregated. The first model of true mass distribution is around this construct. It is an ability to access millions of stores, cut through both urban and rural markets, and to service all classes of consumers from rich to the aspirants. This model works the best in industries that sell goods of mass consumption and daily use. Availability is an overarching consideration in the distribution chain. Customer experience is not vital and all kinds of shops sell the produce at almost similar prices. This model is heavily dependent on the brand pull as the key differentiator. Fast moving consumer goods and tobacco firms, for instance, use this manpower-intensive model, or its variants in different permutations and combinations. The essence of the model is to use an intermediary for local distribution and

---

[4]"What Does A Trillion Dollars looks like?" *Tillmanspeaks, Blogspot.com*, 28 January (2010), basis slide show of www.cnbc.com

break this large country into smaller, more manageable pieces. In return, the distributors earn a healthy return on their investments made. The company is isolated from the credit risk and day-to-day operational management. The downside of the model lies in managing dilution of the brand with outsourced manpower, representing it at the retail end, the cost of one more layer between retailers and the company, and the fact that by its construct it is impelled to fundamentally underserve sophisticated, discerning, and affluent consumers. The centre of gravity of this model is around reach.

A strong and intelligent variant of this model is a mix and match of direct distribution with distributor-led mass distribution. Increasingly, categories realize that all retail is not equal. This gets heightened in products where buying frequency is not as frequent, the ticket size of the product being bought is high, and purchase processes are more involved. Substantive business comes from a handful of points of sale in such categories. In consumer durable, for instance, just 2,500 retailers would mean 70 percent of the business. In mobiles, 2,000 shops give three-fourths of the business. The industry supplies direct to large retail shops. It also endeavors to better control customer experience in these high velocity outlets by deploying their trained merchandising manpower. And companies, for other small shops, continue to use distributors to break bulk.

INCLUSIVE DISTRIBUTION: PASSAGE TO THE RURAL HINTERLANDS

Home to 800 million people, which makes 70 percent of India's population and 12 percent of global population, rural India is an enormous market. Since 2000, per capita GDP has grown faster in rural areas than in its urban centers: 6.2 percent CAGR versus 4.7 percent. Nielsen estimates the rural FMCG potential to be as much as $100 billion by 2025.

Rural consumers have diverse buying habits. They buy often but buy small. Credit could be an important ingredient in commercial interfaces, and relationships play a significant role in purchase decisions.

Corporate India has struggled to create a sustainable and profitable business in these high frequency markets. Many MNCs don't even wish to walk that path. They would rather wait till consumers graduate to their product line up and prices. Half the televisions sold in India are still cathode ray tube (CRT), not flat panel. Given unreliable electricity, half the refrigerators sold are direct to cool not frost-free. MNCs do not participate in this market as this is at variance with their current technology platforms, and they await consumers to graduate to their globally synchronized line up of products.

Companies that, however, recognize the enormous opportunity of rural markets are experimenting with various go-to-market models to garner their share of this business. They convert deemed problems into opportunities. Rural markets are huge, spread over more than half a million villages. They recognize that only 17 percent of villages account for approximately 60 percent of rural wealth; hence, they prioritize. Price is a barrier; the products are tweaked to deliver value at more reasonable price points. *Tanishq* has a range called Goldplus, for instance, designed for the preferences of semi-urban and rural India. Consumers have seasonal income, and they tend to buy in smaller quantities; FMCG companies have sachet packs and telecom companies sell recharges for as low as ₹10. Hinterlands are media dark, but there is abundance of attention; *Colgate* would do a free oral health checkup and *GlaxoSmithKline* salesmen would use tablet computers to educate customers about their products. Reach is an issue; companies use a combination of hub and spoke distributors to reach hinterlands. *ITC*, the largest distributed brand, uses multiple distribution approaches to reach the last mile—traditional distributor vans to serve customers directly; sub-distributors in defined geographies to provide intensive distribution focus; direct reach through two- and three-wheelers to seed activities in villages with high market potential, and its well-known parallel sales and marketing platform known as eChoupal and Choupal Sagars for consumer activation activities. Relationships are vital in rural commercial transaction; Project Shakti of HUL employs locals to sell their products; density of demand is thin, and companies aggregate it at the village or a higher level or simply ride on another existing distribution network.

Consumers, whether rural or urban, want to save, borrow and use financial products. However in rural areas and in even many parts of urban India, formal banking doesn't exist. In what is essentially a branchless banking, *FINO PayTech* accomplishes mass micro transactions using technology such as biometric readers, and deploys many thousands of business correspondents who become the front end for delivery of these products.

The three sisters, The-four-brothers, Juliana's are some of the interesting names given to *sari sari stores* (the word means "variety"), an institution in Philippines, not very different from the construct of mass market shops in India. These are an extension of a typical home. Estimated to be about a million strong and accounting for substantive retail sales, these are neighborhood convenience stores. Mostly managed by women, they are tiny and allow people to buy in economically affordable quantities, even on credit. Cigarettes are sold by the stick and cooking oil by the cup.

Whether it is mom and pop stores of India or *sari sari* in Philippines, it is fundamentally an arm's length relationship with the manufacturer. There will be a distributor in between, even a sub-distributor as well if it's a remote village. China has a rural distribution challenge not unlike other Asian countries. The urban markets are relatively saturated, and infinitely competitive. *Haier* has experimented with new business models to reach rural hinterlands, and is a stunning success story. Abandoning third-party dealer networks, they have invested in self-owned exclusive stores in tier 3 and 4 cities. Customers can also buy over the phone, online, or from a catalogue. Such is the strength of their distribution and service capabilities that many other companies now pay a tariff to use Haier's network of shops for distribution of their products.

Maruti Suzuki now gets one-third of its business from rural India, compared to 4 percent in 2008. For *Hero MotoCorp*, 40 percent of the market is rural. Substantive part of insurance sold by *LIC* is in these markets. For me, it is reasonably tough to visualize a successful company 20 years hence, even 10 years hence, without a true rural game plan.

ADVOCACY MODEL: INFLUENCE THE DECISION-MAKER

The real issue with labyrinthine last miles is that there are so many influencers involved in the sales process that often one doesn't know who owns the customer. The value chains are long and circuitous. There are many participants who shape this chain as goods change hands. It is not easy to decipher the magnitude of influence each participant has. In an ideal world, compensation must get linked to the effort made, but it's easier said than done in this case.

Cipla is an incredibly smart company. It is next only to Wipro in wealth creation over 20-year horizon post-liberalization. It's a $1 billion pharmaceutical company that has consistently outpaced market growth and has a healthy OIBDA margin in the 1920s. As I walked through corridors of their corporate office, I wondered what it is like to sell pharmaceuticals. Consumers know very little about medicines and would rarely ever buy a product different from the one recommended by their doctor. The stockiest of pharmaceutical companies is practically an organized trade union body. They dictate terms to manufacturers. There are many generic versions of drugs, perhaps lower in active formulation but somewhat comparable to branded drugs in performance, quality and intended use, and thousands of factories that produce. Organization structures in pharmaceutical companies have been historically hierarchical, with multiple layers. Then, there are regulatory and ethical issues that perhaps no other industry faces, in terms of magnitude like drug companies all over the world do.

Cipla tasks its medical representatives to work with doctors. Creating a right relationship with medical practitioners is a challenge and an imperative. Medical representatives educate doctors on products, disseminate scientific knowledge, and indoctrinate on drug safety. Independent doctors are counseled on how to run an ethical practice. The company maintains an enormous control on what thousands of their representatives are doing, whom they meet, what they sell and how. Many drug majors are experimenting with e-detailing in addition to what their medical representative does. Treading the thin line between push sales and pull, Cipla puts no pressure to sell into trade. There is consequently no last week skew in business we see in many companies as a norm. The trade accounts are clean, trade disputes are non-existent, bad debt is as good as zero, and the supply chain is distinctly efficient. It's a model that challenges the traditional role of sales as a function, which has believed their only job is to push products. The center of gravity of this business model is in creating an ecosystem. This can be best described as an Advocacy model, wherein there is someone in the middle of the value chain, a doctor in this case, who endorses the brand. Pharmaceutical companies look at the last mile as a revenue driver. But they see it as a result of market activities, and not an end in itself.

DIRECT TO CONSUMER MODEL: MOVE SELLING FLOOR TO THE CONSUMER

> My husband, eight years ago, asked me to choose between family and my government job. Government job is so difficult to give away. My father was angry that I was being asked to make such a choice. I however went with the family, and left my secure job. But in these long years I have lost my independence and self-respect. For every small thing I have been dependent on my husband; I don't drive, he has to be requested to take me around, I want money for personal expenses, I have to literally beg.

The above lines have been quoted from a meeting which the author attended at Gulmohar Park, New Delhi, in June 2014. The meeting was conducted by a franchisee of a well-known direct sales company. About 50 women have assembled at a weekly sales meeting. I am the only man in that room observing what works for one of the finest direct sales companies. Most of them are middle aged, a few in their 60s. Despite the knowledge that only a scattering of them will strike big in this profession, each has come with a hope to make it colossal and be able to live their dreams. We are sitting in a basement room in South Delhi. This is where in the past a single family would live in an idyllic bungalow across tree-lined streets. The bungalows have been replaced with builder apartments having multiple families, and their maids and cars, even pets, jostling for the same space. "Now I have found my feet. I am proud of what I do. Soon I will buy a car of my own, I tell my husband I don't need your money, here you can take some from me," says the monthly winner addressing her fellow salespersons. If there is one industry that returns dignity and independence to people, it is direct sales. Products that need to leverage power of relationships and entrepreneurship make use of this model.

"All human beings are born entrepreneurs. Some get a chance to unleash that capacity. Some never got the chance, never know that he or she has that capacity,[5]" argues Dr Muhammad Yunus, Founder of *Grameen Bank* in Bangladesh who transformed millions of lives using microcredit as the leverage. To validate the assertion that giving an opportunity to livelihood is more powerful and dignified than pure play gratuity, a 100,000 beggars were given non-interest bearing micro-loans, and prodded to sell small merchandise as they went around begging. A good 10 percent of them became full-time salesmen, and many others started active part-time sales.

Project Shakti of HUL explores an identical spirit.

With some 48,000 Shakti Ammas and 30,000 Shaktimaans, HUL reaches over three million households in 100,000 villages in 15 states. Project Shakti has been replicated in Pakistan and Sri Lanka. In Pakistan, the Shakti Amma is called 'Guddi Baji' (Urdu for 'doll sister'). Guddi Bajis, who are trained to provide beauty care services, sell brands such as Lux and Fair & Lovely. During visits to rural customers' homes, they also teach them the importance of hand washing, educating girls, and registering births and deaths. In Sri Lanka, they are called 'Saubhagya,' which means good luck. There are nearly 2,000 Saubhagya entrepreneurs in Sri Lanka and 1,100 Guddi Bajis in Pakistan.[6]

[5] Peter Greer, *"The Poor will be Glad, Joining the Revolution to Lift the World out of Poverty,"* *Zondervan,* Quote of Muhammad Yunus, 142.
[6] Ajita Shashidhar, "Empowering Women–and Men," *Business Today,* July 7 (2013).

An oft-quoted mantra of Hilary Hilton "Zig" Zigler, an American author, salesman, and motivational speaker, is that every sale has five basic obstacles: no need, no money, no hurry, no desire, and no trust. Direct sales leverage the power of human interaction to counter these obstacles.

Let us consider another direct distribution model, selling of insurance. Unlike the case of so many consumer goods where there is a product to touch and feel, life insurance is an industry where the product has no physical features. It's a piece of paper. A promise to pay most likely when you won't be around to see if the promise has been honored, let alone personally benefit from the same. It takes an extraordinary human to knock on doors they have not known. Agents in this industry work on variable pay and have to look for new customers every single day they work. People are at the heart of this last mile, much more than many other categories where brand, quality of product, and other business drivers have a more definitive influence on sales. It's amazing that some sales people with just a laptop and a phone can generate a million-dollar income selling insurance. Indeed they have a round table of the finest financial services salesmen called Million Dollar Round Table (MDRT). Based in the US, the MDRT Annual Meeting has been described as a one-of-a-kind event, unrivaled in the world of business. Every year, approximately 4,000 of the world's top performers gather for one of the greatest gatherings of financial services professionals in the world.

World over, newsprint is a declining business. Only in a few countries does it get delivered at home in the mornings. In India, however, a system of direct distribution has ensured that it has become a part of our morning habits. We do not have to each day make a purchase decision, the newspaper lands up at the entrance door daily. Over 300,000 vendors distribute 55 million copies every day, in person, across 5,000 towns. We are a rare country where the newsprint industry continues to flourish.

The direct distribution model also works in enterprise sales and key account management. An extreme form of direct sales is one with zero intermediation. Marketing methods such as direct mail, telemarketing, direct response advertising, online, and mobile involves no in-person, face-to-face interaction between buyer and seller. In a way, sales and service are integrated into this highly personalized way of sales. It has its own challenges, of high churn in manpower and prohibitive costs by virtue of being personalized. It has always been a challenge to scale up such models to the size of the market opportunity.

VALUE CREATION MODEL: FUSION OF BUYER AND SELLER

The value creation model starts where advocacy ends. Advocacy model recognizes that point of sales is exactly as it states, a point of sales. It, therefore, focuses on creating demand through advocacy for retailer to service. The value creation process integrates seller and buyer, fuses their capabilities, and generates a last mile that's both collaborative and profitable. The center of gravity in such sales models is the end customer and not intermediaries.

This co-creation can take many shapes and forms.

- At the base of the pyramid is a process wherein *a single face is presented to a client,* and aggregation benefits ensue. Let us consider an example. Enterprise customers buying computers struggle to put together disparate and fragmented components of the system—printers, scanners, routers, and so on. Value added reseller, as such sellers of integrated products in technology are called, packages all software and hardware necessary for an effective system to run. The reseller will also provide training, maintenance, and technical support. Just one local number to call, these are people who understand business better than help desk of a company, often located in another continent.
- The second rung of the ladder is where buyer allows the seller to *leverage its infrastructure for mutual good.* Many e-tailers now do what is called incubation. They allow their suppliers to establish online stores. The suppliers make use of warehousing, people, and systems capability of e-tailers.

Suppliers, in this case fashion designers, come with their single biggest strength, their design and creativity, which for an e-tailer, fundamentally a distribution setup, is difficult to possess otherwise. Put together, these two independent entities create, end-to-end value chain for a customer.

The top rung of the ladder in the value creation is when the two entities, buyers and sellers, *merge their processes and capability*. In the traditional motor business, paint companies used to supply paints to automobile manufacturers. This structure traditionally has had distressing consequences. It is one thing to supply a can of paint, and quite another to make it work on a production line, which is unique to each automobile manufacturer. Supply chains as well used to be inefficient because while car manufacturers would want to respond dynamically to take off their vehicles, paint companies, used thus far to a more reliable forecasting in their core business of selling paints for homes, found it impossible to build flexibility and latent capacity in their rigid factory schedules. Soon both entities were replicating many processes, both had warehouses, and they ran supply chains independently for the same product. There was limited ownership of quality, and the managers in the two entities routinely blamed each other for product failures. Even research to predict future color trends was done separately by both the buyer and the supplier. All of it changed when automobile companies and paint companies agreed to work in conjunction. Instead of buying cans of paints, the buyer now pays a fixed rate on per car basis. There is a system of bonus and penalties to encourage collaboration and contribution. This has enforced buyers to make products that meet quality specifications first time right on the shop floor and to enhance the economics of their product formulations. The paint representative is nowadays a technical resource who resolves manufacturing glitches on the shop floor. The seller singularly manages the supply chain, more reliable because they are aware of the cost of missing production schedules.

Value creation leverages a capability that goes beyond physical forms of products or services, creating something that individually could not have been produced, certainly not of similar quality, or at the same cost. It requires deep alignment, understanding of customer's business and their agendas, and an ability to collaborate. In the process, negotiations move away from price cutting to value creation, from selling features and benefits that don't necessarily suit buyers to co-creation of a product or service. Indeed for most B2B, the last mile is sales of the solution, not a product. Integration of the last mile processes can create an entirely new value curve.

SAPIENCE SELLING MODEL: SELL INSIGHTS AND KNOWLEDGE

Land, labor, and capital, Adam Smith believed, are the source of the wealth of nations. Over time, land as an asset class lost its preeminence, and capability to produce goods using manufacturing became the new fountainhead of wealth creation. A large part of the wealth that was created in Europe owes its origin to manufacturing using turbine-propelled machines. However, now even this stands diluted and Europe's hegemony is lost as many companies can make similar products. Only through an experienced and innovative application of *knowledge* can firms now hope to outperform their counterparts and maintain their competitive position.

If value co-creation takes off from where advocacy ends, a step ahead, and fuses capability of buyers and sellers, then the concept of Sapience Sales is the next push ahead. In all the last mile models thus far, there is a buyer who knows what to buy. There is already a purchase specification. Only the seller has to be finalized. Sapience selling is a sales process that starts even before the customer has fully figured out the problem. The buyer knows they have an obstacle, but they do not fully comprehend either the magnitude of the issue or the solution. The seller also does not have a pre-manufactured product. The seller uses many open-ended questions, intuition, and experience sharing to enrich the process of selling and to arrive at an appropriate solution.

Software sales would fall into this category. The buyer harnesses the intellect of seller representatives to take their business to the next level. The seller representatives are subject matter experts. They have the trust of the buyer. They aren't just order takers. They are not afraid to challenge buyers and will speak their mind. And this is precisely how they bring value to the entire sales process.

I did go on a sales call with a representatives selling software solutions. The presentation made by the seller representatives was crisp. It answered three questions; credentials on why they should be here, the kind of work the seller has done in organizations similar to the buyer, and an assessment of what business challenges and context the buyer has. Erudite and knowledgeable, the seller representatives did not try to overtly push any solution. The tonality was still probing, some hypotheses, but no hard sell. It was, I think I can help you, but let's understand the context of your issues. The potential buyer appeared to be aware of the market, the competition, and was in control of the entire sales process. The buyer was concerned about how the new system would integrate with their technology architecture and how exactly it would solve their business problem. At the conclusion of the meeting, I asked the seller representative with whom I went, what would make the buyer make the final call to buy. His answer: "It's finally all about money, and how well it can be spent. I have to show the client the value in making the right call."

THE NEW AGE MODEL: LEVERAGE NEWER TECHNOLOGY AND MEDIA

"Look at these bed sheets, aren't they cute, with Disney characters… aah here is Mickey mouse, our favorite, the mischievous Donald Duck and for the daughter at home, in pink color," goes the voice of a live anchor at *Homeshop18*, an on-air retail and distribution venture, which has live anchors that perform on television and demonstrate products. They have a control room next door. Every show is monitored for its efficacy. On the screen, one can see critical metrics— numbers of calls received, orders booked, stock sold, and everything. It's a fantastic way to engage customers and not merely sell. We all talk of lead times to play out our strategy, larger companies say it takes months to know if what we do is working as intended, at live shows the report card is out even before the show ends.

A sales model like this has turned on its head all incumbent issues that make India a treacherous and complex market. In a country with poor infrastructure of roads, Homeshop18 delivers at home; their detailed demonstration of products on television bridges the enormous gap in our retail to educate consumers and to sell product features that companies have designed. They have successfully used one thing Indians love, their television sets. 170 million households have a television set, roughly a third is what Homeshop18 reaches, and has built sizeable viewership around it. Delhi is their biggest market, destroying the myth that only small town people would show an interest in such buying. They sell a range from saris to jewelry to mobile devices, and indeed would be the largest retailer in many of these categories. It's no surprise, when I last visited them, they had 7.5 million consumers in their customer relationship management (CRM), 47 percent repeat buyers, and a transaction every five seconds.

Close to 20 million room-nights are booked every year in 192 countries with a company that doesn't own a single hotel room. There are people with underused homes, and *Airbnb* simply lets them get paid for its occupation by short-term guests who find prices and space lucrative. The entire concept of shared consumption for profit is leveraged on the Internet platforms, without touching any brick and mortar distribution structure.

Telecom Regulatory Authority of India (TRAI) reported that about 325 million Indians went online in March 2014. This number is close to 351 million Indians who read a newspaper, and about half of the 800 million people who watch television. It does take many years to create the distribution muscle of the incumbent leaders, and costs money that can drain any new entrant. Is there a contrarian business model that explores the power of the Internet or television broadcasting and completely bypasses the traditional brick and mortar distribution models? In a world of a billion consumers, and high costs of the last mile, coupled with India's largely youth population, and being known as the IT capital of the world, digital seems a sensible solution. A brand like Xiaomi in mobile devices was launched only online. Their first offering got sold out within 38 minutes. The digital space cannot be ignored, yet very few companies leverage it in the real sense. Most brands see it as a competitor that dilutes market prices of their products. They would rather protect traditional distribution structures and keep the entry barriers high for any competitor since brick and mortar distribution structures, unlike digital, are difficult to replicate.

III

THE AGENDA FOR TRANSFORMATION

The quest for the right last mile model has been elusive. Companies end up pursuing almost all opportunities simultaneously. But they find it difficult to define precisely what each model will do, and how. Let us consider a bank. They have a physical asset by way of a branch manned with sales people, a call center for telephonic access, thousands of feet on street soliciting customers directly, Internet access, and perhaps some other channels. Yet all these appear to be selling identical products at similar prices. There is little to discriminate one channel from another, what it does, and the purpose of its existence, even though this access comes at dissimilar costs to the bank. And therein lies our biggest opportunity. Let us explore this further.

There are four key variables that should form the foundation for anchoring an appropriate last mile construct. These four variables are: the number of interface points, complexity of sales, contribution size (ticket size revenue less ticket size cost), and the imperative for value creation in the selling process. A mix of these would define what model works best. Each has a defined role and purpose, costs and opportunities for growth, the kind of products each channel sells may also be different, and the nature of marketing mix has to be channel appropriate.

This is illustrated in Figure 2.2.

This is, however, a starting point. When it comes to channel design, manifold choices confront a company. Legacy routes to

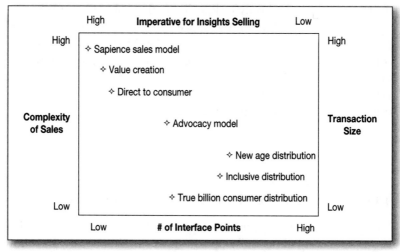

Figure 2.2   The Last Mile Grid
Source: Author's own.

market, however, prevent the companies from considering the most efficient path to the market. Customer typology is usually missed out in channel designs. Companies have multiple kinds of customers, each varying in the complexity of the transaction, and the value of the transaction. And the tasks for the companies are variable too. By definition, channels are not equal in the capability to perform all market tasks. Just as markets are segmented into innumerable parcels, and marketers then design distinct products for each segment, a heterogeneous base of customers and resellers like India's also needs many more differing routes to service than we see traditionally in the companies. A sample grid like the one in Figure 2.3 can become the basis for defining the right routes to the market.

The last mile is execution intensive but fundamentally it's a strategic asset in a country like India. The enormous spend on the last mile must deliver more. It should create a competitive advantage, build enduring partnerships, and deliver experience and trust to our consumers.

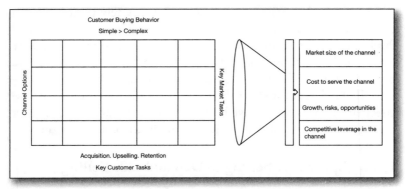

Figure 2.3   Channel Choice Grid
Source: Author's own.

Once we agree to deploy a strategic instead of an operational lens on the last mile construct, the filter that we use to determine the right agenda for ourselves alters. The filter we have used to arrive at transformation agenda is as follows:

- Is it strategic and competitively differentiated?
- Is it value accretive?
- Is it execution savvy?
- Is it the intrinsic trait of winners, though in varying proportions?
- Does it fundamentally unlock more consumers, or usage, or both?

There are large themes at the last mile. All of them can collectively transform a company. The rejuvenated last mile constructs, to truly make an impact, must be seen as in the following six transformative themes.

From Mere Availability to a Strategic Asset in a Company

The task of the last mile is now beyond linear, high frequency selling that focused singularly on more land grab, to a value accretive and competitively differentiated route to the market.

Indeed the last mile is now one of the very few places where a company can add value. Much else has been already imitated and duplicated by the competition. From technology to products, there is not much to discriminate between business rivals in the things we buy as customers. The arenas companies worked so hard to be superior all stand replicated by their competitors. New points of discrimination and competitive leverage, contemporary and customer centric, are needed for companies to get ahead, and to stay there.

From Supply-side Selling to Demand-side Selling

If sales is a consequence of demand and supply curves intersecting at a price point, as traditional economists say, and if you ask sales people whether they are on the demand side or supply side, chances are the job they do is more about liquidating goods and services their companies have manufactured. They act and sell pretty much from the supply side. They *talk* demand, but they *do* supply.

In a country where, across categories, there are more non-users than consumers, it is time to uplift the role of distribution from a pipe that carries goods to a capability that can sire new demand. In the process, companies would expand market for their products and consumers who currently feel disenfranchised will enter the consuming class and get an opportunity to lead a better life. As will unfold in subsequent chapters, the power of the last mile is immense, and generally under leveraged thus far by most companies.

From Frankenstein to Tightly Secured Value Chains

Mary Shelley had written a book in the early nineteenth century, published when she was just 20 years old, in which a man by the name of Victor Frankenstein discovers a method of creating life, and in doing so creates a monster that he then abandons. Considered to be one of the earliest examples of science fiction, the monster's life is a living hell from that point forward, and he eventually sets out to get revenge upon his maker.

The success of many brands, at times, creates a Frankenstein, and leaves the window open for competition to come and grab a share of market that a company left unattended. Disproportionate profit margins, low barriers to entry, a fractured *last mile* value chain that passes through many layers that add costs but not value, and in the process taking away the wealth of customers to profit a few middlemen, are some of the paramount reasons competition thrives. Indeed across categories from cement to water, from steel to mobile devices, one can see companies ignore value by virtue of their existing business constructs, at times for the right reasons, but often for low motivation. Somewhere, somehow many brands assume that their consumers are passive with Pavlovian loyalty, and they will buy irrespective of the price and character of their value chain. Left unattended, this can grow into a Frankenstein's monster and cause relentless damage as new competition replicates similar products, but with a refreshed value chain.

From Product-driven to Customer-driven Agendas

Consider this:

> During the Maoist era, Chinese consumers sought four functional status symbols; bicycles, watches, sewing machines, and radios, known as the four things that go round. As expectations rose in the 1980s, Chinese hoped to purchase six big things; Videocassette recorders, televisions, washing machines, cameras, refrigerators, and electric fans. By 2000, consumers desired even more expensive items, with air conditioning units becoming the most sought after product by consumers in the country's eleven largest cities. Demand also rose for personal computers, mobile phones, color televisions, microwave ovens, and video equipment. Since then, modern Chinese consumer desire has expanded to include experiences, such as education, leisure travel, and cultural events.[7]

The pursuit of unbridled growth has created a challenge in that companies spend disproportionate effort and time in seducing the new customers for old products, rather than nurture the old

[7] Karl Gerth, *As China Goes, so Goes the World* (New York:Hill & Wang, 2010).

relationships for new, contemporary, and sensible product transformations in line with growing aspirations of the people. Obsession with customers and how to serve them, therefore, must not be less than one with brands and products.

The strict definition of the product is what keeps companies to sell identical features and designs, perpetuating margin pressures as rival brands jostle for the same customer with identical offers. Successful companies reconstruct their market. They charge their teams to instead sell solutions, move into adjacent markets, or merge the power of different product categories into one, as they traverse the same path at the same velocity as their customers. Marketing for them is not about what they "do to" customers, it is about what they "do with" customers.

From Hollow Bravado to the Power of Making Things Happen

The Anglo-Zanzibar War began at 9:00 AM on August 27, 1896. The conflict arose when the British disapproved the succession of Sultan Khalid as the new ruler of Zanzibar. "By the end of 25th August, Khalid had his palace secured with almost 3,000 men, several artillery guns and even a modestly armed Royal Yacht in the nearby harbor."[8] Despite that, this war is officially documented as the shortest war in history. It lasted 38 minutes.[9] Zanzibar had no capability to execute when the moment of reckoning arrived.

Exceptional execution of an ordinary idea is behind profitability of a vast majority of companies.

"We make great decisions, but nothing ever gets done." "We have been talking of the same issues for so long, we do wonder if these will ever get fixed?" "What our competition has done was always known to us, it is not a surprise." Statements like these aren't uncommon, often heard in the corridors of corporate offices. Companies differ in the insights they have on business, and they differ in what they do with these insights. Execution is an even

---

[8] Ben Johnson, "The shortest war in history," www-historic-uk.com. Accessed on August 04, 2015.
[9] The exact time is disputed, different sources report it as anywhere between 38 to 45 minutes.

bigger challenge in India given headwinds of heterogeneity and enormous scale. India entices and intimidates simultaneously.

From Automation to Inspirational Power of Technology

On May 11, 1997, an IBM computer by the name of Deep Blue beat Gary Kasparov, the chess Grandmaster. But then he was pitted against a machine that could process up to 200 million chess positions per second. The next day, the *New York Times* reported as follows,

> In brisk and brutal fashion, the I.B.M. computer Deep Blue unseated humanity, at least temporarily, as the finest chess playing entity on the planet yesterday, when Gary Kasparov, the world chess champion, resigned the sixth and final game of the match after just 19 moves, saying, "I lost my fighting spirit.[10]

In the battle between humans and machine, well the machine had won.

The computer is increasingly doing complex tasks that require the capability to process enormous information and even deploy judgment. The machines of today are trying to replicate, at times even better, human brains. While this enormous role spurred by the capability of automation and algorithms is debatable, days when computers were used to merely replace mundane manual activities with a tech savvy interface seem archaic compared to capabilities of a technology in these times. Organizations of all sizes are challenged to make sense of huge amounts of data from mobile devices, sensors, and social network. The belief is that technology will be cheaper, accurate, and objective, and will do many jobs better than humans.

"Think about it: Twenty homes in North America today generate the same amount of traffic that the entire Internet produced in 2008. The Internet is pervasive, and growing at an ever faster pace, taking up more energy, more bandwidth, more time."[11]

---

[10] Bruce Weber, "Swift and Slashing, Computer Topples Kasparov," *New York Times,* May 12 (1997).

[11] Jeff Stibel, *Breakpoint: Why the web will implode, search will be obsolete, and everything else you need to know about technology is in your brain* (New York: Palgrave Macmillan, 2013).

The spectrum of influence of technology on business is evolving. Many companies, our experience shows, have a technology that does "mostly operational" functioning as supporting information reports, executing basic day-to-day functioning and managing technology assets. However, progressive business teams recognize opportunities to leverage IT investments as enablers of business transformation.

How we harness technology is an issue as vital as what technology can do for us.

CONCLUSION

All these are massive changeover propositions. These will all resonate in distinctive forms in subsequent chapters.

In the first two chapters, we have described the imperative for the last mile, and the financial implications of the last mile capability on companies. We have chronicled the India context, the seven last mile models that work currently, and the transformation agenda. There is a case for companies at present ingrained in doing better what they do best, to cross-pollinate and acquire new competencies.

Let's return to the large picture. India is a market of good fortune. Its billion populace is hungry for opportunities, their aspirations are large, and they confidently seek new prospects. We need a framework to unlock the abounding potential of these consumers. For that it's important that we comprehend the concept of "Demand" in emerging economies before we get to "supply side solutions." The demand in terrains like India is not yet mature, in many categories still tenaciously unavailable, it is hardly homogeneous, and the customers are somewhat inexperienced as they explore brands and cutting-edge technology.

Winning India's billion consumers gets scoped out in the next chapter.

PART II

REVITALIZING THE
LAST MILE
TOOLS AND FRAMEWORKS

PART II

PRACTICE ZONE, USE
LANDMINE
TOOLS AND FRAMEWORKS

3 The Five Knots of the Last Mile

Imagine you are in Shanghai. You are on the Zhongshan road, also called the Bund, a Persian name that literally means the embankment: It is Shanghai's famous waterfront running along the western shores of the Huangpu River. Once a muddy towpath, with tall reeds where boats docked, the Bund was where the foreign powers that entered Shanghai after the opium wars, built distinctly European-style trading and financial houses. Jews from Baghdad, for instance, including the famous Sassoon family, one of the wealthiest families in Asia of those times, had dominated Shanghai's business in the early twentieth century.

Not far from here is the somber bronze statue of Chen Yi, the Chinese communist military commander and member of the People's Liberation Army. His vantage position offers uninterrupted views. Across the river, on the east side, is the towering and the ambitious skyline of Pudong, dotted with skyscrapers and ultra-modern architecture, lit up every night in flashy colors. And straight ahead, perpendicular to the statue, is the Nanjing road, linking the Bund with the famous People's square. Chen Yi can see the world around him has changed beyond recognition since the days of the liberation army. This expanse is now home to every American and European brand, West-inspired colonial hotels, neon lights, giant television screens, and an estimated 2 million visitors each day. From the vast Apple store to the persisting purveyors of "massage" and peddlers of fake watches, Nanjing road is the ultimate symbol of the distance China has travelled toward consumerism.

If you want to see what economic prosperity does to material aspirations of the people, China is an undeniable example.

As the rest of the world looked, first in disbelief, and then in awe, China has become today perhaps the largest consumer of everything from automobiles to fashion. In 1993, private ownership of cars in China was 50,000.[1] Today, one out of four vehicles is produced in China, and an estimated 35 million privately owned passenger cars ply on the roads. The young Chinese customer has taken to technology-propelled *Baidu* and *Taobao*, *iPhones*, and *Wechat*, with consummate ease. In most parts of the world, the wealth is with the older generation, while it is the young who use the computers. In China, both the wealth and the mouse of the computer are with the same generation of young consumers, thus creating the world's largest Internet commerce market. The rural population of China is aggressively buying durable and housing. "McKinsey, a consultancy, forecasts that consumption by urban Chinese households will increase from 10 trillion Yuan in 2012 to nearly 27 trillion Yuan in 2022."[2] Karl Gerth, author of *As China Goes, so Goes the World*, has the following to say:

> Consumerism implies more than the increased purchasing of more goods. It refers as well to the orientation of social life around consumer products and services, to the entrenchment of consumerism into the everyday life of a society in which one converses and communicates with others through things bought in the market.

A good 5,000 miles away from Shanghai, roughly at the same time, the Communist Party in China came to power, at the stroke of midnight on August 15, 1947, a new nation awoke to light and freedom. Under subjugation for centuries by invaders, kings, and princes, and 90 years of British rule, India chose the path of democracy based on universal suffrage. At the time of independence, India had a population of 334 million, literacy rate of 12 percent, and average life expectancy of barely 32 years. For a full

---

[1] Stephen Stares and Zhi Liu, eds., *China's Urban Transportation Development Strategy*, 1995, Proceedings of a symposium in Beijing, November 8–10 (1995).
[2] "Chinese consumers: Doing it their way", *The Economist*, Mianyang and Shanghai (January 25, 2014).

five decades leading up to independence, the growth rate of the economy was below 1 percent. The first union budget, albeit for seven and a half months, presented by R.K. Shanmukham Chetty, had provided for revenues of 171 crores and expenditure of 197 crores, of which 92 crores was on account of defense. The finance minister was highly apologetic about his transgression in presenting a rupee 25 crores deficit budget. "If these special factors are taken into account it will be seen that we have not been living beyond our means or heading towards bankruptcy", he had explained in the context of a deficit caused by extraordinary expenditure on rehabilitating refugees post partition of India.

India and China, in terms of the Gross Domestic Product (GDP), were almost equal-sized economies in 1980. GDP is a good measure of a country's wealth, but in the case of China, it has been plagued with controversies, and therefore a reasonable indicator to consider is per capita GDP, measured in terms of purchasing power parity, and expressed in terms of a single currency, the US dollar in this case. Measured thus, *IMF World Economic Outlook 2014* data suggest a 40 times enhancement in the living standards of the people in China from the year 1980 to 2013, versus a progress of 10 times enhancement in India in the same period when both countries, within some years of each other, chose to abandon state controlled development and place trust in private enterprise. Admittedly, China had a superior human index at the starting point compared to India. They had more literacy, higher life expectancy, and greater sensitivity to gender equality, which contributed immensely in their journey toward being a manufacturing capital of the world. It is abundantly clear that India has much ground to cover on material improvement in the standards of living. But India's path to development is a lot less interventionist by the state and driven by the rule of law. The pole position taken by information technology, software, and pharmaceuticals, industries propelled by intellectual capital, in the global arena by India is a good early indicator of the future potential.

Different companies in India have pursued the quest for billion consumers variously, and most got into the fray after promise of level playing field in the early 1990s post-liberalization. Some companies consider India as a serious opportunity; many feel a billion is just a number of warm bodies, mostly without a wallet worth talking about. The universal truth however is that in every category, there is unexplored fortune. Holding the key to this treasure is an enormous range of customers. They are the young college-going kids who have a smartphone, a Facebook and Twitter account, and sip coffee at Starbucks, even though the pocket money is limited. They are the young executives who have just started out in life, but aspire big, they do not see savings, unlike their parents, as a virtue, but effortlessly take loans and use credit cards, and in many ways define why growth in India, unlike China thus far, has been fuelled almost singularly by way of domestic consumption than investments, particularly in infrastructure. They are the middle-class housewives who manage household expenses prudently, create a disposable income for themselves from fixed monthly budget, and have begun to experiment with beauty products, but not as often or as regularly.

And then there is another India that most companies don't really know how to reach profitably and make a business sense of. These are the urban poor and consumers living in far flung rural markets. It is their first flush with discretionary incomes. They want to spend, but carefully. They are value conscious, unfamiliar with a whole range of products and brands, not comfortable walking into self-service modern format stores as they continually seek trust and tend to rely on retailer recommendations.

Many companies in India that could not understand the aspiring populace have quickly understood that 1.2 billion people do not make 1.2 billion consumers.

China and India are together forecasted to drive more than half of the global growth in GDP over the next few years. But as we saw in the first chapter, growth is not democratic; it does not benefit everyone evenly. Nor does it open up for all categories of goods naturally, and in the same proportion as increases in disposable incomes. It is not even uniform geographically either since people's indigenous attitudes vary across regions in India. To illustrate the case of regional disparities in consumption, consider the case of the state of Punjab, where the demand for status products like mobile phones, home décor, and durables peaked much earlier than in most other parts of the country. As per published numbers, even in 2008, among all states, excluding some metros that had an independent license, penetration of mobiles in Punjab at 48 percent was the highest, and almost all other states were just half of this number. The journey from latent to actual demand, many companies assume, is a natural path as disposable incomes rise. That's not entirely true.

In this context, as depicted, there are two ways the last mile can be seen. The first is as an aggregation node. It assumes that there is demand for our products and services, there is a steady trot if not a rush toward consumerism, and the last mile ought to be constructed in such a way that it fulfills the demand that is being sired with more consumers entering the middle class. This thought is akin to a pizza delivery model, with the last mile being equated to the delivery boy. Gains will ensue but no real differentiation or a sustainable competitive advantage can occur. With time, if not instantly, all sensible competitors will get to the same spot. Most concurrent last mile models tend to find their center of gravity around this structure, which is no more than plumbing a pipe to the market. The task of any business in India, however, must be not only to serve demand, but also to create one. The second approach, therefore, is focused on the procreation and harnessing of the demand. Thus far, it has been an assumed responsibility of communication and advertising to open these floodgates. The rationale is correct, except that, as we will see in many cases put forth by it and in isolation, communication impacts only so much. One reason, among many, is that our consumers do need hand holding. Someone has to help them make a choice, and provide confidence that the promise made by the product will be kept. Even in premium categories, à la cosmetics and smartphones, where one assumes customers are so savvy and affluent that they go to shopping aisles and pick up products, it takes advisors in shops to inform, assist, advice and then close business. We are a country made up of unseasoned shoppers, mostly new entrants to the consuming class. We buy when we feel comfortable, when we trust the provider, when we are sure that the offer will positively impact our life and make us feel good. High-touch engagement at the point of sale, therefore, is indispensable. And that's why the last mile is needed to unlock true demand.

Every Turbonator Company, irrespective of their domain category, has first grown the category by unshackling the demand. In the process they have improved their market position.

Incumbent companies grew at an average Compound Annual Growth Rate (CAGR) of 9.7 percent in sales revenue over a 20-year horizon after the market reforms. The Turbonator companies have grown by 14.9 percent, roughly 50 percent better. What is interesting is that in the first five years, till 1998, both grew at a similar pace, a double-digit growth, but then Turbonator companies took off. They have been accelerating the gap every five years. A similar data holds true for cash and profits from operations. Turbonator companies have grown operating profits at a CAGR of 18 percent and cash at a CAGR of 16 percent in the last two decades.

The concept of a nautical mile is based on the circumference of the earth, and is equal to one minute of latitude, almost 500 feet longer than a land mile. The fifteenth century sailors had no Global Positioning System (GPS); they needed a standard to know as to how fast they were getting to their destination. They used equipment available then, an hourglass, a rope, a piece of wood, and created the first maritime speedometer. Though now measured more scientifically, the speed equal to one nautical mile an hour at sea is still called a knot.

Markets in India are enormous, each knot will open one more layer of demand, some obvious thus far, a lot hidden in the current construct of last miles. A billion consumer market, heterogeneous and still developing, has pools of revenue and profits to be unveiled almost like layers of an onion. Each knot differs in intensity of competition, profitability, lifetime value of demand, and scale of customer traction. The profile of the customer varies, and neither the construct nor the task of the last mile is identical in the various knots. As I worked across categories, five distinct knots were discernible, and companies do differ in their ability to unlock value in each. Let's have a look at each of the knots, and what it does, to begin with, as explained in Figure 3.1.

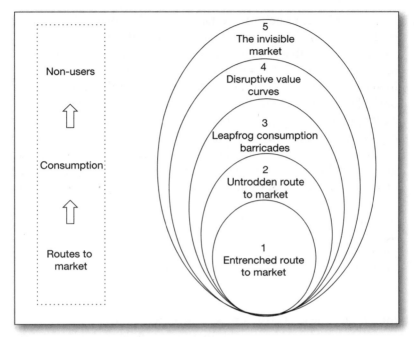

Figure 3.1   Five Knots of the Last Mile
Source: Author's own.

THE FIRST KNOT: ENTRENCHED ROUTES TO THE MARKET

The existing route to the market is an obvious and important first knot. It may have a disparate construct and vary by category, but a structure by which customers get to buy products and services does exist. Every company each year also talks about a step change in the availability of their products. Generally, what they have in mind is a duplication and amplification of current routes to market. Who can deny that it has to be the first step? Let us consider a new company that sets foot in the market. If they follow the first knot, as they almost always do, this new, unseasoned and inexperienced company will join the quest for the most competitive and aware constellation of customers. Intermediaries, who sense that the brand power of a new player is yet to be firmly established, will demand their pound of flesh by way of credit and discounts. Nonetheless the advantage for an entrant is that of being in the most concentrated pool of current subscription for their kind of products and services, with minimal effort needed in educating customers or in the establishment of the last mile capability. However, so long as all companies within a category just focus on the first knot, the leader will enjoy uninterrupted advantage in both cost to distribute and velocity of cash.

Contrary to perception, the first knot itself is neither staid nor given. It holds only so much consumption and is indeed racked up by burgeoning competition, and with time it does get to be increasingly less profitable to operate in. Business history shows that there is a global precedence as well to shifts in markets that have been tectonic. In many parts of the globe, just to expound on this point, corner stores gave way to supermarkets, then to shopping malls, thereafter to discount stores and big box retail, and now increasingly to online retail. India may not change so dramatically, but change it will. Even a minor shift will alter market shares of brands and the cost structure to distribute.

All forward-looking paths in the last mile, beyond the first knot, in varying scale, are bigger and better organized. For companies the challenge of this plausible shift is real, even hard. Small stores and small clients have hardly any negotiation power. A larger sized intermediary or a client is expensive to engage with. These intermediaries are knowledgeable; chances are they know cost structures of manufacturers intimately. They would not hesitate to sleep with competition, worse create, and sell own labels. While this journey is reasonably uncontainable, there is another likely development that will restore, to an extent, power to companies. In the next few years, diversity in the first knot will become sharper. This will be impelled by the growing power of newer and bulkier intermediaries, while the old intermediation points, currently made up of smaller interceders, will also mature into many more subsets, each unique in size and customer typology.

The agenda for a company is clear. They would need to learn to manage diversity in their intermediaries and clients. It will be strenuous to run one size fits all last mile models that we have had for so long. This is a new reality. But the reward is immense for companies that know how to tame this heterogeneity and multiplicity. One of the illustrations will demonstrate the power of the same. A beverage company used to sell its produce at identical prices and in not too undifferentiated ways across its shops. They decided to segment mom and pop outlets. A few outlets were on the main road where thirsty customers would pick up a drink on the go. Some were in a neighborhood where a family would buy to stock for a week or a few days. Yet some more were the shops where college kids would get together after a game of cricket. A shop is not a shop. It is a venue where customers of differing needs, predispositions, and backgrounds congregate. This information was employed to segment points of sales. Outlets where customers just grabbed a drink needed to focus on non-returnable bottles put in a vertical stand from where it is easy to retrieve; family shopping means larger package size. College kids need an environment to chill and chat. In such outlets, promotions and display mix are markedly young and peppy. Sustainable innovations like these integrate the product with its customers.

We have so far looked at how unfolding events are likely to impact companies. Ability to see the large market in granular parts, and deploying a last mile solution apt to each typology, is a key choice. Let us now consider what is going to happen to our existing channels of distribution, our first of the five knots, and what possibly they can do to remain viable. These channels, particularly those wherein competition is intense or structural changes may impact the category itself, are likely to struggle in the future with both growth and profit margins. Newer arteries for distribution of goods already encroach on their market. Some manufacturers sell direct to customers. Many international brands offer worldwide shipping. Online commerce is gaining customer trust. Consumers are being encouraged to buy second hand products from sites like *OLX* and *Quikr*. As all these trends gain traction, demand will shrink in traditional channels. The other encumbrance will be on profit margins that will get squeezed by competition. Online display of prices, just to emphasize the point, for instance, now by *Amazon* and the like, cuts degrees of freedom for many channels that thrived and profited from the obfuscation of critical data points from their customers. The path-breaking work, *Fortune at the Bottom of the Pyramid* by C.K. Prahalad, has proven that poor people pay a premium on everything from the price of rice to the cost of credit versus their richer counterparts. An important reason for sustained poverty of the poor is lack of transparency and non-disclosures in the market place.

Existing channels will increasingly find it difficult to charge only for pass through of products. We have to imagine them in future as Value Added Resellers. They must bring value to the transaction that is unique to them for customers to prefer them to competing suppliers. My bookshop I find is a befitting example. It is not a large shop, unlike many big box retailers in this category who, unable to pay for high rentals, have had to shut the shop. I rarely find a title missing. The man at the counter knows intimately about most books and has a word to say about many of them. The display is limited but intelligent. Contemporary titles and books are prominently visible. The shopkeeper knows the online price for most books and does not hesitate to discount. As soon as a new title hits, and if I have bought those kinds of books, an email and SMS are sent out. Retailers who wish to thrive in future will be pushed to know the products and offer expert guidance. The common thread in non-conventional last mile models that work well are their ability to explain to consumers the product and what it can do for them. All this has to be done in an environment that is non-threatening and non-condescending.

The truth is that there are many companies that struggle with the first knot itself. Only a few genuinely excel at it. Execution of the first knot entails mastering the science of the subsisting business model. The companies within industry vary in their effectiveness, the costs, and the extent to which they leverage their selling capability despite vending not so dissimilar products.

THE SECOND KNOT: UNTRODDEN ROUTES TO THE MARKET

The second knot is where one forges new nodes of delivery, taking advantage of convergence in channels of distribution. The product, the price, and the customer value proposition do not alter in this instance. Chemists selling fast moving consumer goods in addition to medicines, data access products being sold from computer channel and not only mobile shops, auto rickshaw drivers selling mobile recharges, *Homeshoppe*—like media leveraged channels using the power of television to sell many products into hinterlands—are all instances of value being delivered by a new route. Newer nodes of delivery create incremental demand for brands that are first to unravel these, though they are unlikely to sustain this advantage over time.

Let's look at the last mile for customers seeking to buy a computer. Knowledgeable staff, complete range of products, better prices, and one-stop availability of peripherals and software would transpire as top reasons for customers to choose a point of sale. In almost every city, there is a so-called computer market. Hundreds of small establishments jostle for business. These offer best prices given the competition in their neighborhood, and one can get everything needed there, from printers to software. These small shops, however, fail to offer shopping ambience and trust. Large format retail stores in this category are a reasonable choice for customers. The computer is not a product one buys frequently; hence, even if the bigger stores are far and few, it is not a deterrent to a customer. These big box stores can reproduce the value curve of smaller shops, and indeed perform better on some other critical parameters that are meaningful to customers.

Consider another example. It is a well-heeled assumption that people do not like to buy insurance; they have to be sold one. Therefore, agents are needed to explain products in detail. This has kept distribution machinery in insurance both prohibitively expensive and limited in size. *PEP* is the single largest retail chain with over 1,500 stores in South Africa. They now also sell insurance products in partnership with Hollard Group Risk. Their products are focused on the specific needs of customers. Similarly, a low cost appliance store, *Casas Bahia* in Brazil, sells unemployment and personal accident insurance. Additional policy benefits include a lottery ticket and pharmaceutical discounts. Insurance is offered and explained to customers by their sales staff during the appliance sales process. Claims are also processed in store by Casas Bahia, thereby preserving the interests of clients and not only companies whose insurance they have sold. These are instances of a meaningful extension of channels for products that have been traditionally sold by insurance agents.

Floundering profitability in the existing lines of business, soaring costs in putting together the infrastructure needed to make goods available, and poor value addition by points of sales thus far, and hence ease of substitution, have contributed to encourage both brands and channels to seek polygamous relationships. These new nodes do give an advantage to the company that moves in first, but only so long as competition does not ride on the same channel. Brand shares change, with disproportionate allowance to the first mover. If one, however, takes a helicopter view of the industry as a whole, the gains for the entire category will be marginal. It will recruit only those customers who earlier would not buy for last mile deficiency. Barring enhanced availability, the remainder of the value curve for a customer magnifies only in a limited manner.

THE THIRD KNOT: LEAPFROG CONSUMPTION BARRICADES

The third knot is where one builds last mile capability to diffuse components that inhibit current consumption. It doesn't open new channels of distribution, as much as it kicks in usage.

Many a category in India suffers not only for want of enough customers, but also because the existing customers do not consume enough. Some parts of the differential between international benchmarks and India in per capita consumption numbers can be explained by purchasing power disparity, but there are other inhibitors at play too. Across categories enhancing usage is a serious opportunity for growth in companies. Neilson has the following to say on the fast moving consumer goods business:

> Compared to regional counterparts, FMCG spending in India is far below peers on a per capita basis. In 2011, Indian consumers spent just $31 (USD) per capita on FMCG products, significantly less than consumers in Thailand ($214), Philippines ($161), and China ($128). Even among urban Indians, where income is higher,

FMCG spending reached just $65 per capita. Benchmarking to China alone pegs the FMCG upside at 12 billion dollars—or an additional dollar for every three dollars in FMCG sales today.[3]

Unlocking consumption itself will propel revenues of companies. Consider this, what is the one thing that prevents us from getting our house painted? Not a do-it-yourself market, it is the hassle of engaging with contractors, running around for material, and turning our home upside down that holds us back from doing up our homes as often as we would want to. Paint companies have set up painting solutions, giving customers an end-to-end service. They offer color consultancy, trained contractors, and their own supervisors to ensure quality and timeliness. The increasing and now noticeable contribution of this service is a testimony to the fact that a new value curve has been established, and some revenues that would otherwise be lost, stand retrieved. In a similar manner, eTailers fill the last mile value gap that was holding back consumption. There are customers who find shopping a real inconvenience. For them there is nothing exciting about breathing polluted air and maneuvering traffic to be able to shop. A large range, better prices, and delivery at home are the new value curves set up by the Internet retailers. The Internet-propelled retail is willing to accept cash at the time of delivery, and many now deliver merchandise the same day as well, thus further diluting leverage of brick and mortar structures.

The insurance industry has for long been run on emotional benefits. People buy from people they know. Yet there is a distinct distrust in the entire process. The feeling is that the broker or agent, for their gains, takes customers for a ride. Therefore, while the last mile exists by way of direct sales, it again inhibits, postpones decisions to buy. A testimony to customer resistance is the way term insurance, the most legitimate life protection plan, is increasingly getting bought. Customers chose to buy it online. Term insurance now gets sold almost like a commodity, a pure play functional offer that competes

---

[3] "India's growth story is still unfolding," *Nielsen Insights,* November 28, 2012, http://www.nielsen.com/in/en/insights/news/2012/indias-growth-story-is-still-unfolding.html

on price. In response to customer defiance, some of the insurance companies now ask their agents to carry laptops. A needs assessment is done of customer's financial goals, as it always was, but now the machines, and not the agent, propose an appropriate product, each unique to a customer. The rationale for the product and what it will offer as benefits in times of exigency is transparent. Illustrations demonstrate how the product will perform over time, and what returns a customer is likely to earn. This has substantively neutralized distrust in the agent, an inhibitor in buying decisions, and hence unlocked to some measure the blocked pipe to consumption.

Consider *Maruti Suzuki,* the giant in automobiles space. They know that close to 40 percent of car buyers are first-time buyers, and impediments to purchase have to be marginalized. Maruti has driving schools, including lady instructors, to teach people how to drive. They have hundreds of videos in local languages that are shown in vans which traverse rural markets extensively; and they know that the concept of equated monthly installments works well for fixed income salaried employees, not so much for farmers with inconsistent income for whom they have innovative financing solutions. It is no surprise that more than a third of their business comes from rural markets, even for a category as expensive as an automobile.

The third knot is a fundamental shift compared to the earlier two. The two initial last mile competencies were focused on amplification of the power to distribute. The third knot seeks to unlatch triggers to consumption. It does not expand distribution as much as it grows consumption.

THE FOURTH KNOT: DISRUPTIVE VALUE CURVES

A new generation of companies recognizes that they can create growth by combining assets they have with two critical levers thus far underutilized, one entrepreneurial capability of people and second technology. An alliance of the power of people and technology with whatever we are doing has the force to deliver a holistic solution to the problems we face, and craft a new business model, beyond the mere alteration of some features in our products.

It is possible now to store cash and use it to transfer to someone else, or to pay utility bills, even shop at merchant establishments using just a mobile phone. Airtel Money, Nokia Money, and some others facilitate these transactions. *IndusInd* bank even allows their customers to withdraw cash from ATMs using just a mobile. Safaricom's M-PESA is now being used by most adults in Kenya, and being replicated in many other parts of the world. It does away with the requirement to have a bank account, a serious issue for the urban poor and rural customers. With M-PESA, the user can buy digital funds from any of their thousands of agents, send the electronic cash to any other mobile user in Kenya, who can then redeem it for conventional cash at any agent point. Rapid mass-market penetration of mobile phones has created opportunities for new business models to emerge, as with a mobile phone there is now a means to count, identify, and reach out in a purposeful way to the vast majority of people.

Argos was founded in 1973 and is now the UK's leading general merchandise retailer. The customers can check stock availability and reserve goods through the "Ring & Reserve" call center and the "Text & Take Home" (SMS) services using, respectively, their fixed or their mobile phone. They have access to catalogues on all screens, mobiles, television, and computer. A customer specifies what they want, pays the bill, receives a ticket, and then has to wait to pick up low-price home and electrical goods that arrive by conveyor belt from the rear of the premises. With 700 plus stores, Argos has learnt to incorporate the emerging technologies with this somewhat unusual sales and distribution method. Migration from high-engagement retail stores to low-touch, self-service channels in some instances can yield an entirely new value curve at the last mile, thus positively impacting consumption.

Let us go back to our earlier example of a paint company in Chapter 1. The customers wanted a large range of shades to choose from, but paint companies had no way to walk that path as a large assortment would have severely blocked their cash. A range of business models was deployed. Fast moving stocks were kept closer to points of sale, and those with lower velocity and predictability were aggregated at fewer warehouses, and supplied to order.

It still never truly satisfied customers. But once paint companies made their retailers as part partners in manufacturing, with the factory manufactured base being converted into exact shade using a tinting machine at the last mile, enormous value got released. In the process, four benefits came about. *One,* the customer could now access thousands of colors giving them the exact shade and tone they wanted. *Two,* stocks availability became as good as 100 percent and revenue loss due to stock-outs disappeared. *Three,* for a company, and for their trade, substantive cash that was blocked in inventories, got released. *Four,* at the last mile, the quality of conversations changed. Customers concentrate more on enormous range they could choose from, rather than haggle on prices alone.

In all the above cases, technology has been incorporated at the last mile to directionally alter the value curves.

THE FIFTH KNOT: THE INVISIBLE MARKET

"Can you imagine what the air would cost if someone else provided it". Signed by God. "If you missed the dawn I made for you today, it does not matter. I will make you another tomorrow." Signed by God. "Put yourself in my hands, and see what I can do." "Please don't drink and drive. You are not quite ready to meet me yet." "If you think Mona Lisa is stunning, you should look at my master-piece in the mirror." These are headlines of an absolutely gripping *God's billboard campaign* launched some years ago by the Church of Singapore in the face of dwindling church attendance.

The fifth and final knot is in the conversion of non-users.

An appropriate way perhaps to deal with non-users of our products and services, and to seek answers for enlisting them is to first step back and identify with the concept of poverty. It is a bit of diversion, and an extreme way to illustrate non-users, even incorrectly suggesting that people who do not consume our products, are necessarily poor, but it is a determining instrument to build a perspective. All we have seen thus far is economists and governments trying to fix a numerical value to the concept of poverty. Either people are above that number, or below it. A study by Oxford Poverty and Human Development Initiative on multidimensional poverty shows that income measures alone do not capture deprivations in non-income dimensions. "Multidimensional poverty is made up of several factors that constitute poor people's experience of deprivation – such as poor health, lack of education, inadequate living standard, lack of income (as one of several factors considered), disempowerment, poor quality of work and threat from violence."[4] True poverty is both an economic status as also helplessness or lack of influence over the forces in one's life. Economic power can be delivered by doles and subsidy, and often by reducing prices these customers have to pay, the power of which innumerable "sachet stories" of consumer brands have aptly demonstrated, but empowerment of the disenfranchised is a bigger issue, a resolution of which deeply impacts fortune of the society and sustainability of what business does. It is beyond the realms of tinkering with products, and just their price. Bereft of empowerment built in business models at the last mile, its impact on current non-users is minimal in the larger scheme of things. All-embracing business model that can make a difference in the lives of non-users are what profoundly impacts and sustains what companies do.

Mechai Viravaidya is popularly known as "Mr. Condom" in Thailand. An MBA from Australia, he was stuck by poverty in his country, and concluded that population explosion had to be controlled. It's not Thailand alone; population control has been on the agenda for decades across the globe for sustainability of the planet. The real hindrance to population interventions has been to bring about change without it being seen by people as an invasion of their privacy. People should, in an ideal scenario, willingly restrain proliferation. Historically there haven't been enough customers for such ideas. The norm of the day was to employ doctors to spread the message of population control. But there were not enough doctors to give gravitas to this purpose. And doctors were seen by people to be prescriptive and not empathetic. The *PDA*, the organization founded by Viravaidya, then galvanized nurses and midwives to

[4] Oxford Poverty and Human Development Initiative, "Measuring multidimensional poverty: Insights from around the world," *Oxford Poverty and Human Development Initiative.* http://www.ophi.org.uk/policy/multidimensional-poverty-index/. Accessed in June 2014.

spread the message of population control. It served well the limited purpose, but the numbers were still too small for the reach they needed to tackle an endemic issue. PDA then put to use millions of shopkeepers at the last mile, enrolling them in the task of propagation of knowledge and the product. At one time, their distribution was better than the largest of multinational consumer brands. Condoms blowing contests, Ms. Condom beauty queen and other innovative activities on the ground were designed to appeal to the Thai sense of fun. Even monks were reportedly enlisted to bless condoms. More important, it destigmatized the entire concept of condom usage. By its choice to proliferate distribution and knowledge like never before, and spread inspiration, Thailand has achieved one of the steepest drops in population control, with the birth rate dropping from 3.3 percent in the 1970s to 0.8 percent by 2000, from 7 children per family to 1.5.

We may need to validate with more research, but at the forefront of transformation in markets like China is detailed segmentation that companies in China do versus ones I have seen anywhere else, and the velocity of their innovations. It is not unusual to find up to 80 market segments identified and products catering to them. Perhaps there is a big learning here for companies seeking to make a difference in the lives of current non-users. Most companies in China did not get carried away by segmentation models of the West where demographics, ownership of assets, and attitude of people tend to converge more than deviate, thus condensing the range of market segments.

Haier, the company that in 2011 had the highest market share in the world in white goods, is an amazing success story in appliances. They have washing machines that can clean even potatoes and peanuts, a boon for their rural customers. For cold regions, they have ones that can operate in freezing water; for hinterlands impacted by mice, they have special wiring-enabled washing machines; for poor grid power areas, inbuilt voltage stabilizers; and for students a small machine that can fit in their college dormitories. Most of us are not farmers that our clothes need a heavy-duty wash. Haier has a washing machine that cleans a single change of clothes. It conserves water and electricity, and is a big hit in metros like Shanghai. This ability to understand what a customer wants as distinct from one-product fits all approach has been supplemented with an enviable distribution channel. At the heart of this last mile revolution is *Goodaymart*. When it comes to low income, less developed, rural markets, all companies tend to outsource distribution to third parties. Not Haier, they have a franchised route to market where they have partnered with local entrepreneurs. "*Goodaymart* has set up over 7,600 county-level, 26,000 town-level exclusive stores, and 190,000 village-level liaison stations. It established delivery stations at over 2,800 counties, deploying more than 17,000 service providers, thereby realizing sales reaching the village, delivery reaching the doorway and service reaching home."[5] Their front end sales teams, technicians who go and repair products and call centers, are tasked to come back with what customers are saying, thus helping them get insights that otherwise require a great effort to unravel. Many products, including the famous washing machine for potatoes, owe their origin to the voice of a customer thousands of miles away from their headquarters. They have also built an enviable go to market, and enjoy commanding market shares.

> The Haier team asked the obvious questions. What are we doing? Why are we doing it? What are the alternatives? Almost no one had asked these questions because the traditional 5,000-year-old system had hardly changed. What they discovered through very careful analysis was that, at a certain scale, it became much more efficient to substitute a circular for a radial distribution system. Once they had that idea, the rest was easy. Implementation was not easy, of course. But, conceptually, the redesign was easy.[6]

Other brands and categories now increasingly employ The Haier highway into mainland to sell their produce, and even Haier reportedly aspires to get half the turnover from non-Haier sales on the formidable last mile they have built in rural China.

---

[5] http://www.haier.net/en/about_haier/brands/goodaymart/
[6] Marshall Meyer, "Going out by going in," *The Haier Model: Using Rural China as a classroom for overseas growth*, Knowledge@Wharton (June 26, 2014).

CONCLUSION

Shashi Tharoor in his *India: from Midnight to Millennium and Beyond*[7] puts it succinctly:

> At the stroke of midnight on August 15, 1947, a new nation was born. It has 17 major languages and 22,000 distinct dialects. It has over a billion individuals of every ethnic extraction known to humanity. It has a population that is 32 percent illiterate, but also one of the world's largest pools of trained scientists and engineers. Its ageless civilization is the birthplace of four major religions, a dozen different traditions of classical dance, and 300 ways of cooking a potato.

It is not unusual to see companies work at multiple knots at the same point of time. The first knot is an amplification of the existing last mile. The second knot enlists similar nodes of distribution to increase the numbers of intermediation points, improve availability, and gain share from the competition. The third knot unlocks consumption and removes blockages in consumption. The fourth knot creates an entirely new value curve by innovating current ways of influencing customers. And the final knot seeks to convert current non-users, and uses an enormous range of comprehensive business models for the purpose. There is nothing sequential about it. Demand does exist at each stage, though the quantum may vary from one knot to another for each category.

A billion consumers, spread over 3.3 million square kilometers, multiplied by the diversity and heterogeneity of India, need innovative solutions. The next chapter explores strategic paths pursued by the Turbonator companies in their pursuit of the demand of a billion consumers.

---

[7] Shashi Tharoor, *India: From Midnight to the Millennium*, (New York: Arcade Publishing), 1997.

4

Sextant Arcs of Turbonators

Alice in Wonderland[1], a novel written in 1865, the story of a girl who falls through the rabbit hole into a fantasy world populated by peculiar creatures, has a delightful exchange between Alice and Cheshire cat. It goes something like this.

> "Would you tell me, please, which way I ought to go from here?" "That depends a good deal on where you want to get to," said the Cat. "I don't much care where," said Alice. "Then it doesn't matter which way you go," said the Cat. "So long as I get somewhere," Alice added as an explanation. "Oh, you're sure to do that," said the Cat, "if you only walk long enough."

Temptations galore. You see massive market opportunity. You see many other companies and categories getting bigger and making money. Some of them have pioneered new markets, a few sowed the disruptive seeds, and many simply replicated what has worked well in other parts of the world. Yet you are flummoxed by a simple question—what is the best path to market perforation?

There are always alternate routes that can get the company to widely the same space. Early in the strategy-making process, the management must grapple with the issue of what directional path a company should take. Shepherding the company to one path versus another, in making this choice, the company stands pledged to its destiny. You can replace people, change products, buy the latest technology, but the directional path, once adopted, is generally difficult to reverse.

---

[1] Lewis Carrol, *Alice in Wonderland,* (United Kingdom: Macmillan), 1865.

Imagine you are a sailor in the seventeenth century, and tasked to move from point A to B. All you have is a vast sea, and you are required to navigate. Once you are out of sight of land, everything looks the same, and it gets worse at night. How would you know which direction to steer the ship, particularly when the shore is no longer visible?

Ocean navigation undeniably was inaccurate and dangerous for centuries, till the year of 1731 when John Hadley invented a device by the name of Sextant. The instrument got its name from the fact that it is equipped with an arc that is one-sixth of a circle. This device is used at sea to determine the distance of the ship from equator, or its latitude as is popularly known. The rest is accomplished by determining the time, the date, and the longitude, which is found by comparing local time with Greenwich. The sextant was the instrument whose invention paved the way for modern navigation and allowed sailors, who were afraid of venturing beyond the sight of land or such familiar position, to go into hitherto lands. While GPS has altered modern-day voyages, most large ships, even now, carry a sextant, a handheld instrument used to measure angles between the sun and the moon and the horizon, as a backup to their GPS systems.

Set out to "unknot" the market, and release unexploited growth opportunities, the Turbonator companies have chosen an array of strategies to win in the market. If you are in waters like a ship, there are various paths you can take to get to the destination. In my observation, as I worked across categories, what these successful companies have deployed can be summarized in terms of six sextant arcs, or paths, available to them:

- *Surge Ahead*, doing better what they do best, replicating the proven success formula with a machine-like consistency; or
- *Grow the Core*, keeping the same core but enriching and fortifying the essence of the root proposition; or
- *Trim Sails*, eliminating costs, processes, and historical way of doing business to come up with a refreshed value chain: or
- *Go Upwind* by leveraging the four key "bullish" secular trends in the market-acompressed discovery process about brands by the Internet savvy young generation, increasing purchasing power, conspicuous consumerism, and rapid urbanization.

- *Go Uncharted* into thus far exclusive and unequaled territories; or
- *Escape Velocity,* basically generate so much of market momentum that it decimates the centrifugal force of gravity.

Demand is unknotted only when either an existing customer value proposition is amplified, or a new one is sired. The strength of these innovative approaches, as you will experience while going through them now, is that these create opportunities for both a company and its customers.

Each path to success must meet a criterion for a company to invest in its development. The criterion is five-fold.

1. The *Scale* of the arc: It must have a scale and profit pool to justify investment in people and distribution structures.
2. The *Growth* potential of the arc: Even if it's a slow burn, the candle must burn bright in some time horizon.
3. The ability to bestow *Competitive* position: It must be an arc wherein one can win and create a sustainable competitive advantage.
4. The *Realism* of the arc: Realism in pursuing opportunities comes when companies get into what is in synch with their vision and capabilities. It's not a mere vision statement that is enough to succeed, as indeed many wishes don't come true. It involves an understanding of where an organization wants to go, but tempered with its capabilities and the context of the market.
5. The *Sustainability* of the arc: Sustainability is the net positive impact of what we do with society, people, and their lives. Look around at companies that have survived and prospered over time. Companies, categories, and ways of doing things that endure the test of time are those that add value to the people they seek to serve.

Each arc of success necessarily comes with a set of numbers, on each of the options. These numbers display market size, investments, growth, contributions, and competitive position over a predefined horizon of time. These six arcs are pictorially depicted in Figure 4.1.

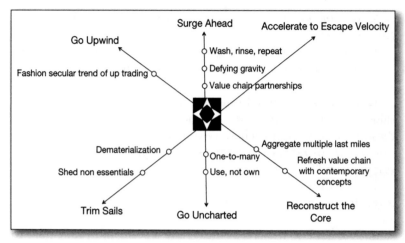

Figure 4.1   Sextant Arcs of Turbonators
Source: Author's own.

SURGE AHEAD: DO BETTER WHAT YOU DO BEST

Turbonator companies, without exception, excel on parameters that matter to the category they are in. Over the years, they have kept on perfecting the same. They never believe what they have is splendid or as good as it can get. Whether it's the ability to improve the velocity of stocks, or reduce bad debts, or innovate products, or cost of distribution, or create a large footprint, or the quality of execution, whatever it is that propels the industry, and gives sustainable competitive advantage, Turbonator companies keep on working at it.

Every industry has a proven success formula. Turbonators happen to execute it better than anyone else. Our work suggests that they are getting sharper at it than their competition. This widening gap is what reflects in their superior performance on cash and profits, even ahead of the relative difference in revenue growths.

There are multiple approaches toward building repeatability. One is the prolific engine of multiplication, breeding a proven success formula, best described as *Wash, Rinse, and Repeat.* The real issue with the emerging markets is that they compel brands to compete at levels they have never before, a challenge that many global brands particularly struggle to overcome. Hence, the second approach is the one that beats the odds, we call it *Defying Gravity*. Finally, the traditional concept of business as "winner takes all" does not provide sufficient propulsion in emerging markets. It is, therefore, important to leverage the collective power of *Value Chain Partnerships* in the quest for growth.

Wash, Rinse, and Repeat

Agra, the sixteenth century capital of the Mughal dynasty, home to a monument such as Taj Mahal, is also a big trading center in the state of Uttar Pradesh. I was on a market visit to Agra. Not far from the Fort railway station, where I got down from the train, is Kinari bazaar, the traditional wholesale and retail market of Agra. The sales representative met me at 9.30 on the dot, in the morning, and we started to navigate the unyielding traffic on his motorcycle, with I tightly tucking my knee, and he weaving his way around with an authority that I have only seen exhibited by heroes in south Indian films. The scene that hit us was one of unending small shops in every conceivable narrow alley, their merchandise flowing into the streets, brand signage carelessly whimpering for attention, cloth banners displayed right in the middle of the road, mish mash of electrical cables creating an art even Picasso could not have imagined, a temple every 50 feet, often right in the middle of the road. But behind all this is the energy and excitement of an Indian bazaar that is difficult to describe unless you experience it.

I started the market visit. Our man was carrying a rugged hand-held smartphone. It had a list of retail outlets that needed to be covered. These were also color-coded depending on whether the retailer had done any business in the month or not. The smart-phone device was equipped with past purchase data, stock out information, status on receivables, and other analytics pertaining to the outlet. Algorithms had converted gigantic pieces of data into information that had meaningful commercial value. The sales order was transmitted instantaneously to the distribution center, and the process of replenishment started usually even before the salesman had left the outlet, thereby cutting time to market, high costs, and avoidable inaccuracies in replenishment. Marketers knew that many purchase decisions were made at the shop itself. A while later, an activation representative walked in with a laptop. His job was to operationalize the agenda on visibility, promotions, and customer engagement. As per the guidelines, the material was stacked, and product promotions and point of sales got displayed prominently. The store was now equipped to service customers. This process was repeated shop after shop every day as per a predefined market beat.

As I set out to analyze this market visit, I deciphered three forces at work that deliver the fortune. *One*, a business must know the sweet spot wherein consumers can be hunted and mined repeatedly for value. In short, the companies must have a success formula that works in the market. *Two*, the power of the success formula is in its execution. The formula is rarely ever a secret. After all it's played out day in and out, often for decades, with some refinements, but nothing radical. But it is people and processes, metrics and technology, culture and values that conspire together to change the quality of execution in one company versus another. *Three*, the revenue is scalable when instructions on success formulae are unambiguous, scripted, and closely supervised for its quality. The sales representative, with whom I worked the market, did the same task, day in and out, without any dilution of effort or intent. Once a success formula had been discovered, it stood institutionalized by way of a process, a way of doing things. Just like the label on shampoo bottles that says what's so obvious; wash, rinse, and repeat, creating a perpetual cycle.

Defying Gravity

Super 30 is the name of a coaching institute in Bihar that trains its students for Indian Institute of Technology (IIT) examinations, a passport to the best in engineering education. More than half a million students write IIT exams each year, and less than 2 percent are admitted. What is unique is that Super 30 is committed to coaching only the poorest of the poor that otherwise have no resources to have an equal opportunity for success. Among the successful students are children born into families of cobblers, roadside vendors, tailors, impoverished farmers, and the like. What their success demonstrates is that a frenzied teacher plus committed students who study 16 hours a day is equal to life out of poverty. Everything else, that we would otherwise believe is a decisive additive to success, pales into oblivion when there is a sense of purpose and direction. The *TIME* magazine has ranked Super 30 as the best school in Asia for 2010. Anand Kumar, the brain behind the brains that make it to IIT, has been on record explaining his underprivileged background, and how he strongly felt the inspiration to stand up and be counted.

Far from the images of thatched Super 30 institutes fighting the sweltering heat of Patna with a dozen odd ceiling fans, there is another India. Large format stores, contemporary and chic, often in shopping malls, are rapidly growing in confidence and customer traction, thus tapping the appetite for contemporary shopping. "Why do customers come a long distance to shop here," I ask an innocuous question to the shop head, seeing the store filled with weekend shoppers. The reply I get is that it is driven by the availability of a range under one roof and trust in their brand. It is logical; a high value and low frequency purchase does tend to gravitate toward aggregation nodes like big box retailers. But then can aggregation alone ever be a sustainable advantage? Can't, for instance, online e-commerce do it on a bigger scale. Started by a former English teacher, last known *Alibaba* was selling 800 million items through 6 million vendors and had sales of $420 billion in China. Amazon has been selling 230 million items in the US. Internet commerce can easily wean away urbanized and rapidly proliferating online customers. No category is safe. Not even a category like foods, which many would consider as the last bastion of the brick-and-mortar structures. This is what *Taobao*, part of the Alibaba stable of companies, does in China. "Users will be able to pre-order rice from suppliers in China's rice bowl provinces in the north. After about 5 days of drying and processing, the rice will be shipped to users allowing them to taste the first rice harvest of the year. Taobao estimated that this direct-shipping model cuts down on warehousing and other costs, reducing the amount of time it can take for a bag of rice to go from field to home from 3-6 months to within two weeks."

To be fair, big box retailers in India are doing much more. They provide a better shopping ambience, carry larger trust, have formalized return and exchange policies, and deploy private labels to engage value conscious customers. But the store team itself seemed detached and disengaged, efficiently carrying out tasks for the day, but not really trying to make a difference. How exactly do they leverage all the customer data they have. Do they figure out why customers buy one product but not another at the store? Do they know of which products their next-door small shop out prices them? Do they know what percentage of catchment they attract, or what merchandise to expand for a specific store, or what "catch phrases" in their point of sales advertising work better? How do they execute the value of probably the last bastion in differentiation, and possibly the best defense against the inevitable onslaught of online sales, the customer experience?

Last miles have been historically associated with just the supply side. Front-end jobs run the risk of descending into lowest common denominator, which is only a warm body. If we turn it upside down, and say that the last mile is equal to demand generation, jobs and job incumbents will begin to steer worthwhile insights.

Super 30, the story we started with, has a stupendous success rate. The institute takes in only 30 students every year. Launched in 2001, 308 of 360 students have made it to IIT. This uncommon consistency is driven by a sense of direction and purpose despite unfathomable challenges that less privileged students of Super 30 encounter on a daily basis.

Value-chain Partnerships

Finally, the traditional concept of business as "winner takes all" does not provide sufficient propulsion in emerging markets. A network of relationships and partnerships propels a business. The imagery of corporate success, perpetuated by management theories on competition, and many not so fulsome movies, is one of savage competition, subterfuge, selfish pursuit of profits. Partly legitimate, but nothing can be farther from the truth. The success in a billion consumer market can't be driven by just competition; it has to be propelled by collaborations and intense network of value accretive relationships.

Let us consider an experience that demonstrates why success is an entirely collective act. About 70,000 babies are born every day in India, one baby every 1.25 seconds, 27 million in a year. Each one of these babies has to be inoculated for polio, a highly contagious virus known for paralyzing its victims. Roughly four doses are recommended at different age points. Prior to 1978, the year when oral vaccination was introduced, nearly 500 children were paralyzed every day by polio. But here too the last mile is daunting. The sheer scale, lack of education, community resistance, and insanitary living conditions in many parts have been thus far enduring obstacles.

> India developed micro maps, breaking regions down by neighborhood, by street, by the house. The goal was to make sure no child fell through the cracks. The government employed global positioning system and geographic information system technology to track mobile populations. It even set up vaccination booths at railway stations.[2]

"The immensity of the Indian campaign can be hard to grasp. There are more than 700,000 vaccination booths in every campaign led by 2.5 million vaccinators."[3] India has been free from polio, for the last four years.

Four execution initiatives enable Value Chain Partnerships agenda to thrive. *One,* a robust partner value proposition, a give and take that's fair, while the remaining value accretive to end users. *Two,* the entities need to have a common view on processes and key data points. They must be seized of the same issues. *Three,* there has to be a continuous investment into skills upgradation. It is not about growing big, it's about growing together. The *fourth* is

---

[2] Elizabeth Stuart, "India's successful polio campaign," February 13, 2014, www.globalpost.com/health.

[3] Esha Chhabra, "The End of Polio in India," *Stanford Social Innovation Review* (Summer 2012).

commitment to key partnership principles of equity, transparency, and mutual benefit.

Whether it is *Wash, Rinse, and Repeat*, or *Defying Gravity*, or *Value-chain Partnerships*, it essentially amounts to perfecting a recipe that works in the market. It is flourishing the genetic endowments of a company in the best possible manner. The value propositions become efficient, but these do not fundamentally reconstruct and transform.

In the next five of six sextant arcs, value curves do alter, each arc progressively deepening the impact on markets and society.

RECONSTRUCT THE CORE: REDEFINE THE CORE PROPOSITION

The core customer proposition does alter over years in every single industry. Companies that grow together with their customers live a long life. Companies that grow apart from their customers become history. Making the customer value curve *contemporary*, synchronized to the new reality, or *aggregating* smaller parts to offer users the value of a bigger piece is a potential route to remain relevant in the market.

Make the Last Mile Contemporary

Consider *Jumbo King*, the chain of outlets that sell *vada paav*, the unassertive Indian version of burgers. A reasonably large market, with about two million pieces being consumed daily, it has been thus far a completely unorganized business. The last mile made up of hawkers selling it on portable stalls created a gaping hole—it wasn't hygienic, there weren't enough flavors, and it left an after-taste of having consumed something down-market as compared to multinational outlets that sell fast food. It's a perfect recipe for rejection by population turning increasingly young. Inevitably located next to a railway station or a high traffic location, Jumbo King changed it all with their contemporary outlets in a clean environment. Their back end is standardized and controls quality, and the front end has standard equipment. They serve this humble snack in innumerable flavors from 53 outlets at the last count.

"In addition to making profits, our aims are constant development of new hand-woven products, a fair, equitable and helpful relationship with our producers and the maintenance of quality on which our reputation rests," says the credo of *Fabindia* founder, John Bissell. A British, Bissell, came to India in 1960, fell in love with an Indian girl and made this country his home. *Fabels* is their recently launched contemporary wear range. For a company that is known for ethnic Indian wear, they are hoping their voguish jackets will look as cool as traditional kurtas did, and fire the imagination of the new generation of shoppers. Of course Fabindia realizes that most new buyers are young and indigenous wear is worn on special occasions alone. There is a need to connect with the new generation. Hence, the makeover.

Enterprise sales have been conventionally built around large sales forces which do face-to-face selling. The buyers are profoundly disaggregated; they vary in size and scale, usage practices, and geography. Growth in the past inevitably meant increasing the size of the sales force. Given that we have an estimated 50 million small and medium enterprises, almost as large as China, proliferation of enterprise products beyond major industrial hubs is a tenacious task. A disruptive new way is being embraced. There is no need for sales teams to knock on every door to discover one that is in need of what they make. Small-to-medium customers can now research, learn, seek help, and even buy online. Software suppliers are the first to offer this. Cloud positioned trial packs enable buyers to check out products before buying them. Digitally facilitated sales models now allow a representative to know the customers who have visited their online site, or taken freebies. This gives the representative a list of enterprise buyers who may have value for their products, and a representative can capitalize on this information to expand their market. This is as far as it can get from days of cold calling so integral in the legacy B2B models, to leads that are now warm.

Aggregate Multiple Last Miles

The real issue with the last miles in India is enormous disaggregation. It made sense when the availability itself was the cause to consume. But today, it has reached the levels of being dysfunctional.

An infinitely small-sized point of sales and interface will never have the resources, people, or capability to be value accretive to customers who seek economy of effort and consistency of experience.

Let us now consider precedents where aggregation has unleashed a cutting edge, topical value chain.

General practitioners, commonly called family doctors, in medicine have traditionally been our first point contact for any ailment. They could handle most of our day-to-day conditions. But a family doctor is unfortunately a depleting breed. No more than 10,000 fresh, trained doctors take to general medicine in a year of the 40,000 graduating students in medicine in India. Not too many general practitioners want to start an independent practice any more, fully aware of their inability to be a one-stop family medicine solution for their patients. The aggregation in the delivery of medicine proposed by newer, corporatized hospital chains is concentrated either in tertiary or specialized care. As a result, primary care patients are compelled to access higher order and more expensive hospitals, and undergo a battery of tests for not so serious ailments. Often we run the risk of seeing a neurosurgeon for a headache and a gastroenterologist for a stomach upset. *Nationwide* is a family doctor based clinic. They run a chain of primary health centers. These operate from corporate offices or residential complexes. Equipped with lab-based services, a pharmacy, 24 by 7 access to doctors, a wide range of health plans, and an option for home visit for elderly patients, nationwide clinics fill the huge gap between fragmented general practitioners and super-specialized hospitals.

An identical issue confounds hundreds and thousands of small and medium enterprises. They do not have the capability and resources to market their wares. The orders they get are by word of mouth. This impedes their growth agendas. *IndiaMART* helps 1.5 million registered users when last known go viral. They have created a platform for buyers and sellers to find each other online. At the last count, 10 million enquiries were getting generated, of which an estimated three million would fructify into a commercial transaction.

Disaggregated businesses face head winds. These are expensive in the absence of economies of scale. The cost of marketing is prohibitive for small producers. From a customer standpoint, these do not offer one-stop solutions. Over time, as we have seen in many industries, Goliaths will ease out Davids. Aggregation into a meaningful construct has created value and inclusiveness, even a recipe for survival of smaller but purposeful businesses, that otherwise were lost.

Come to think of it, so much around us is of value, but their last miles have outlived their resonance. The reason why new value curves propelled by the last mile alterations are needed is that the customers generally move faster than companies and providers of services.

None of the examples given above plays on price or even product, as much as on experience.

TRIM SAILS: ELIMINATE THE NON-ESSENTIALS

How the Mighty Fall is a work by Jim Collins. It is, simply put, a study of failure and mediocrity based on "more than 6,000 years of combined corporate history."[4] He found that one of the key reasons for the failure of companies historically has been "undisciplined pursuit of more." It's not complacency, but over reaching that leads to dilution and compromise. As a disposition we always add more as we grow.

Greg McKeown, the best-known advocate of the concept of essentialism, has the following to advise:

The way of the Essentialist means living by design, not default. Instead of making choices reactively, the Essentialist deliberately distinguishes the vital few from the trivial many, eliminates the nonessentials, and then removes obstacles so the essential things have clear, smooth passage.[5]

Henry Ward Beecher, the American clergyman born in 1813, best known for his support for the abolition of slavery, did say, "In

---

[4] Jim Collins, "How the Mighty Fall: A Primer on the Warning Signs," *BusinessWeek,* May 14 (2009).
[5] Greg Mckeown, *Essentialism; The Disciplined Pursuit of Less* (New York: Crown Publications, 2014), 7.

this world it is not what we take up, but what we give up, that makes us rich."

There are two significant ways last mile value chains have been made to become lean and mean in the process, creating larger markets and customer absorption. The first of these is by *Shedding Non-essentials*, and the second is by the pursuit of *Dematerialization*, a process of conversion of physical assets to digital entities. These deliver a lean and more potent value curve to the customers.

Shedding Non-essentials

What exactly is a non-essential in the value chain is an eternal quest. Some companies have diluted overlapping layers used to move the product around, a few have done away with processes that deviate attention from productive tasks, still others have integrated themselves with their buyers in a bid to remove duplication of similar activities being done by the two entities.

The most classic instance of dilution of layers of distribution and resultant inefficiencies is the famed Dell model of selling directly to consumers when everyone else was using intermediaries. In the process, a significant cost advantage and product customization were accomplished, giving them a leadership run for many years in a category where such ramp position changes rapidly.

Similarly *flat without brokers* is a Mumbai-based setup that delivers exactly as it states. Tenants and landowners interact, build trust, and negotiate directly with each other, and among each other in case of shared accommodations, without any brokerage. Banks that want to reach financial products to deep rural areas, but understand that the cost economics is adverse, have done away with the single largest deterrent, the expensive physical infrastructure by way of a bank branch. They use services of *business correspondents*. Grocery shop owners, public telephone booth operators, retired teachers, village functionaries and other franchises pad up to bat for banks as business correspondents, who sell financial products apart from whatever work they do. There are no fixed costs; people are paid for service actually delivered, thereby eliminating the major disincentive to the cause of serving rural markets.

There is a chemical company that doesn't wish to be named. They sell to hundreds and thousands of manufacturers. Their big buyers are few in numbers, and these buyers bargain hard for best prices. The small and marginal users are more profitable. However, supplying small quantity and delivering service in a category like chemicals is tenacious. The company has been losing this more profitable business of small purchasers due to its inability to grasp low volume but high complexity business. The chemical company then decided to change its tactic. They shed their interference in areas that were beyond their core competence. Their distributors now supply direct to undersized manufacturers who need chemicals. The distributors are able to source from multiple producers and, thus, ensure a complete range of products for their clients; they physically handle all materials, including mixing, blending, and repackaging them as per customer needs. The chemicals company has gained immensely by vacating the turf they were adding no value to, and the small customers are satisfied with one-stop solution to their buying needs.

It is not only parts of a product that can be deemed non-essential. It can also be processes. Consider a mobile device company in India. Their sales people used to squander effort with their distributors just to extract sales orders from them. The financial investments in devices business are large; the market runs on credit and the range of products are enormous. All this made the task of persuasion of distributors for sales orders fraught with enormous pain at the end of the frontline salesmen. The company decided to turn the process upside down. The system algorithm automatically arrives at replenishment needed at each intermediary point on the basis of actual off takes. No sales orders are procured. The material is only replenished to the level of stock norms. By doing away with a process that fundamentally detracts from the real task of sales, the sales force now has the bandwidth to pursue demand generation activities.

Dematerialization

Dematerialization refers to the reduction in the quantity of material required to serve. It means doing more with less, simply put.

Electronic greetings, e-books, music, money, games, software, stamps, shares of companies, and many services have witnessed, with time, substitution of physical flow by digital flow. Material flows are usually more expensive than information flows because physical movement entails costs of handling, loading and unloading, people, insurance, warehousing, shipping, returns, spoilage, and damage. Hence, whenever possible, substituting information flows for material flows cuts cost to serve.

Imagine you are in the business of moving containers on the sea. Nearly everything in this world is transported by ship. It is not a surprise that world trade globally has been growing at almost twice the rate of growth of the economic activity as measured by the world GDP. "If the containers of the Danish company *Maersk* were lined up, they would stretch 11,000 miles, more than halfway round the planet. If they were stacked instead, they would be 1,500 miles high, 7,530 Eiffel Towers."[6] Shipping containers, used for moving material around the globe, is a capital-intensive business. Companies heavily depend on leasing containers as a means of transporting materials across international borders. If you send a container from port A to port B, the probability of having a consignment ready at port B when the first consignment is delivered is low. Multiply this problem with millions of such containers at sea; it is impossible to match demand and supply, a critical imperative in ensuring returns on capital intense assets like a container. *Synchronic Marine* has deployed a neutral global container database. If I need a container to ship material, all I will do is go to their online portal and find out who has surplus containers anywhere in the world, and lease it. It is perfectly natural for even competitors to lease containers to each other.

Telecom companies used to sell paper recharges. Often retailers would be stocked out of the exact denomination of recharge that a customer wanted. Telecom companies too were constrained in the past. They could not offer a large range of products, since the retailers resisted complexity perpetuated by innumerable paper vouchers of different denominations for different products. Electronic recharges, delivered on air, put an end to all these issues. The retailer is now never stocked out, and is not required to manage hundreds of

---

[6] Rose George, *Container Shipping: The Secretive Industry Crucial To Our Existence* (United Kingdom: The Telegraph, September 6, 2013).

denominations in paper. It allows even a small time retailer to sell this product, as the investments that were earlier spread over innumerable denominations are now in one electronic wallet.

Equivalently, consider an electrical wholesaler who has to sell an enormous range. A purchase clerk would in the past dutifully note down lengthy orders from hundreds of retailers. The retailer had no visibility of stocks and, therefore, was forced to work with higher levels of inventory as a buffer to shortfalls in replenishment. There is now a new online software application. The retailers now share the same technology platform as their wholesaler and, therefore, have real-time access to stock availability. All orders are transmitted via a mobile, and retailers would know fulfillment levels instantaneously. This transparency enables retailers to cut the inventories they were forced to keep and redeploy the cash in growing the business instead.

Just follow where the cash goes, either yours or of partners working with you, and chances are you will find ways and means to shed non-essentials, and thereby free constraints on growth.

GO UPWIND: FASHION THE SECULAR TREND OF UPENDING MARKETS

At times we say that India in a few decades from now will be as big an economic superpower as China currently is.

Curious about why China has done so well, the International Monetary Fund (IMF) had examined the source of the nation's economic growth and arrived at a startling conclusion. It is not more capital, as was widely believed, that singularly led to the economic growth in China, validated by the reasonable stability of the capital-output ratio. It was not labor either in the most populous nation that has precipitated double-digit GDP growth for most of the last three decades. It was an improvement in productivity of people that accounted for 42 percent of incremental growth in China.

Prior to the 1978 reforms, nearly four in five Chinese worked in agriculture; by 1994, only one in two did. Reforms expanded property rights in the countryside and touched off a race to form small nonagricultural businesses in rural areas. Decollectivization and higher prices for agricultural products also led to more productive (family) farms and more efficient use of labor. Together these forces induced many workers to move out of agriculture. The resulting rapid growth of village enterprises has drawn tens of millions of people from traditional agriculture into higher-value-added manufacturing.[7]

Though this is not the full story of China's transformation, but the limited point here is the deep transformation in the society, attitudes, and occupations of people that accompany economic rejuvenation.

In 2013, China accounted for almost 30 percent of the world's economic growth. Brazil, Russia, and India, the other three nations of a forum called BRIC everyone thought would drive the global markets, collectively accounted for less than 7 percent.

Huaihai road in Shanghai, often likened to Tokyo's Harajuku, is known as the fashion district of Shanghai. Featuring everything fashion-related from clothes to accessories, the street is dotted with huge malls and major shopping outlets. If you care to look into developments in retail in China, or the way people dress up, or the assets they own, surging incomes go in only one direction—these propel demand for better quality and superior value products. The secular trend of the market is up trading. Either the brand will lead consumers up that path, or the customers will find another companion brand on the journey to improve their life.

The Boston Consulting Group (BCG) and Confederation of Indian Industry (CII) have examined in detail the shape and size of consumption expenditure, and its expected evolution from 2010 to 2020. They have broadly identified four household segments; Affluent (6%), Aspirer (14%), Next Billion (30%), and the remaining half of households as Strugglers. The report suggests that as one moves up the income ladder, the share of spending on food as a proportion of total income declines. A struggler spends 42 percent

---

[7] Zuliu Hu and Mohsin S. Khan, "Why is China growing so fast", *Economic Issue Number 8*, Page 5, International Monetary Fund copyright 1997.

of income on food; an affluent spends less than half of it. In the decade ahead, therefore, all categories from telecommunication to apparel will grow, most around 3.5 times the current level, and foods will grow at a lower rate of 2.4 times the current value. Should this come true, a lower number of 28 percent of households will be "struggler" households in 2020. The contribution of "affluent" to consumption that is currently at 24 percent, from just 6 percent of households, will grow to 39 percent in 2020.

Trading up is not about luxury products. It is also not about affluent consumers alone. Whether trading up beats trading down is liable to vary by product category, trends in disposable incomes, and with the value being offered.

GO UNCHARTED: FRUGAL, CONSTRAINT-DRIVEN INNOVATIONS

The pattern of growth across nations in the world has been changing for some time. Accelerating rates of growth in emerging economies have challenged the hegemony of the developed economies of the past. An article in *The Economist* in 2013 best summed up remarkable variations in growth and its impact on the world.

> This year will be the first in which emerging markets account for more than half of world GDP on the basis of purchasing power, according to the International Monetary Fund (IMF). In 1990 they accounted for less than a third of a much smaller total. From 2003 to 2011 the share of world output provided by the emerging economies grew at more than a percentage point a year. The remarkably rapid growth the world has seen in these two decades marks the biggest economic transformation in modern history. Its like will probably never be seen again.[8]

The attractions of the emerging markets are obvious—expanding populations, booming middle class, and limited competition by way of domestic competitors. However, success in these markets is not a guarantee. The issues that face the emerging economies are

---

[8] "Emerging Economies, When Giants Slow Down," *The Economist*, July 27 (2013).

very basic. Resources are short of need. Solutions are unlikely to be off the shelf. Everyone isn't going to become rich. Not in a hurry in any case. These markets, therefore, call for constraint-driven innovations.

We have assumed that products can be consumed only if these are bought and sold even if sparsely used. The first approach is to amplify the numbers of people who can share the scarce resource, *one-to-many* as is called. The second manner to go into uncharted terrains is to *disaggregate usage from ownership*. After all Mahatma Gandhi did say, "The world has enough for every one's need, but not enough for everyone's greed." Ownership perpetuates greed particularly in products sparsely used. The way to grow and get to a billion wallets may well be by taking more people to consume what you produce, in the process making lesser by way of revenues from individual customers, but leveraging the collective value of a large mass of such customers.

One-to-many

Imagine a world where constraints in infrastructure impede levels of consumption, and hence limit growth and diffusion of such products and services to people. People who live in populous nations understand how finiteness of resources impedes progress. There has to be a means by which we separate delivery from infrastructure constraints and enable many more people to simultaneously consume.

Let us consider the case of education. A UNICEF India report states, "90 million females in India are non-literate. 20 per cent of children aged 6 to14 are still not in school and millions of women remain non-literate despite the spurt in female literacy in the 1990s."[9] The real issue is its last mile constrained by inadequate infrastructure. There aren't enough schools and colleges. Because classrooms are limited, only a handful of children can get higher education. No doubt that in most parts of the world, college education is prohibitively expensive. The supply is far short of demand.

---

[9] UNICEF India.

NIIT Cloud campus does not have brick-and-mortar classes, they have cloud classrooms. There are live and interactive real-time classrooms powered by their synchronous learning tools and technology. Access to the best quality teaching, and teachers, lessons on demand, online assessment, laboratory exercises in machine rooms, is some of the revolutionary features. They offer more than 100 courses to half a million students already.

Distinctly superior in cost economics, this concept holds significant value in proliferation of what we make to consumers who need it.

Use, Not Own

Companies necessarily assume that their business is manufacturing, whether of a product or a service. And the way to make money is by selling these things to a buyer at a price. Buyers have also presumed that they have to own something to be able to consume it, such has been the power of consumerism that has impacted the entire world.

Human needs in this scenario where everyone aspires to own the best are in excess of means. A proxy way to look at this is the public debt of the governments, symbolic of expenses that exceed their capacity to generate revenues. They have spent money that has not been earned. The governments in the world as a whole have run a public debt of $54 trillion at the last count. India's entire economy is less than $2 trillion; the US economy is $16 trillion, just to put this number on public debt in a perspective.

A range of online services, from cars to accommodation, bicycles to household appliances have emerged, thus far largely in the Western world, wherein the customer rents the service for the period they wish to consume directly from buyers who have no use for that product at that point of time. Airbnb and *RelayRide*s are classic examples in this direction. Many software suppliers give out bulk packs for multiple simultaneous users at a discounted price. The Internet makes it easier to aggregate buyers and suppliers. And online social sites help establish trust. This idea, in a spirit of collaborative consumption, enables millions of people to rent things to each other.

In all these cases the transformation is real, from selling of products to commercial collaboration.

ESCAPE VELOCITY: YOUR COMPANY'S FUTURE BEYOND THE TIPPING POINT

In physics, escape velocity is the speed that an object needs to be traveling to break free of planet or moon's gravity well and leave it without further propulsion. For example, a spacecraft leaving the surface of the Earth needs to be going at seven miles per second, or nearly 25,000 miles per hour to leave without falling back to the surface or falling into orbit. Escape velocity in business alludes to the momentum needed for an idea to surge.

Telecom, when introduced in India, used to sell only post-paid connections. Customers had to settle bills after the billing cycle. Some of them would not pay up as well. Since companies were taking the credit risk, only so many customers who could demonstrate proper financial paperwork could take the credit and own a mobile connection. The market was limited; a few shops plus some direct sales agents would do the telecom business. A small-sized business, however, taxes a customer for scale disadvantage. Costs, and telecom is capital-intensive, are defrayed over a smaller pool of subscribers in a diminutive business; hence, average call tariffs were high. Indeed customers paid even for receiving an incoming call in those days. A fast forward many years hence, prepaid as a product was launched, whereby customers paid upfront for what they wished to consume. More important, the size of recharge went down to as low as ₹10. A customer could now freely choose how many calls to make. The product did not come with pre-defined contours like fixed rental in this case. The distribution was democratized and even a roadside tobacco shop was now eligible and financially capable to be a point of sales. Instead of a few shops that used to sell, there was now hardly any street or an alley that did not have a retail point propagating telecom products, carrying brand signage, and enticing customers to their consuming class. In one go, the industry exploded its distribution and customer base. The escape velocity was reached. In the decade between

2000 and 2011, the subscriber additions had grown at a staggering 73 percent CAGR.

The telecom story is unique in being able to create an ecosystem, a larger business model, and an astounding engagement with the customers. The secret sauce to viral growth is to get customers buzzing. The contours of cellular development, which perhaps hold some lessons, may help unknot other categories with enhanced urgency.

Dr GNS Reddy is, similarly, attempting to give people in villages means to a better livelihood. He has created a technology loop for farmers in Karnataka. Each farm has an enclosure where cows are fed nutritious diet. They are milked by automatic suction, and the milk is sent directly for refrigeration. Automation enables remote monitoring. Each cow has an identity number and is monitored centrally for quality. Vans come in the evening for collection of milk from farmers. The milk is processed as per European standards for organic milk and is sold in the nearby urban markets. The manure collected is used to generate electricity in a biogas plant.

> Focusing on farmers whose major crop are small orchards, Dr. Reddy shifts their farming practices to use the free ground to grow fodder and other crops and to introduce automated organic dairy farming. He supports farmers to invest in cows, milking and chilling systems for the milk, a biogas plant, and a sprinkler system for the farm. To run this technology, the cow manure is funneled into a biogas plant that provides electricity to the entire farm. Equipped with technology and the energy to run it, Dr. Reddy has handed over the dairy production and manufacturing chain to the farmers and made them the managers of operations and marketing for their farms.[10]

Unlike the "mopping up" operation of other milk companies, this is an uncommon, self-sufficient, sustainable business model.

---

[10] Ashoka India, *Investing in new solutions for our Worlds' toughest problems*, http://india. ashoka.org/fellow/gns-reddy. Accessed on August 04, 2015.

CONCLUSION

To get to escape velocity, an occurrence where billion hearts are abuzz, entails working an entire lot of things in collaboration. I would say these are (a) a business idea that addresses a genuine need of its customers; (b) a sense of pride in ownership of the product or service by its users; (c) a product that is not pre-manufactured but can be cut to the size of the wallet, thereby encouraging diverse consumers to purchase; (d) a market system that eliminates any form and kind of transmission loss; (e) local presence by way of an entrepreneur who disseminates knowledge and confidence, and has stakes in success; (f) continual engagement with your customers, a means by which you are top of mind, an easy and a useful presence in their lives; (g) preferably prepaid as a mode of sales, it removes legacy issues in collections of debt, which inevitably restricts the proliferation of products.

Let us, in conclusion, summarize our key arcs.

Sextant Arc	Key Theme	Key Action
Surge ahead	Efficiency propels market gains	Do better what you do best
Grow the core	Inclusive, contemporary value curves	Reinvent the core customer proposition
Trim sails	Refreshed value chain	Eliminate the non-essentials
Go upwind	Better products and services	Fashion the secular trend of upending markets
Go uncharted	Innovative value curve	Frugal, constraint-driven innovations
Escape velocity	Substantive momentum, transformative value curve	Your company's future beyond the tipping point

The word success in Google search yields about 1,070 million results, reflecting how incredibly important it is for all of us. Soccer yields less than 755 million results, just to put it in perspective. But to get there, and remain there in the long term, is a process, not an end state, an institution, not rhetoric. None of the companies we know got it overnight. For them, it's a reward for years of hard work in the market, and with clients.

Early day boats with just sails, irrespective of how big their hull was, could only go so far from the shore. It needed revolutionary Turbonation technology to transform the industry. Companies and business are no different in India's billion consumer market at this point of time. Beyond availability and land grab, the traditional center of gravity in the last mile models thus far, they all are in need of propulsion to transform the pace of diffusion of products and their impact on the society at large.

And at the core of the transformation process in a company is a machine, an engine, what we call Revenue Turbine. The revenue turbine is the instrument to bring the strategic path to life. The task of the revenue turbine is to unknot the demand, deliver scalable revenues, and to be strategic in its quest for competitive differentiation. The process of getting to such a revenue turbine is detailed in the next chapter.

5   The Revenue Turbine

Why is a question of yesterday. How is a question of tomorrow.
—MARK ROLTON

As a manager, you would want to build more value in your enterprise, become the measure others hanker to emulate, deliver prosperity to the shareholders who have put faith in you, and help shape a company that is an employer of choice for bright minds. But the questions are: what drives the company value? Why does the stock market reward some companies with dizzying multiples in valuation and discount most others?

Predictable, growing, profitable, and long-term sustainability of revenue performance is at the core of trust a few companies have with their stakeholders. One can say that revenue is just a number, a numeral. Indeed one among many statistics. But this one figure is an affirmation of the character of your business. It reflects the faith and engagement of customers with your brands. It is the abiding substantiation of superiority of your strategy and execution over your competition. It is the corroboration of trust and commitment of your employees and business partners. If there is one number that says it all, amid many measures that are indicative of a company's performance, it is the quantity and quality of revenues in a company. "Over the long term, revenue growth powers 75 percent of total shareholder return (TSR) for the upper-quartile value creators of the S&P 500."[1]

The challenges in the emerging markets like India are uncommon and mammoth. The opportunity is large, but many companies can testify that getting customers to part with their money isn't that

---

[1] Rich Hutchinson, "The Go-To-Market Revolution," *BCG Insights,* May 2 (2014).

easy. Market penetration numbers will corroborate that there are more non-users than consumers across most categories. Even those who consume are young and inexperienced, and many still flirt with competing brands. The quantum of their usage is low. Replacement frequency for products that come with expiry dates is lethargic. While in every category there is a traditional channel of distribution, the new ones are growing exponentially, progressively threatening old and entrenched ways of trade. From the Internet commerce to modern trade, there is a recalibration of channel power. In the past, a relationship with intermediaries and clients could get our business; today, the same transaction needs more legs to stand on.

India is a growing market, but this growth is neither uniform nor universal. The tasks it demands for a company are diverse. To be successful, a company needs to cultivate users, deepen usage, grow category, be unique and differentiated versus competition, invest just ahead of the curve into right channels of distribution and growth segments, nurture right markets and right tasks, and given the size and complexity, run business like a well-oiled machine capable of repeatability.

Historically constructed sales machine, as the name suggests, is just a sales machine, and now, in the context of diverse and complex tasks in the market, needs to be upgraded to drive revenue agendas of a company. A precision machine, *Revenue Turbine*, as distinct from a sales machine, inspired by an 1884 invention by Charles Parsons of a *Turbine* that dramatically altered shipping and power generation industries, is what is needed to systematically, in a process-driven way, enable companies to comprehend, and indeed execute, the large India agenda. The idea must be not only to access billion wallets, but also to make a difference in the lives of the people company touches, which in turn will endow the brand with the capability to replicate this success again and again.

LIFE PATH NUMBER 4

People with number 4, as in numerology, are the worker bees of the society. They are determined, practical, down to earth, cerebral, and known to put in long hours of work. Transformations, not surprisingly, as one looks at the world around, are often a four-step process, and call for diligence and persistence. In the world of Buddhism, a religion with more than 300 million followers, enlightenment goes through four steps, before culminating into "Arhat," the ultimate point of perfection. The world of psychology similarly has four steps of competence, starting from unconscious incompetence to conscious incompetence to conscious competence, and finally unconscious competence, a culminating rung wherein the individual has had so much practice with the skill that it becomes a second nature.

Revenue Turbine also goes through four steps of development. These four steps provide a framework that directly and indirectly controls a company's destiny and its market valuations. More important, it's an assessment of the work needed to get to subsequent steps. The prize at the end of the cycle, akin to enlightenment, is full realization of organizational capabilities.

PROPELLING THE LAST MILE WITH A REVENUE TURBINE

A revenue turbine in a company must be visualized as a machine, an engine, which is charged with the responsibility to deliver the company its strategy, and to unseal the latent demand of a billion customers in the market. Companies do vary in this capability. The four steps in the development of the last mile capability, as I worked across multiple businesses are: amorphous, growth, performing, and leading. Firms are liable to be at either of these, often also straddling in between varying stages, but the center of gravity of their last mile would lie at one step or another. These four steps together make the last mile maturity model, as depicted in Figure 5.1.

It is fair to expect that firms with an amorphous last mile are unlikely to be opening the fourth or fifth knot of demand. They would be preoccupied with trying to stay afloat, fending off competitors in the existing market space. This, among other things, is what happened to incubators in their epic battle with Turbonators. The tasks an organization has set up for itself and the capability of its last mile must be synchronized for outcome to be delivered.

	Amorphic	Growth	Performing	Leading
Processes, and Practices	Unstructured Processes Decisions are arbitrary driven by hierarchy!	Basic distribution processes are defined. Functional capability is in place	Advanced processes like sales forecasting tools, inter-functional coordination and practices	Real time information, established business practices, trust and transparency
Goals/ KPIs	Quantity focused internal targets	Value focused internal targets	Revenue and market share targets	Revenue, market share and profit/ contribution targets
Organization dynamics	More than 5 levels of hierarchy, Structure is informal and direct	Formal processes but task driven	Strong functional structure with formal processes	Structure is business unit, accountable to customers, less hierarchy
Cost of Go To Market	Higher than the market	At par with the market	Lower than the market	Significantly lower than the market, gives a distinct advantage of costs and cash velocity versus competition
Performance	Inconsistent	Meets internal targets	Meets internal target and grows better than the market rate	Leads market, consistently gains revenue market share, predictable and repeatable revenue capability
Planning Horizon	Less than 1 year	1 year	Up to 3 years	5 Years plans, with strong spotlight on current year performance
Automation	Limited Automation	Real time visibility of the Key market data. Contemporary Processes particularly in supply Chain and customer interfaces	Networked systems with business partners, tech as a differentiator	Cutting edge technology, effective use of algorithms, mobile apps, Global Positioning Systems, etc.
Treatment of Metrics	Ad-hoc management of data	Basic management of information. Some processes exist to make decisions basis data	Functionally capable metrics	Incisive and market leading metrics, three and sixty degree view of the performance
Fundamental Construct	Basic Sales Apparatus	Evolving Sales machine, focuses on availability and client development	Sales practices actively develop business for the company	Sales practices grow the category, procreate demand, convert nonusers

Figure 5.1   The Last Mile Maturity Model
Source: Author's own.

FORGING A REPEATABLE AND PREDICTABLE REVENUE TURBINE

The problem with steam engines, in use before the invention of turbines, was conspicuous. These were used to drive pistons using pressure and not the velocity of steam, thus losing substantive power and entailing prohibitive costs. The principle of subdividing the whole expansion of the steam into a number of stages so that only comparatively moderate velocities have to be dealt with, still forms the basis of all efficient turbine designs. Like Parsons, our Revenue Turbine follows stages. Methodologically each step unlocks a part of the value.

There are seven stages in the formulation of a Revenue Turbine. These seven stages are as depicted in the Figure 5.2.

Step 1: The *Revenue Turbine* Blueprint

We need to know where we are at present in the last mile, and what is the farthest point in the opportunity funnel that we need to travel to. We operate in a world where our partners and customers actively make a choice. This exercise is therefore conducted not only for us, but also for the industry leader, and other relevant competitors. The tool we use to extract our current state is a *benchmarking* exercise. Benchmarking tells us where we stand, and can be a stunning confrontation with reality. What we now need is the farthest point of trajectory to know how far and where the business needs to go in a defined frame of time. We need a map of the future. The tool used to discern the future is the *Opportunity Arena*. It defines the future we intend to pursue and build a winning position in.

Benchmarking

Let's begin with benchmarking that tells us our current state.

At a conceptual level, a company must have an advantage in the market. A company must be doing something that uniquely solves the need in a market, and the competition must be disadvantaged in replicating or imitating it. Without these two simultaneous

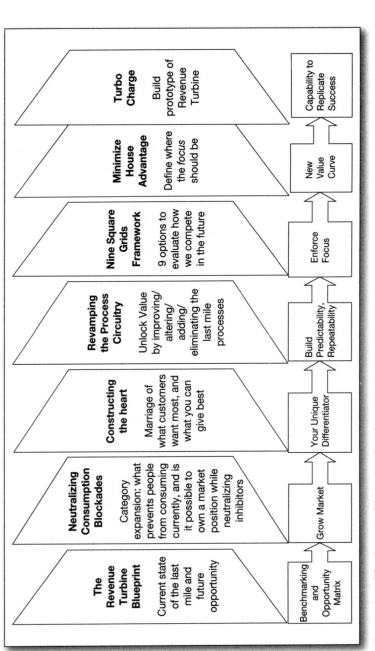

Figure 5.2 The Revenue Turbine—Roadmap
Source: Author's own.

preconditions being met, the business case for an enterprise will have serious issues in its endurance. We, therefore, need to benchmark competencies and output parameters that give sustained and unique advantage to a company. The advantage a company can have broadly can be of five kinds:

- *Constitutional,* wherein your stature in the market defines your ability to compete. Leaders always live the proverbial nine lives. Structural advantage is a pole position that bestows market leverage.
- *Delivery difference,* whereby your actions/capabilities in the market create perceptible and sustainable contrast with the other competitors. For instance, in a market perpetuated by radio cabs, *Uber* and *Ola* launched an asset light, mobile-application-based taxi service, and wriggled out a substantive share of the market at the time of the launch.
- *Value,* whereby your people capability, intellectual capital, processes and managerial competence give your customers a better value.
- *Market foresight,* that alludes to the company's capability for a winning streak, to continually upstage and out think their rivals in the future as well.
- *Category builders,* a handful of companies understand that ability to grow the industry, and their dominance in the newer but faster growing niches, is the best way to make the competition increasingly irrelevant.

It is said that the brain stores information in patterns and associations. This first step in spawning a transformational revenue turbine is to benchmark visually. The result of this exercise is an optical map of where one stands versus industry average and the leader. The choice of competition and the choice of parameters are critical because often these do not even lie within industry boundaries. Hence, the lens of a customer and not a producer is suggested. It will not be sensible for a PC company today, to illustrate the point, to disregard the ecosystem of other screens, when conducting this exercise.

The parameters have been carefully chosen. These are the parameters wherein top-level differentiation is valuable, and should be attempted. It cuts across industry boundaries, though one can always include any industry-specific variable if that variable impacts success in the category. The benchmarking for market advantage is as depicted in Figure 5.3.

Put together, these parameters provide a comprehensive picture of the current last mile capabilities. These parameters have an elaborate worksheet attached to it, and when scored with real data, it generates a visual panorama. This panorama tells the top-level storyline of both the industry and your competition. One such illustration, done for a client, with its results, is reproduced here, as shown in Figure 5.4.

Each advantage calls for a different set of competence and capabilities. More important, a challenger in the market cannot be a me too, but must occupy some distinct advantage. If you are infirm versus the leader in each of these four potential market advantages and have no real plans to circumvent the legacy disadvantage, it is quite likely that the future will not be different either. The center of gravity must reside somewhere, there has to be competence that is unique and differentiated.

Opportunity matrix

The purpose of any strategy exercise must not be to arrive only at budget numbers as remnants but to determinedly juice out all potential opportunities in the market.

Seeing the future is a tough task. Multiple prisms may be needed to arrive at the best-case scenario. We employ *four* different ways to make an attempt to read the future.

- The first framework to pinpoint opportunities is around *Market Growth and Structure*. To construct future, trajectory as the basis is applied. Not all changes are discontinuous and disruptive. Most have trends. Buried deep into those trends is the right ammunition to look ahead. It's crucial, therefore, that we delve into the history of our markets and segments, see their evolution, and deploy insights thus gained to

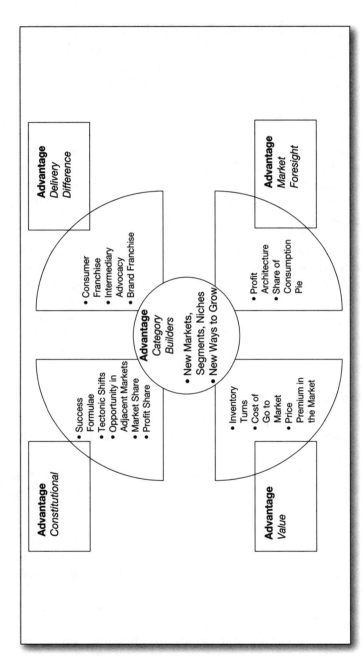

Figure 5.3   Benchmarking for Market Advantage
Source: Author's own.

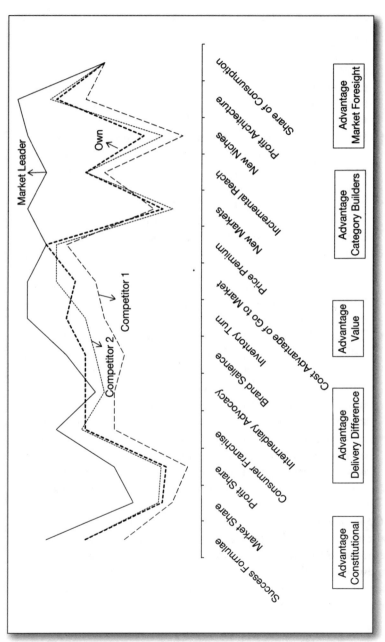

Figure 5.4   Benchmarking for Market Advantage
Source: Author's own.

predict future. The data that we think through can consist of the lead indicators, lagging or coincidental indices, a bit like views from within a vehicle through the windshield, the rearview mirror, or the side window. All are important for us to remain on course. A business finally is an intricate balance between future opportunities and past capabilities, and this framework accomplishes just that.

- In the second subset of the opportunity matrix, we bring in *Competition*. In particular we ask about the big moves recently made, or proposed. Customers make choices. We must be the choice they make.

- The third part of opportunity matrix is in *Foresight*. It is an assessment of big changes that are anticipated in a horizon of three to five years. The developments can be in the construct of products (new segments) and some may be already underway in another adjacent category, not necessarily yours. The transition can also be in the way markets are currently being serviced. The purpose of this exercise is to take note of developments in our markets, customers, and technology.

- The fourth component in the opportunity matrix is what we call *Market Pathfinder*. Think of answers to these three questions. Who are our customers? What do they need from us? And what can we be uniquely good at? These are the qualitative parameters that validate our success formula, reflecting why consumers, clients, and influencers buy us, and will continue to. And more important is the messaging convergent across different touch points in the value chain. A brand has a strategic position; hopefully, it is differentiated. But does the same positioning echo all the way to the consumer?

Opportunity Matrix, therefore, is a blend of quantitative and qualitative, past and future trends, market and our strengths, all integrated into one framework. Given the times we live in, a framework like this, when applied, will reveal a future likely to be different from where one stands today. The blueprint for an opportunity matrix is shown in Figure 5.5.

Market Growth and Structure

	Today -5 years	Today -3 years	Today	Today +3 years	Today +5 years
Industry Growth					
Industry Revenues					
Industry Profits					

Foresight

- New products
- New channels
- New markets
- New potential partnerships
- Sell complementary products
- New technology
- New processes
- New ways to sell
- Ways to enhance supply chain capability

Competition

- What new entrants have entered industry, and what are they doing
- Big competition moves made recently
- Potential competition moves

Market Pathfinder

- What did we set out to accomplish as a business
- What do we do best
- How are we perceived by our clients
- Insights on target consumers, target channels, target intermediaries, and their needs
- The differentiating reasons consumers buy us
- Reasons to believe, the proof to trust our claim

Figure 5.5 Building an Opportunity Matrix
Source: Author's own.

Step 2: Neutralizing Consumption Blockades

There is a striking data. The Turbonator companies have had the best growth when the categories they are in grew the most.

Growing the category is perhaps the most underrated management concept. When Maruti Suzuki sets up its own driving schools to train more people, including women, to drive, or when McDonald's separates vegetarian kitchen from a non-vegetarian for Indian customers, they are determinately neutralizing reasons why people do not consume what they produce.

Ask any customer service department that is charged with the responsibility of growing wealth from the existing customers, anywhere between 10 percent to 30 percent of the company wide margins come from the customer service departments.

If a product category is not perforated enough in the market, or consumers use it sparingly, and replace the product infrequently, this dilution in the value of consumption transpires for many reasons, unique for each category. It can be because of issues in constructs of products, or in their delivery, or in their ability to connect and engage customers, or even affordability. We look at these triggers to consumption. We put this information through a funnel seeking data points on what inhibits, and a potential role the last mile reconstruction can make to help the cause of getting more users, and usage. The Grow Market framework is depicted in Figure 5.6.

Step 3: Constructing the Heart: Five-E Model

To build a heart is not something natural to a company that so far knows how to build machines and deploy technology. We attempt to build the heart for a revenue turbine using what is described as Five-E Model.

Once you start thinking of a business in terms of relationships rather than for-profit transactions, the obvious question is: what can you give your customers that they can't get elsewhere?

The voice of stakeholders is presumed in a company, but often not heard loud and clear. Our next step in the construction of a

Industry/Category		Current Status	Inhibitors	Best Practice(s) from another category	What needs to change?
Product Construct	Motivation to Consume				
	Velocity of Innovations				
	Benefit to Customers				
Delivery	Availability				
	Service Ecosystem				
Customer Connect	Experience				
	Engagement				
	Ease of Relationship				
Adoption	Affordability				
	Efficiency				
	Profit Recipe				
	Market Concentration				
Trust	Transparency				
	Accountability				
	Digital Connect				

Figure 5.6 Neutralizing Consumption Blockades (Grow Market)
Source: Author's own.

revenue turbine brings in the perspective of key stakeholders like customers/clients and retailers/intermediaries. After all, the heart is something that should resonate with the community we intend to serve.

Consider this case. The seeds of revolution in communications in India were first sown in the mid-nineties when the government allowed private firms to offer mobile services. The first licenses were given for four metro towns in 1995 and for 18 other geographies in 1998. At the time of liberalization, state-owned firms had a monopoly of the Indian telecom market. They had a stranglehold on fixed line and the best quality of spectrum for mobility, a key ingredient to profitability and customer satisfaction in telecom. Private operators, despite no visible differentials in technology, went about painstakingly setting up what they called *Match Box Distribution* (implying that telecom should be sold from every outlet that is capable of selling a universal, low value product like a matchbox); while state-owned setups continued to remain challenged in the arena of service and availability of their products. From which shop to buy products of a state-owned Telecom Company is an unfathomable mystery even today. For a business that was recruiting new customers by the millions in a month, who needed *convenience* of product availability and a point of service, it is indeed an unpardonable lapse. Not all private operators are currently listed on the stock market, but if they were, approximately $120 billion of wealth by way of market capitalization has been created in this sector since the mid-nineties. There is no other sector, barring perhaps information technology, which has accumulated wealth of this magnitude post-liberalization. It's safe to say that state-owned setups have more or less missed a substantive part of this newly generated wealth.

Some years hence, but not too far away, insurance market too was opened up to private competition. The best of national and international brands rolled in, with the next generation products, global experience, strong brands, and superior ability to service. However, more than a decade and a half later, the state-owned *Life Insurance Corporation* continues to dominate. Private players have sliced away some share of the market. No more than 30 percent, however, is split between 24 players who originally came to India. These firms certainly did not walk away with the market, unlike the case of telecom. The Life Insurance Corporation did not dilute its stranglehold on one key driver to success, which is at the heart of this business. With one million strong agents in a business procured predominantly face-to-face, *basis relationships and trust*, the Life Insurance Corporation continues to be an industry leader by far.

Our work has shown that there are five drivers that matter to key stakeholders. They are decisive in the construction of a heart for companies. These cut across industry boundaries, though these may differ in the intensity of impact in one category versus another.

Empowered Pricing is an intuitively right parameter in a society that still has pangs of guilt with conspicuous consumption. India is a value sensitive market. Not only trickle down of wealth to the poor has been slow, the buildup of conspicuous rich, unlike in China, has also been slow. It's difficult to imagine a business in India with scale but not capable of delivering the best value. We do know a brand like *Xiaomi* took just four years in China to upstage entrenched global brands. *Micromax*, a homegrown company, as of now threatens the biggest global brands in mobile devices. Micromax is a half-billion-dollar business, growing rapidly and successfully, and straddles a range of price points. They strongly believe that the Indian model of value sizing products is exportable to other parts of the world. That explains their international forays, and indeed many brands of India, from *Bajaj Auto* in automobiles to *Bharti Airtel* in telecom services, have replicated successfully the India value story in emerging markets across the globe.

Empowered pricing need not be confused with the lowest prices. It has to be seen in the context of perceived value. For many gadgets, like those of Apple, for instance, the same customer is willing to pay a higher price because of the firm conviction on the product and brand superiority.

Exceptional Reason to buy is a key customer trigger in the purchase funnels. Consider *Apple* once again, a company that reportedly rakes in half the global profits on mobile phones, despite just selling an estimated 5 percent of global volume sales of mobile devices. Marta Kagan has written a fascinating blog titled "7 reasons your brand will never be as awesome as Apple." These go something like this. Your product kinda stinks. You are not pretty enough. You break your promises. You don't care enough about your customers. You are spread too thin. You need to grow a pair. The last of these is a deal breaker; you don't have a good reason "why." Everyone knows what a company does. Why it does what it does, and how, a clear and compelling reason, and how it will change the world, is what catapults brands to leadership. Consider these consumer propositions. Brooklyn based *Mast Brothers* create handmade chocolates. They personally source best cocoa from all parts of the world, and make small batches, with sophisticated tastes, wrapped in colorful custom papers, and sold from specialty food shops. *Fleisher's* is a butcher shop. Their meats are organic, of grass-fed animals, free of antibiotics or hormones. *Amada* makes press brakes for wide bending range. Their patented slit-crowning feature ensures consistent angle accuracy. The customer proposition in all these cases is unique, compelling, and easy to communicate.

Power messaging enables sales conversations that can create opportunities. The most effective and compelling B2B marketing case studies, for instance, are those where the focus is clearly on the business implementing the solution, not on the company who sold it. These work even better when buyer testimonials advocate as to how the brand helped them find a solution. The reason for acquiring a brand has to be apparent to all, including customers, employees, and trade partners, even competition.

Elucidation selling is increasingly a differentiator that both consumers and retailers seek. It is pronounced in B2B selling. Many years ago, the sales representative was the only fountainhead of information. They would meet customers, armed with savvy marketing literature and polished communication skills, and sales would happen. Times have now changed. Stakeholders have access to more information from the Internet, competition, and market. They are more than half way through the selling process by the times this representative meets them today. It's not about telling basic product features or prices; chances are customers know it already, and they know for the competition as well. For sales to happen, what is needed is an ability to give compelling insights to an informed buyer, to address obstacles to closing sales, and to offer solutions rather than information. Sales machinery made up of representatives that add value to their stakeholders, and help grow a market, builds a kinship and relevance that's tough for the competition to replicate.

Ease of Relationship is the next factor. Research has suggested most repeat purchase decisions people make are out of habit. We do not stand in front of shopping aisles every single time and make buy decisions. Habituated buying decisions are a reality. If customers prefer to be on autopilot, when making a buy decision, the implications for a company are clear. We have to make it uncomplicated and effortless for our customers to continue to buy our products. Ease of relationship at the last mile comes from ease of availability and ease of doing business with a company. *Availability* is a great imperative, not surprising, given the scale and complexity of India. It's an ability in the supply chain to deliver the right product at the right place and time. Retailers and clients want easy availability to free up their cash that can get blocked into inventories, and for customers, in any case, it's more like a hygiene factor. In our experience, we have seen most brands that sell more are also available more. This parameter also alludes to ubiquitous distribution. Any cola company will tell you that the reason their delivery trucks roll out at 6 AM in the morning is to make sure that their millions of points of sales are stocked up. They know in an impulse buy category, being first, and being universal, leads to market share.

Empathy is the final factor. Theodore Roosevelt once said, "Nobody cares how much you know unless they know how much you care." Though pronounced with service brands like healthcare, hotels, and banks, it is, simply put, an ability to identify with the needs of your customers, before, during, and after the transaction. In our view, empathy comes from multiple sources, but in the construct of last miles, it has essentially three levels for a company to engage with. One is when companies move from a singular focus on internal targets to outcome and impact. If Amul concurrently develops both market and society or when the e-Chaupal of ITC empowers farmers with information, they are going beyond the call of their sales targets, and building a relationship difficult for the competition to replicate with ease. Two, when brands educate customers about how usage of what they produce can improve their lives, again a bond is established with the customers. And finally when a brand offers a sustainable livelihood to people while selling products, it again connects deeply (Project Shakti of Hindustan Unilever).

The Five-E Model is created for both consumers and any influencer (for example, retailer, distributor, and doctor) separately. Since the weight of each variable may vary from one category to another, a weighted score is the driven-basis importance of that variable. Emanating from this grid, we should be clear, what the sales tasks are and what the last mile system must do to deliver strategy.

The Five-E Model populated with real data, for self and competitors, looks like this, as shown in Figure 5.7.

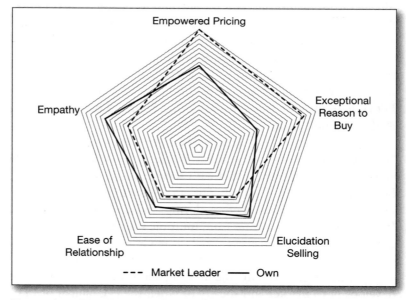

Figure 5.7   Five-E Model (Your Unique Differentiator)
Source: Author's own.

Step 4: Revamping the Process Circuitry

Have you wondered how with a mere switch you can turn on gadgets like lights, televisions, and computers? In all of this, you are completing an electric circuit allowing the smooth flow of electrons through the wires.

The Last Mile is a process. It is made up of business partners, intermediaries and influencers, complex supply chains, enormous cash entrapped in the value chain, and hundreds and thousands of people tasked with ensuring efficient availability. Extraordinary companies have converted this process into a science. They break down the entire last mile into meaningful, discrete, sequential components. The purpose is to bring to sharp attention what we are doing in each section of this process, and if there is an opportunity for doing things differently, with more efficiency, or lower costs, or both.

Our research has a conclusion. The Last Mile costs the companies half of the profits they earn from their customers. And the Turbonator companies enjoy a cost advantage of 5 percent to 8 percent in their last mile costs over an average cost of other competitors in their category. The Turbonator companies are prudent in the manner and quantum of what they pay for the selling of their produce, their supply chains are robust, and their cash velocity is superior to their rival's. To reach this stage of financial superiority, these Turbonator companies have put to question, in granular detail, what they do in the market and why.

The sample framework is reproduced herewith, in Figure 5.8.

Step 5: Nine Squares Grid Framework

As an invention, the Parsons' steam turbine is unique, and has lasted since 1884. The main feature that distinguishes earlier steam engines from turbines is that in the engines, the steam has to be contained by, and act against, a piston. In the turbine, the steam's action is kinetic, generating motion as a result of its own ability to expand. Parsons installed three parallel-flow turbines of different pressures to reuse the same steam in quick succession. Each turbine was connected to a separate shaft that drove three triple-bladed

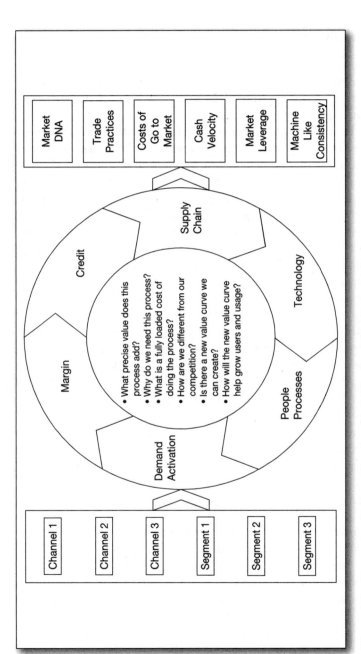

Figure 5.8 Revamping Process Circuitry (Build Predictability, Repeatability)
Source: Author's own.

propellers. By setting a series of turbine wheels on one shaft and limiting the pressure drop between adjacent wheels, Parsons was able to reduce shaft and peripheral speeds to acceptable limits. By allowing steam to expand across the turbine blades, he was able to improve performance further; and by introducing the steam between a pair of coupled but opposed turbine sets, he avoided thrusts on the end bearings. Electric generators then worked at about 1,500 revolutions per minute (RPM), while Parsons' turbine worked at 18,000 RPM.

Everything we have done so far must now be made to help build a prototype Revenue Turbine.

Like a turbine, multiple parts of the framework need to be optimized and synchronized for efficiency. In an exercise of this kind, many options and ideas come to the forefront. It is a natural and covetable outcome of the process. As a practice, we finally engage with multiple data points, insights, and trends. These pertain to today and the future, to competition and us.

For Turbonation, a right set of inquisition on the current state and the future is called for. The process to help in this turbonation is called Nine Square Grids. The purpose of this grid is to help:

- Unleash a new value curve
- Arrive at points of differentiation versus the competition
- Arrive at points of parity that have been missed thus far
- Unblock inhibitors to consumption
- Bring focus to the strategy and execution,
- Define the change agenda, both directional, and in quantum of revenues and cash

The framework for the *Nine Squares Grid* is as shown in Figure 5.9.

Step 6: Minimize House Advantage

We may think that all games in a casino are simple games of luck and offer equal opportunity to win or lose. Therefore, any machine in a casino is good enough to play. But that's not the reality.

	Add	Subtract	Multiply	Divide	Eliminate	Exponential	Equivalence	Uniqueness	New
	What will we do more that we do well?	What will we do less that we don't do that well or is less relevant?	What will we rapidly proliferate?	What will we split into smaller parts to enhance focus?	What will we stop doing?	What will we grow exponentially?	What will we seek parity with the industry standards or the leader?	What will we do unique, and can be a differentiator?	What will we do that we have never done before and is vital?
Benchmarking									
Opportunity Matrix									
Neutralizing Inhibitors									
The Heart-5e Framework									
Process Circuitry									

Figure 5.9 Nine Squares Grid (Enforce Focus)
Source: Author's own.

Casinos operate to make money. If it were a game of luck alone, they would have even chances of winning or losing. Casinos are in the business of taking your money. In order for casinos to make a profit, the games offered must have an inbuilt advantage for the casino. Otherwise it will become a game of luck, and casinos can go broke. This inbuilt advantage is called House Advantage. But all games in the casino do not have the similar magnitude of advantage. A seasoned, knowledgeable casino player, therefore, plays games that come with least house advantage, like a blackjack. This gives them the best shot at making money in a casino.

Surgical precision on choosing right markets to compete has contributed substantively to make a hitherto unknown company overtake the heavy-duty competition. Detergents business is a good $2.5 billion market in India. It has attracted the best-known MNC brands, and most of them have been around for decades. *Rohit Surfactants Private Limited (RSPL)* has had humble beginnings in the small town of Kanpur. Their brand, *Ghari* detergent, on the basis of some recent numbers has become the largest selling detergent. Unlike most emerging brand stories that are centered on the price being the biggest differentiator, Ghari has been much savvier. They hardly compete on the price. What has helped Ghari is the Pareto principle, the size of its home market Uttar Pradesh, where it enjoys a dominant position. The adjoining markets the company expanded into—Bihar, Madhya Pradesh, and Punjab—along with Uttar Pradesh account for a third of the total consumer products market. In the initial phase, instead of chasing market share across the country, even in a category as universal as laundry, the group decided to deepen distribution in a limited area. They picked up geographies with the largest population and chose to gain a disproportionate share in these markets. And it's only recently that they have ventured nationwide with close to 4,000 distributors at the last count.

Many companies today suffer from an attention-deficiency hyperactivity disorder. From processes to products, markets to customers, complexity is a natural outcome of growth. The quantum of activity is infinitely more than the quantum of results. They end up creating and hoarding things that make no meaningful impact on their purpose, profits, and customer base. Deciding what not to do is as important as deciding what to do. The best example is the management style of Jack Welch who was known to be ruthless in his views of "fix it, sell it or close it" when a business did not meet the strict criterion of being either number one or two in the industry.

Step 7: Turbo-charge

The data we have, and the options we generated on the basis of the data using Nine Squares Grid delivers a new value curve. This is the proposed *Revenue Turbine*. The net output is a comprehensive list of changes we will make in each component of the Revenue Turbine, and delta impact on revenues, profits, and cash in a defined time frame.

The process of Turbonation enables us to conceive a new market place. The process does generate a distinctly competitive construct. Comprehensively, it revitalizes each element of the last mile constructs, and in the process delivers a superior value proposition to our stakeholders.

CONCLUSION

Steve Jobs had said in the Stanford Commencement Address, "You can't connect the dots looking forward, you can only connect them looking backwards." It is never enough to have data. It is quite likely that your competitor will have the same information. The difference is in the ability to arrive at the central, binding thought. This task is difficult, which is why only a handful of companies and entrepreneurs get it right.

Companies that see the big picture instead of small differences, those that deploy insights rather than data, do shape the future.

David Rosenhan, Professor of Psychology and Law at Stanford, pioneered the application of psychological methods to the practice of legal processes. One of his widely acknowledged works is "On being Sane in Insane Places." This experiment was done to determine the validity of psychiatric diagnosis. As part of the research, healthy and normal people were sent to a total of 12 mental hospitals. These pseudo patients were told to feign illnesses like hallucination and others. On the basis of self-declaration of these people, and some preliminary tests, the hospitals readily admitted them as patients. Apart from feigning illness, the pseudo patients were instructed to behave normal and answer everything honestly. After admission, these patients did tell the hospital that they are now feeling normal. The hospital staff, however, did not even notice the difference between the normal and the insane, and prescribed antipsychotic drugs. On an average, these mock patients stayed for 19 days in the hospital and were prescribed a total of 2,100 pills.

In the next stage of the experiment, the hospitals were made aware of their "over diagnosis," and the mistake that they had made by admitting normal people as insane. Professor Rosenhan agreed with hospitals that he would again send impostors. He actually sent no one the second time. But of the 193 cases that came to these hospitals in the normal course, 41 were considered impostors implanted by the Professor, and sane, and 43 were considered suspects. In the zeal to correct the earlier aberration, the hospitals had swung to the other extreme and were now diagnosing the insane people as normal.

It did prove that the method by which psychiatrists extract information and arrive at a diagnosis is flawed. The source is self-declaration, undue focus on a small set of data points, and disregard for other critical variables.

Incumbent companies suffer not because they have lesser market data, but because they do not connect the dots, they look at discrete pieces of information, and perhaps not too many such pieces to be able to craft out the larger market game plan. By itself, the data have limited use.

The success of *Revenue Turbine* is not in its fabrication. It is not in the numbers that it uses, or the insights that get uncovered. Challenging companies pit themselves against others in the same ecosystem, they strive for identical clients and customers, and they have an equivalent access to macro data. The success is in being able to leverage all this information to craft out your unique position in the market and in being meaningful to the customers. There has to be a seamless story that scripts what we do in the market and with our customers. And like any good story, there must be a hero, a fall guy, a fascinating plot, and a fitting structure.

Thus far this book has been focused on tools and frameworks to build a strategic and market apt last mile. But the uncommon challenges in emerging markets like India call for operational and commercial capabilities that are fundamental to success. There are non-negotiable, decisive, must do, indispensable competencies. There are four such mission-critical competencies. We start, in the next chapter, with the first one, what we call Zero Calorie Value Chain.

PART III

DELIVERING THE
LAST MILE
MISSION CRITICAL(S)

6 Zero Calorie Value Chains

Lohmanplein is a residential neighborhood in Den Haag. In the middle of a string of apartment blocks is a shopping center. On a cold winter night, I walked to the supermarket there, ALDI. It's a food retailer, a hard discount store. I expected to find a drab, down-market outlet that ordinarily characterizes stores where low price is the biggest reason for customers to come. I was surprised to see a bright, happy supermarket, a big ALDI sign in red at the entrance, and a reasonable mix of shoppers, endorsing the fact that superlative value triggers loyalty that cuts across classic segmentation. This chain of supermarkets had begun when the brothers, Karl and Theo Albrecht, who own it were tiny; their mother had opened a small store in a suburb of Essen. The father was initially employed as a miner and later worked in a bakery shop. As you walk through the aisles, you are struck by the fact that there aren't too many of the familiar brands you are accustomed to seeing in supermarkets. ALDI does not sell brands. They have what is called private labels. They zealously make sure that the quality of these private labels, manufactured by or for them, is better than, or at par with leading brands, but at a deeply discounted price. No more than 1,300 items, unlike larger format stores whose count reaches 30,000, are sold, bringing to question intense segmentation and complexity in business being perpetuated all around us. ALDI's, with over 9,000 stores in the US and the Europe, is an astonishing growth story. It has conquered every market which they have entered. Their success is a testimony to the fact that even in more developed parts of the world, there are more customers who care for "value" than those who don't. It's a privately held company, and financial numbers are at best estimates. It's believed that their annual turnover exceeds Euro 50 billion. On top of the Forbes list of German billionaires are the founders of this discount chain. The family is worth 35 billion Euros, when last reported.

I first saw such private labels in London way back in the 1980s. Their packaging had struck me. These store brands would just have the category name printed in colors of blue or green on a white paper and pasted on cans and cartons. At least visually, these looked more like the remnants of the World War military supplies. Private labels have come an incredible distance from those times of just being a low cost alternative to national and international brands. The retailer who sells such private labels, often under its own store name, has a natural advantage over national brands. They know what their customers shop and why, the pack sizes that move, the promotions that work, and the products that remain unsold on shopping aisles. The big retail chains are increasingly putting this data to good use by running their own innovation funnels way ahead of some global brands. Faced with one economic crisis after another, a high inflation, low interest rates on deposits, and a belief that store brands are almost as good in quality, customers progressively endorse store brands over the much advertised but expensive big brands. Indeed ALDI isn't alone. It is an extreme. Schwarz group of Switzerland, Tesco PLC, Wal-Mart Stores Inc., Royal Ahold, and Jumbo chain of Argentina, all would have private label contributions close to half of their sales.

After having established the imperative for a new Last Mile in India (Chapters 1 to 3), and a conceptual framework to bring it alive (Chapters 4 and 5), we now move to key levers that secure the market for brands. The first of these is around making sure that value chains exude value and not carry costs and inefficiencies. It resonates well with the central thesis that while India, with enhanced prosperity and an urban shift, will create new consumers over the next two decades, these inexperienced customers are likely to be no less demanding on price than their predecessors. New to the consumption class, these consumers will exercise caution and frugality.

FIXING VALUE, NOT PRICE

ALDI customers do not only love the low *prices*, but they also endorse the superlative *value* they chalk up at the store.

Traditional value chains start with manufacturing and end at the customer. These accumulate costs at each point of interface, and a firm would typically add gross margins expected as a top up before arriving at the final price. The disconnect with this approach is that it takes the price to be a by-product, customers at that price a given, and tends to replicate one model of go-to-market across diverse categories and segments, even if it leaves most customers either over-served or under-served.

In a customer's mind, the "Value" is a tradeoff between benefits and the cost of these benefits. In pursuit of zero calorie value chain, this chapter is focused on expanding the market by right pitching the "value" of products and services. It does not necessarily, and only, imply frugal pricing.

Many categories like software and consultancy services can determine the potential benefit to their clients, and hence do value-based pricing. In such cases, they would take a percentage share of the incremental value that they help create or charge per man hour of the high intellect work put in by them.

Value-based pricing has advantages for a company; it permits the company to pick up all the legitimate dollars it should when they sell their products. Such a "dynamic" price-based product, one that competes on value, versus its counterpart at "static" prices, is compared lesser with competitive offers. It, therefore, best insulates a company from the risk of commoditization and mindless price competition.

Price and value talk to each other if *how* we sell is trumped up to incorporate the benefits that customers truly seek in the products. The benefits a company gives to the customers have to be the attribute they desire, must be uniquely owned, more important uniquely delivered when the customers experience the product. There are many ways to get there, and subsequent part of this chapter will capture some successful *Value* stories.

Let's first unlock the complexity in analyzing and comprehending the concept of price, and the price competition, before we build further on the "Value" agenda.

PSYCHOPHYSICS OF PRICES AND BREAKING THE VALUE BARRIER

Just Around the Corner was a restaurant in London that ran successfully for many years. The restaurant did not have any price list of its own. The customers were asked to pay what they believed was a fair price for the food they ate. Contrary to expectations that the restaurant would be taken for a ride, most customers were fair, enabling the restaurant to run for more than a decade.

We use numbers in our daily life. The ease with which we use numbers hides the complex cognitive process behind the manner we recognize stimuli and make comparisons. This subconscious practice reflects the way human mind approaches the entire issue of purchase and pricing.

Somehow 165 bucks a month sounds better than 2,000 a year for us, though it would largely average out the same. A *"small $10"* sounds more attractive than "$10." Similarly, "$1,099.00" looks more expensive than $1,099. Number 9 in a human mind is a more powerful numeral when it comes to pricing. Research has shown that a price offer ending with 9 will have more takers, even if it's more expensive than a cheaper offer. Also, the human mind notices relative price differentials between offers, not absolute. And that is why the best way to sell an expensive item is indeed by placing it next to an even more expensive item.

In addition, there is a frame of reference in a customer's mind. So long as everyone in the industry, or in complementary categories, charges almost the same, the consumer will neither notice the difference nor question the rationale for such pricing. That is why we will be outraged if we are asked to pay for emails, though we all pay for tiny text messages. Consumers take prices as given. And value chains are never questioned. We believe all colas and all shampoos are priced in a narrow corridor. Just as crabs are exported on the high seas without a lid being placed, so we know that market forces will ensure reasonable price parity among competing brands.

But once someone breaks the value barrier and turns conventional norms upside down, as ALDI did in retail, and *Whatsapp* messenger did to the text, and innumerable other brands like *Southwest* airlines have accomplished, the flight of customers is difficult to contain. This is the Frankenstein monster that I had drawn parallel to in Chapter 2, which destroys the maker itself. Innumerable new business and new wealth, at the core, do not necessarily have new technology or a brand with a long heritage. It's very often a refreshed value chain.

ARCHITECTURE OF PRICE COMPETITION

Let us now consider some businesses around us and look at what happens to the "price" as it gets tossed around the last miles.

Indians buy around $15 billion worth of drugs a year—tiny compared with the US at $400 billion—but the market is growing at double digit annually. Exports constitute about 40 percent of the turnover of this sector. If any industry in India is best poised to be a global leader and has ingredients to succeed in international markets, it has to be pharmaceuticals. But back home, the last mile in a pharmaceutical business is multilayered, expensive, and awkward to the extent of being almost controlled by their own stockist, who stands between them and more than half a million retail pharmacies. In other industries we studied a stockist, an intermediary, though guided by concerns of own profits, finally and firmly represented the brand they were selling, lived by its values and propagated its cause. This is not the case with pharmaceuticals in India. A stockist would typically keep multiple brands, often competing, and these stockists have lobbied themselves into an organized body. Many brands have generic versions of the drug, akin to a private label in terms of market construct, thereby diluting the manufacturer's hold over distribution. An indicative value chain for generic drugs is depicted in Figure 6.1.

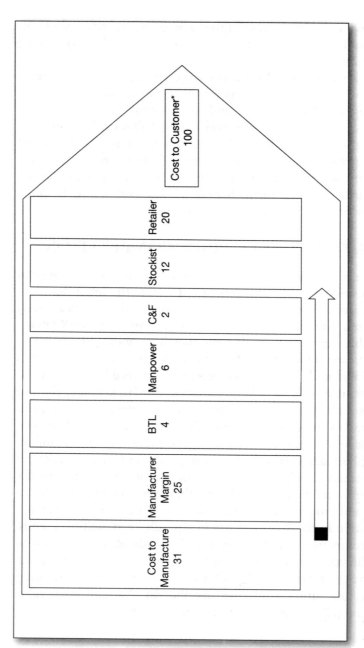

| Cost to Manufacture 31 | Manufacturer Margin 25 | BTL 4 | Manpower 6 | C&F 2 | Stockist 12 | Retailer 20 |

Cost to Customer*
100

*indicative numbers only, may vary by brand/category/company.

Figure 6.1   Indicative Value Chain—Pharmaceuticals
Source: Author's own.

In almost every category in the market, top three or four players make up three-fourths of the industry. In pharmaceuticals, it takes a good 200 of them to constitute three-fourths of the market. The top 10 players, out of about 10,000 manufacturers, have 30 percent of the share. Low technology barriers, moderate capital intensity, high growth, rising insurance covers, relatively weak brands, and good profit margins in pharmaceuticals are the obvious festering ground for competition to swell.

Indeed, the growth of most Davids across categories is motivated by easy money left on the table by market leaders. Let's look at some other categories to understand why innumerable players are able to coexist, almost to the point of bacterial competition. We start with footwear, a $3 billion domestic industry, growing at almost 15 percent year on year. More than 4,000 units manufacture footwear, and close to 60 percent of the business is with the unbranded, unorganized segment. We take an illustration in the case of sneakers and recreate an illustrative value chain for a top brand, as shown in Figure 6.2.

A product that costs X, takes on a magnitude of 3X to 5X, depending on the brand, by the time customers get to buy it.

Let's look at the value chain for another category, the apparel. Few categories have as poor a correlation between cost and selling price as apparel do.

There is a bewildering variety of apparel. The domestic Indian textile and apparel market is estimated to be $60 billion, growing at about 9 percent CAGR. This one is an illustrative one for trousers. A typical value chain moves from fiber to yarn to fabric to garment and then retailers. At every stage, the value almost goes 2X to 3X. The multiples are more stratospheric in case of higher order products like kids wear and fashion brands. This explains why our shopping mall is festered with shops selling apparel, footwear and watches; only they can afford the high rents.

Let's look at a typical illustration from the apparel industry in Figure 6.3.

These illustrations demonstrate why competition proliferates in some categories. We know that flabby value chain is not the only reason, but it is a valid cause for intense competition in a category.

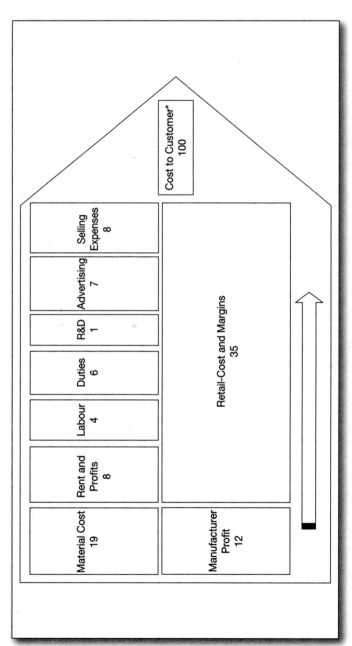

*indicative numbers only, may vary by brand/category/company.

Figure 6.2   Indicative Value Chain—Sneakers
Source: Author's own.

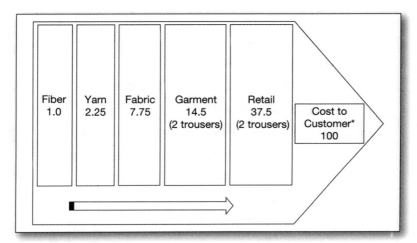

| Fiber 1.0 | Yarn 2.25 | Fabric 7.75 | Garment 14.5 (2 trousers) | Retail 37.5 (2 trousers) | Cost to Customer* 100 |

*Indicative numbers only, may vary by brand/category/company.
Visual representation basis data from "creating and preserving value".
Arvind Singhal, Suhashini Sood, Vishesh Singh.

Figure 6.3   Indicative Value Chain—Apparel (Khaki Trouser Illustration)
Source: Author's own visual representation basis data from 'Creating and Preserving Value in the Textile and Apparel Value Chain: From Fibre to Retail' by Arvind Singhal, Suhashini Sood, and Vishesh Singh; *Textile Outlook International,* January–Februrary 2004.

A good measure of value chain capability, though fraught with a few analytical issues, is to look at the contribution of the top three players in the industry. Some industries have gone through consolidation (cement); a few are so capital intensive that by definition these have high barriers to entry (automobiles), and still others are structurally disorganized (food processing). Notwithstanding issues like these and more that are case-specific, a higher number tends to indicate limited degree of freedom for a new competitor to maneuver in the industry. Inevitably lower concentration of market power among the top three competitors is generally indicative of enough money in value chains, and low entry barriers, to lure newer competitors. A sample of market concentration(s) in India for entire market, including the unorganized sector, is depicted in Figure 6.4.

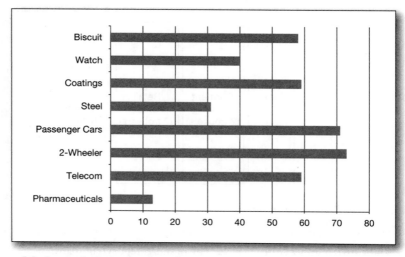

- Market includes unorganized sector too.
- Indicative numbers, for illustration purposes only.

Figure 6.4   Percentage Market Share of the Top Three Brands (Total Market)
Source: Author's own.

POTENTIAL PRICE MOVES

Operational cavities, such as those in the value chain, open up nine potential market options for competition. This is the framework wherein competitive moves are likely to be made taking advantage of a feeble value chain. These potential price-led market maneuvers are as illustrated in Figure 6.5.

All potential competitive moves, however, are not a source of concern, as quite a few of these maneuvers are unlikely to yield significant market advantage to companies that provoke such market moves. The left-hand quadrant is made up of at best tactical battles. Have you noticed that at any time a predator slashes price in sectors like aviation and telecom, the market leader wastes no time in following up? They know well that this pricing move is not based on structural cost advantage. Such price moves are nothing more than a lazy manager's marketing strategy. It could be a liquidation of

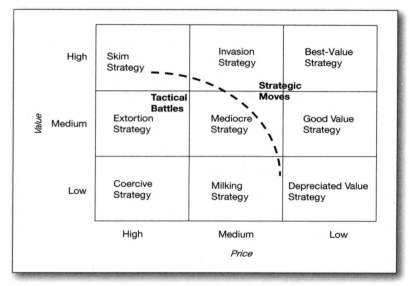

Figure 6.5   Nine Potential Price Moves
Source: Author's own.

excess inventory or a quest for some market share and, therefore, any attempt to wean their customers away should be met head on. The immediate concern is the top right-hand quadrant. A position there by competition can infinitely weaken your business. ALDI is the unquestionable leader in that quadrant. It has the right products, the right quality, and the route to market by way of its own stores, and discounted prices that manufacturer brands struggle to compete with. With low costs as a pivot, a competition like ALDI can shift the ground beneath larger, less flexible opponents and turn the mass and momentum of bulkier companies against them.

THE JOURNEY TOWARDS ZERO CALORIE VALUE CHAIN

Customers are savvy to see the value if it exists. They continually weigh price and performance, emotional connect, and functional benefits, in making buying decisions. Let us look at instances of how companies across categories have successfully leveraged value while pricing their products, resisting the downward spiral on their margins. There are essentially *five paths* that play at either enhancing value in the products we sell, or in eliminating inefficiencies and costs, or a combination of both. In either case, if the price and value is synchronized in our products and solutions, it helps expand the market, endows a winning differentiator over competition, spurs customers' recommendations, and improves profitability.

Path 1: Disrupt Established Ways

Examples from the world of sports will testify that sportspersons who have gone against the conventional wisdom leave an indelible mark on the game itself. Consider the game of cricket. For well over a century, the game has had some unwritten rules: see the new ball through in the first few overs, steady yourself, and don't lose wickets when the ball is dewy and swinging. Flick through cricket archives, there are legendary tales of how slowly and defensively the opening batsmen played. It took Sri Lanka's Sanath Jayasuriya's combustible stroke play to demolish all the previously assumed tenets of the game. Three steps out of the crease to the fastest bowlers, the bat in his hand appeared like a baseball club, and certainly not something that the "Gentleman's Game" was used to. His disruptive innovation revolutionized the game of cricket and led his team to be the World Champion in 1996.

"The art of war teaches us to rely not on the likelihood of the enemy's not coming, but on our own readiness to receive him; not on the chance of his not attacking, but rather on the fact that we have made our position unassailable," so said Sun Tzu, the famed general who led his troops into combat more than 2,400 years ago. Let us consider some examples of companies that have followed the philosophy of Sun Tzu by rendering the competition irrelevant.

Seoul subway is the world's most extensive subway by length, and most used. As I walked through the Seonreung subway station in Seoul, I saw a stunning sight. Instead of glamorous models advertising one brand or another, a familiar appearance on metro pillars turn billboards, here is a virtual display of over 500 of the most popular grocery products. All over the world, grocery shopping once a week is a dreaded task. For hard working Koreans, even more. Tesco was the challenger brand in South Korea, in pursuit of leadership, but they wanted to be a leader without having to invest in more retail space and increasing costs, a capital-intensive path most retailers habitually choose. The idea that emerged was to circumvent the concept of people having to come to the store to shop, instead let the store go to the people. Typically a smartphone is used as a QR code scanner, displaying the code and converting it to some useful form, thereby doing away with the need to type anything on a browser. Commuters on the subway can scan the QR code beneath the desired item they wish to buy via the *Homeplus* app on their smartphone and the item is then delivered directly to the customer's home at the chosen time. It's the world's first virtual store, a pioneer in transforming routes to market, and a game changer for Tesco.

Lei Jun, the founder of mobile devices company *Xiaomi*, has fast become one of China's most celebrated and famous entrepreneurs. He grew up near Wuhan, an industrial city in central China, and studied computer science at the university. Xiaomi is selling smart phones. Xiaomi now sells $5 billion worth of handsets, largely in China, and is fast emerging as a force in many other parts of the world. The local brand launched just four years ago now sells more units in China than Apple and Samsung as per some reported numbers. It is a company that plays by a set of rules very different than the established industry patterns. They sell hep and inexpensive devices direct, on the web. There are no distributors and dealers. For them hardware is just a platform to run services. They endeavor for long product life cycles of 18 months plus, unlike most mobile operators whose product cycle may last just six months. This enables them to initially sell phones at bill-of-material costs, and profit over the longer time horizons when component costs are bound to fall.

One common theme that inevitably disrupts the established ways in the industry is by beginning to think solutions rather than the product. The classic example is *Rolls-Royce* that manufactures precision engines that run airplanes. They have a control room in

Derby, which for a fee, tracks 4,000 odd aircraft engines 24 × 7. This enables scheduling preventive maintenance and real-time problem solving, and is indeed an insurmountable barrier for a new competitor to come. Someone can perhaps take the technological leap and make engines of a similar caliber, but to replicate the entire ecosystem around it, and add value to the product that has already been sold, is an enormous task. What companies like Rolls-Royce and Xiaomi do is to transform the construct of product and services with profit booking not at the point of sale but over the entire length of consumption. This creates a perpetual revenue stream, and, more importantly, an entry barrier for a pure play price warrior.

The best of products can fail if their application by customers is not profoundly thought through. Consider this. The *Gurgaon toll plaza* was the largest in South Asia. But it was a complete mess, till the court ordered its closure. Long queues, a good half an hour wait for the commuters to merely pay the toll, road rage, and violence were a daily phenomenon. Around the same time that the Gurgaon expressway came up, Dubai too started the system of toll called SALIK. It's an electronic system. There are no booths for cash collection or an army of people managing it. Indeed there is no one at the Dubai toll. One is required to have a prepaid card akin to mobile recharges. As you pass the toll, an automatic debit is affected. There are no queues, no stopovers, and easy flow through.

It may be useful to ask a few simple questions in the quest for changing the battlefield itself. What are the existing and established manners of disseminating value to customers? What exactly are feeble and fragile points of inflexion in the current value chain? What does the customer do with our product? What are the pain points for end users? What can you do that is different and value accretive? Is there a way for you to make money out of giving service and solutions to your customers?

Path 2: Establish a Unique Customer Connect

"*Once upon a time*" is the most ingrained phrase in a child's memory, shaped by stories told to him/her in the childhood and continuing to fascinate well into adult life. The competition has data. Chances are it is already doing a price comparison on media. They perhaps have as good a product at a cheaper price. However, the reason clients will choose one is in intangibles—trust, respect, and a bulletproof relationship, things that no one else can touch.

People are best persuaded when you tell them a story, and when they identify with your story. It works because stories build an emotional connect. Facts and data erect a psychological resistance by raising intellectual defense; a story is a way to leave a message that breaks the fortified walls of the human mind. Value chains indeed are best preserved when consumers are connected fervidly with our chronicle. This is a scenario which dramatically cuts into the freedom of a price warrior.

There is enough to learn from consumer goods companies that successfully tell us why every generation of the same product, launched often within a fraction of innovation time, is faster, superior, more hardworking and efficient. Designed by someone cool or endorsed by a celebrity, or being organic, green, ethical is another way to weave a persona, a spirit in the product that consumers can identify with.

B2B business, and not only consumer goods, also have a story to tell. *HP ProCurve* has a strong selling point—lifetime warranty. Many durable products carry such or diluted versions of warranty, but always struggle to explain the same to their customers, so much so that customers today assume that goods purchased by them are as promised, either explicitly or implicitly. It is a challenge for something that has been commoditized to be transformed into a unique selling proposition. To build a story on lifetime warranty, *HP* captured images from manufacturing and testing, and interviews with the senior management. They explained why and how their products could indeed carry a lifetime warranty. All these are hardworking options to enhance the market.

A product is rarely ever bought for its own sake. In a customer's mind, there is a lot more that they seek from the consumption of that product. Just as you have the option to sell coffee powder, or sell coffee, or *sell an experience* as *Starbucks* does. You have the choice to vend fiber, or yarn, or a shirt, or an identity. You can sell rides or you can be a *Walt Disney*.

An *experience* adds life into lifeless products, akin to going three-dimensional in a movie hall. It changes the value like nothing else can. And value of customers engaged with a brand is the toughest to replicate. In the construct between head and heart, customer experience with the brand is the heart. It gives people a social currency; they can now talk about it, share the experience with others, pen a tweet, write a blog, and tell their friends thousands of miles away on social networking sites. *Apple* uses its retail outlets to show consumers its brand philosophy. If you ever notice, their stores are rather somber; long wood tables, nothing ostentatious or unnecessary to distract your attention. All product displays are hands on and interactive. The staff is not tasked with pushy sales we are so accustomed to in most high-end stores. They either greet and direct customers to the appropriate products, or advise and sell, or provide service and resolve problems. Nothing distracts attention from larger than life product displays. Compare this with innumerable competition PCs spread out carelessly in small retail stores, almost compelling one to just discuss price and get on with it.

Experience does not necessarily mean extravaganza or incremental costs. It has to be category appropriate. It must resonate for potential customers. Even simplicity can be, for instance, an equally good experience. A maze of tariff options has kept telecom customers deeply suspicious of their service providers' intentions. It is safe to say that there is hardly any category with as much tariff complications as mobile telephony. *Simpel* of the Netherlands, now a part of T-Mobile, is an example of simplicity in products and tariffs as the core differentiator in this category.

Experience creates connect, leading to favorable predisposition, and more purchases. What experience does is not wrestle as much with parameters that drive quantity of value. It improves quality of the value chain.

The questions to ask are: Why do consumers want our product? What is our story line, why us? What emotional connects can be added to the construct of the product that we sell which are meaningful and authentic? Which class of customers does not consume what we make, and can we become relevant for them?

Path 3: Tame Low Value, High Volume Constructs Endemic to India

The story goes back in 1942, a class four dropout from South India arrived in the city of Mumbai. He started to serve native food on plantain leaves, which all in Mumbai have sworn by for decades. Rama Nayak's *Udupi* restaurants are basic, with no frills. Fine dining adds enormous costs in the food business. The last mile in Udupi eateries is created to deliver the velocity of sales. As soon as you sit down, a glass of water hurriedly appears before you. The menu is limited and within minutes of your order piping hot food is delivered to the table. Just as you are about to finish your meal, the waiter arrives with a bill. Pronto the table is wiped clean to serve the next customer. A long queue of people generally waiting to be seated is suggestive of the value of an experience that puts the core product, the taste of the food at affordable prices, as the bedrock for customer loyalty. The product remains the hero, not fancy furniture, expensive chandeliers, and expensive cutlery so intricately associated with most restaurants.

Mobility is the most distributed and consumed products across all categories, with ownership exceeding 60 percent in most countries of the world. A reliable metric, therefore, to highlight consumption capacity in a country is Average Revenue Per User (ARPU) of a telecom company. Monthly ARPU in India is about $2.5 versus Singapore at $35, European Union at around $30, US at $50, and the Middle East at $12. This, however, doesn't construe that operating performance metrics of Indian telecommunications is not on par with the world. Indeed the large scale does make up substantively for low per capita realizations, albeit with more capital intensity. Serving low value, high volume consumers, the fundamental construct of Indian market, calls for a last mile capability different than the one needed for high value, low volume consumer base.

Consider *QB House*, a story well known. Getting a hair cut in Japan is an emotional experience, a rather long ritual. Every strand of hair is literally pampered. It is cut, conditioned, washed, and then styled. There is a wrapping in shrouds, the consultation, end-less rounds of hot and cold towels, and the shoulder rub. And after a couple of hours of this ritual, the staff would all line up outside and see you off. QB House changed it all by moving the entire concept squarely into a functional arena. QB shops are in nooks and corners, next to high traffic areas like metro stations. They do not have reception staff to accept bookings on the phone. There are, however, traffic lights outside the barbershop. A red light means 15 plus minutes wait, a yellow from 5 to 10 minutes, and green no wait at all. A customer has to stuff money in a machine to get a ticket, the exact denomination if you please, which is then handed over to the barber. When it's your turn, you will be called over, seated, and the barber will politely ask you what kind of cut you want. Simple instructions work, no elaborate directions can possibly be executed. QB gives you a hair cut in flat 10 minutes, and at fraction of a price customers in Japan used to pay earlier.

QB House, started by a representative of a medical equipment firm, now runs a successful business with hundreds of such shops. The belief is that *Getting Asset Light* can dramatically alter cost curves and drive consumption. This story has the gravitas to be replicated in innumerable categories where customers are waiting for a new value curve, lighter and more efficient.

The issue is not only being asset light. It is also being *Asset Right*. Most hotel chains know that their core competency is in the management of a hotel. A hotel is a capital-intensive business. The high price tag of the real estate and the cost of construction is a dampener to anyone who aspires to grow big. Large-sized hotel chains do not own properties that carry their brand name. People with capital own these properties and become partners with hotel names that manage the property to a uniform brand standard. *Marriott*, for instance, maybe owns only six out of 3,500 odd properties that bear their brand name.

Assets are not only about what we sell. It is also about the *Processes* we pursue. Most big processes consume enormous cash and working capital. Let us consider supply chains that have traditionally been seen as a cash guzzler. This view has been perpetuated by the less than efficient cost and cash velocity in this part of organization in the past. Developments in IT, and a change in mindset, have empowered many a business to enhance service levels and deploy cash optimally.

Inventories are reflective of underdeveloped capability to forecast correct demand rather than poor sales. *Supplying to Demand* is often the first way to cut costs and get a larger share of revenues by way of superior availability. But many companies, even today, struggle to catch the tail of true demand for their products. The traditional system of forecast by sales teams has been in the Turbonator organizations replaced by simulated forecasts, or a mix of the two at sales and operations planning (S&OP), and now integrated business-planning forums. Sales data (actual and forecast) are analyzed across hierarchies (products, geography, customers, and time periods) to form the bedrock for simulation. For an organization to get to this stage, some imperatives have to be aligned. Sales teams can't dump stocks. They have to sell to customer offtakes. This removes artificial troughs, which is often the vital cause for cash to get blocked and unwarranted investments in creating flexible manufacturing. Demand networks are more responsive than supply chains. The data are both granular and real time.

We need to populate value chains with real-life cash numbers, and ask ourselves, what do we spend money on in the value chain, and why? What can we do differently to release cash that is blocked? What is our core competence? Are we trying to manage things outside the purview of true value we can create?

Path 4: Atomize Your Business

Jeff Stibel, a brain scientist and an entrepreneur, has the following to say:

> Nature has a lesson for us if we care to listen; the fittest species are typically the smallest. The tiniest insects often outlive the large lumbering animals. Ants, bees, and cockroaches, all outlived the dinosaurs. Single cell organisms have been around since the beginning of life and will likely be here until the end. The deadliest creature is mosquito, not the lion. Bigger is rarely better in the long run.[1]

---

[1] Jeff Stibel, *Breakpoint: Why the web will implode, search will be obsolete, and everything else you need to know about technology is in your brain* (New York: Macmillan, 2013).

This kind of deconstructing the otherwise big picture enables precision targeting, lowers the costs per use, spreads more, and gains larger mindshare.

Value sizing is a science and an art. Different segments of the populace have varying capabilities to pay for broadly the same product. Homogeneous constructs in our products, sold at static prices, adversely impacts this capability to right size our offers to a variety of customers.

Thanks to granular analytics and enormous amounts of data, it is possible to model how value can be atomized for customers and clients. A telecom company segments its customer base in a manner that the right customer gets the right product offer. A consumer goods company can push suitable stock item in the most apt distribution channel. The television serials that run for decades are dispensed in small dosages of one act per day lasting maybe half an hour.

We all know how atomization works with products. Fast moving consumer goods companies have been at the forefront of recognizing segments and offering solutions, from differing pack sizes to variants of the same product.

But let's consider two illustrations of how the concept of atomization has been deployed by the Turbonator companies to create value at the last mile. The first illustration enforces focus at the last mile through the *Channel Alignment Grid*, and the second illustration remits razor sharp last mile execution through the *Growth-and-Challenge Matrix*.

CHANNEL ALIGNMENT GRID

The Turbonator companies have grown their revenues exponentially, a multiple of 15X in the last two decades as we saw in Chapter 1. The geometric growth transpires and the best value is realized when there is an alignment between the three drivers to the revenue—purpose of the product, channel capability, and consumer life stage. Products have defined roles, a purpose to exist. Either it's to acquire new paying customers, or creating an entirely new market, or to up sell to an existing base, or to churn the

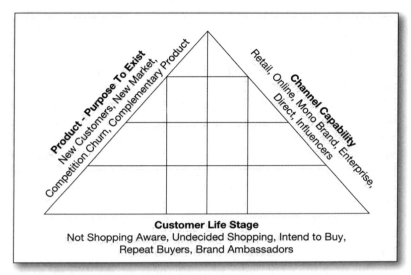

Figure 6.6   The Channel Alignment Grid
Source: Author's own.

customers of competition, or an offer complementary to the existing products. All channels and all clients tend to have a core capability for a handful of these requirements, not all. Customers too are at varying points of inflexion; these are hardly at similar life stages of shopping behavior, from being aware of your products to being your brand ambassadors. Segmentation of market and consumer base is an imperative to marry product needs with channel capabilities and consumer life stage. The framework that delivers an optimal balance between the product, the channel, and the customer life stage is shown in Figure 6.6.

Let us carry the proposition of atomization forward with the second application that targets execution capability.

GROWTH-AND-CHALLENGE MATRIX

Intuition, history, market size, and ease have been the basis of sales representative territory allocation thus far. It has been largely driven by considerations of geography. Companies have petabytes of data available on their customers, what they buy, how, and when, and yet it is hardly put to use for purposes beyond minor marketing tasks.

Consider this, one of the biggest telecom companies in a metro market typically used to create some 20 sub-territories. These were all fabricated by considerations of geography and size alone. Managers would manage it, with layers of supervisors on top. Every representative by construct in this structure is a generalist. It didn't take long to discover that these representatives could not handle all kinds of customer profiles and products. So, parallel sales forces had to be created, one for own brand stores, another for enterprise, yet another for organized retail, and so on. If one includes all kinds of personnel that are in sales, a good 500 outsourced and in-house people manned the business in this one city alone.

This situation went on for years, till the company decided to put to use their enormous data and experience, and micro segment the market differently. They used a mix of parameters like market size, competition intensity, customer typology, and growth potential to arrive at 100 odd clusters or micro-markets. Granularity of data enabled the creation of high-resolution images of the market. These markets are no longer north or south, east or west; instead these clusters have a customer profile (voice or data, premium or low end, etc.), competition intensity (high to low), growth (highly penetrated to nascent), and these now look live with sales tasks and challenges, not merely physiography and topography.

While this improved the visibility of the tasks in the market, there was another issue to contend with. Managers deploy their manpower-based considerations of location preferences and past experience of their people. Territory allocations on the basis of geography like stated above are fundamentally built to "service" the market, not to "win" in the market. Fusion between sales people typology and sales tasks is an imperative in the markets that call for differentiated strategies.

The game of soccer had recognized long ago that people, by their genetic constitution and training, are built for specific tasks. Every position in soccer has a purpose and a clearly defined deliverable. If it takes someone with leadership abilities and deep understanding of the game to be a sweeper, aggressive and focused people make a good center forward. The center back is fundamentally a defender and a winger plays tactical roles that call for endurance, timing, and awareness.

A market can be built with similar principles as soccer, that is, to strongly focus on, and being capable of, winning. A micro-cluster that is in the outskirts of the city would need, to use soccer parlance, wingers to build the territory; a market with enormous competitive intensity and high on opportunity, and size would need a striker to rapidly wean away share from competitors; a cluster with high share and stakes will need to make sure the defense stays intact and, hence, a "sweeper" profile. The sales tasks in each part are different, the market spends needed are at variance, even the product offers stand granular. Not a detailed version, an abridged one, is reproduced herewith in Figure 6.7.

Marketing has been at the forefront of segmentation for long. Indeed their challenge has increased manifold now with an imperative for mass customization in the digital age we live in. It's time to task the last mile to rapidly transcend beyond geographical territories to micro-segments, each section unique in challenges and opportunities for growth, and thus deploy optimum strategy in each parcel of the market.

Path 5: Straddle this *and* that, not this *or* that

The real challenge for companies in India is to find an optimal balance between the value they need to retain as margins, and the price that will attract customers to buy their produce.

As a product, I find pizza to be the shrewdest, and one of the many solutions to the inevitable conundrum of pricing right in order to retain margins but also being affordable enough to attract a larger customer base. The concept of pizza is simple at its core. There is a base, it's common, and it is purely functional. Then, there are toppings. Depending on your palette and the weight of the wallet, you can make a choice. Pizza as a product has effortlessly imbued innovations over time—in its base (thin, wheat), toppings

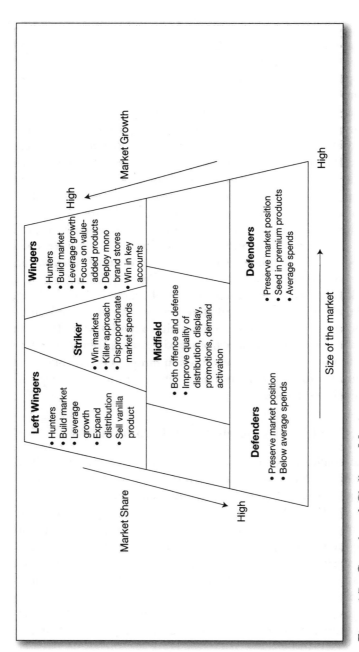

Figure 6.7   Growth–and–Challenge Matrix
Source: Author's own.

(all kinds), cheese (all types), delivery (concept of time), volume (sell whole or slices, size), and experience (take away to fine dining). It is no surprise that pizza is available just about everywhere in the world. It straddles multiple price points at a fraction of a marginal cost. Consumers feel empowered because they are the ones who get the choice and make decisions.

Automobile companies have best attempted to carry the idea forward. They create a base model of a vehicle, and then bundle the features into different versions, almost the way a pizza is generally sold. Many financial service products have also replicated the concept. Insurance, for instance, has a base protection plan, and thereafter riders like accident benefit, critical illness, and the like.

Consider software companies. They have two versions of a reasonably similar product, at different price points: Home and Professional, the assumption being that higher price paying corporate will not wish to be seen using a Home version. Theatres do it all the time by pricing tickets depending on where you are seated. *Old Navy, The Gap, and Banana Republic* are the brands from the same house. These brands straddle different price points; rich people are seduced to buy their clothes at the Banana Republic, while the price sensitive people go to Old Navy. The pizza-like resourceful way is to create segments and make sure that people who can pay money continue to do so, while consumers who are vulnerable to prices are also retained.

Let's consider an example closer home. Till five years ago, telecom companies charged calls on a per minute basis. This meant that customers paid for a full minute even if they talked for a few seconds. In an attempt to find a competitive space in an overcrowded twelve-player market, *Tata Docomo* launched a disruptive market move, per second billing. This could potentially destroy industry margins by a good 12 percent to 15 percent. Therefore, the incumbent mobile operators chose not to react. The long queues to get Docomo connections were a testimony to the power of the superior value of a seconds billing plan. Big players hoped the tsunami would pass. After about four odd months and erosion in their base of revenue-paying customers, they had no option but to reluctantly transition their per minute calls to the per second basis regime. The interesting thing is not this story but two critical facts about it. One, industry penetration grew phenomenally, from just 500 million subscribers in 2009 to 850 million in 2011. The second fact is as to how skillfully incumbent telecom operators went around executing their reaction. Per second billing was available to their customers, but only if they made the effort to call up and ask for it. In every category, there are customers who for mundane reasons like inertia and habit will not move, even if the competing offer is better. Then some corporate customers have product plans that are bundled with freebies. Even today, five years hence, reportedly "most operators now have between 40% to 60% of their subscribers using per second tariff plans."[2] They have managed to preserve some value even in the face of an extreme price move in the industry.

One-third of the world's blind population lives in India. In yet another illustration of segmenting value at one end, and price at another, acknowledged *Aravind Eye Care System* treats poor patients for free, and the richer ones get quality treatment at full but still affordable prices.

When we make products and services, and work in price competitive markets, it may be prudent to learn from a childhood fable. Once upon a time, there was a little girl named Goldilocks. She went for a walk in the forest. Pretty soon, she came upon a house. She knocked and, when no one answered, she walked right in. At the table in the kitchen, there were three bowls of porridge. Goldilocks was hungry. She tasted the porridge from the first bowl, the second, and the third one. These belonged to Papa bear, Mama bear, and baby bear. The porridge she tasted, the chair she sat on, the bed she slept in, and all were more of the same, with difference of size alone. The learning is that the best way is to keep pricing at a simple 3—Regular, Premium and Super Premium or Economy, Regular and Premium, depending on the category, thus taking advantage of the fact that the human mind tends to do the comparison and contextual shopping, and many people will be willing to pay more as well. The best thing about

---

[2] Sunny Sen, "A matter of seconds," *Business Today*, May 25 (2014).

having different price tiers is that it shifts the client's mindset from, "Should I pay you at all?" to "What price should I pay you?"

Next time we trigger a price reaction to a price move, we need to sit back and ask a few questions. Have we left operational inefficiency on the table for the competitor to come and grab? Is the price move a structural advantage that competition has, or is it a land grab tactical move? What is the true value we give to our customers, and how can we make it unique and differentiated?

CONCLUSION

The concept of Zero Calorie Value Chain is based on the competence to discriminate between efficiencies and inefficiencies of processes, costs, and legacy routes to the market.

This is the first of the four bastions of business growth in the emerging markets like India.

As the industries approach relative maturity, most incrementally and a few of them radically, the essential construct of the market changes. In the auto industry, for example, companies are finding that their traditional sales activities are less needed by the customers, who are now going online for feedback on the performance and prices of the cars they want. Consider telecom, a category with the large acceptance and diffusion. The new customers now are not as ample in numbers, or as profitable. The churn of the existing customers has subsided, compared to the prior periods, as the customers have settled in their relationships with the respective service providers. The competitive pressures do exist but a kind of coexistence among rivals prevails given that everyone now has large publicly listed balance sheets to protect. In terms of the quality of the work, the tasks, however, in a Telco have changed substantively. Keeping ahead is no more frenzied acquisition of the new users particularly in the voice business; it involves product innovations, new applications, standardization of processes and quality, building convenience, and experience quotient for the customers. The acquisition-related tasks have been bartered for enhancing revenue from subsisting customers.

Thus far this book has been tilted toward new customers and new markets. But as the market grows, many segments of the market sensibly consolidate too. Where these will tilt depends of the trajectory of the industry structure as it evolves. Our next chapter explores the concept of Customer Capital, the currency to measure our customer centricity, and existing customers as the source of abiding value. More important, it specifies the customer agenda in the India market made up of young shoppers.

7 Customer Capital in the Times of the Millennial Generation

In 2007, Vodafone acquired a controlling stake in Hutchison Essar, the telecom operator, at an enterprise valuation of $18.8 billion. The capital-intensive industry of telecom services at that point of time was OIBDA negative. There were extensive debts on the books of all companies. It has been one of the most competitive industries with the finite electromagnetic spectrum being shared by innumerable fierce operators. Swings in the vacillating regulatory environment, in addition, create a perpetual business cycle of opportunities and threats in this industry. "That Vodafone has won Hutch Essar without a protracted bidding war and at a price below the top of the supposed range of around US$20 billion is positive," noted Dresdner Kleinwort analyst Robert Grindle, at the time of the acquisition.[1] But not all analysts and business media were enthused by Vodafone's move to acquire Hutch Essar at the price tag they paid. "At an enterprise value (EV) of $770 per subscriber and an EV/EBITDA (earnings before interest, taxes, depreciation and amortization) multiple of 16.4 for FY 08, this deal has certainly not come cheap for Vodafone."[2] The Average Revenue Per User (ARPU) was about $8, with a reasonably high churn in subscribers. The ARPU since then has slid to under $3. In terms of conventional arithmetic, it was an extravagant deal. What Vodafone legitimately purchased into was the quality of 22 million consumers Hutch had, the confidence in lifetime value of those subscribers, and a punt on the future growth in an emerging country like India.

---

[1] *Vodafone Group Wins India's Hutch Essar*, Quote in the China Post, February 13, 2007.
[2] Krishna Gopalan, "Dialing into India," *Business Today*, March 11 (2007).

The investor confidence in valuations of a company is driven by their assurance on revenues and margins from the existing customers in the future, and the structural business model. On an average, our stock exchange has a multiple of 16X, in simple language, signifying that the punt on current earnings is a multiple of good 16 times. For our Turbonator companies, this multiple is 24X. This confidence, at the core, emanates from the quality of customers and clients the business has and the ability to generate a lifetime of value from them.

A business with an intrinsic capability to measure customer equity knows that upwards of 75 percent of their balance sheet in a year is driven by customers already on the books of the company. Telecom, direct to home, insurance, B2B business, airlines, all have the ability to measure revenue, contribution, and lifetime value of their current customers. The sales teams in hotels secure contracts from long standing key clients who generally fill two-thirds of their room nights. Retail business does publish two sets of numbers, one for same-store sales and the other overall finances. And it is the same-store sales that analysts track closely, because that's the authentic barometer of the quality of growth in a company.

If indeed business success is based on customers we already have, we need to examine as to why is it that business strategies are not based on them? Why is the attention largely around new markets and unknown customers?

The answer I find is reasonably straightforward. The truth is that most companies do not even measure the value of these customers. Inevitably companies that do not measure the financial value of their existing customers will rarely bother too much about them. In such companies, customers are presumed to be passive recipients of service. This still reflects the old economy wherein choices were non-existent, and we all should be thankful for getting something. Because one is in the business wherein consumers need advice and help, where products break down and have to be rectified, hence service departments exist. In this kind of construct, the company and its customers aren't like two peas in a pod, with identical goals. The entire transaction is underpinned by near term commercial considerations.

Such relationships, antipathetic as they are, are unlikely to secure future earnings for a company that cares little beyond a mere supply of goods or a service, and investors in the stock market will perpetually discount such brands.

Customers have two distinct buying personalities: indifferent and engaged. The personality that surfaces during particular buying decisions depend on the type of value customers seek. Most businesses are optimized to sell to the indifferent personality. In this buying mindset, customers are focused on practical features such as price and convenience. As a consequence, customers' relationships with sellers are often adversarial.[3]

The last mile has been habitually seen as a one-way street, a unidirectional movement of goods and services. As soon as the product or service reaches an intermediary or a client, the role of a company ceases to exist. Users become anonymous, the value chain hazy, and control on customer experience gets fragile. Attrition or churn of customers is a natural consequence in circumstances such as these. Ironically, faced with a depletion of revenues of customers who abandon it, forces the company to focus even more on new acquisition to an even larger in attention to the existing profitable customers. A business like this is like a bucket that leaks. It has to be perpetually refilled. Consider this, a company that loses value of the existing customers by 1.5 percent a month, a fairly realistic number across categories that measure this number true, will be left with 40 percent of the first year value by the fifth year; a company that loses by half as much, 0.75 percent per month, will have about 65 percent of the value intact in five years. Simplistically if every customer gives equal revenue and if a new acquisition costs same months of payback period, and assuming no costs on retention of customers, the company with 0.75 percent churn per month will be ahead on profits by 25 percent versus the company at twice the rate of customer attrition.

---

[3] John Todor, *Addicted Customers: How to Get Them Hooked on Your Company* (California: Silverado Press, 2007).

THE CONTEXT

The purpose of this chapter is to help create a framework that harvests the wealth of the existing customers. In a growing economy that is regularly fabricating new customers who enter the spending class, it is easy to miss out the concern for the existing customers. If some customers stop using our products, it really matters less, as many more are available.

This chapter seeks to answer three pertinent questions. What is unique about the customers in India? What currency should be used to measure the value of your existing customers? And how does a company build aforementioned customer value?

Before we get to this inquest, let us step back and look at the context in which the customer story thus far has played out in India. This is our starting point.

At an overly simplified level, for the purpose of this work, we can divide the development of the business in India into three phases. *Phase one* of the business was propelled by the ability to merely supply, that too, largely essential goods. Availability was the competitive advantage. Ability to get licenses and capital to build factories became a source of wealth creation. This phase died somewhere around 1970s, and all it has left are a few business houses that diversified their business portfolio to new age products, and some of these traditional business houses are doing rather well, but many of them which didn't move as rapidly as the markets did, are a poor shadow of their heyday glory.

Then came *Phase Two*, the boom fuelled largely by easier access to capital, a liberalized regime, and competition from a new breed of entrepreneurs. Television was born. The Indians took to television like duck to water. Money followed eyeballs. Brands took over our lives. If the media spend was large and/or advertising effective, consumers presumed trust in the brand. And brands did inform, impress, seduce, and cajole us to reach our wallets. It is the concept of *Lovemarks,* as Kevin Roberts would say, the result created by the trinity of mystery, sensuality, and intimacy. Great brands have the power to touch our hearts and change us, because at the core these are a symbol of what we are, invented in response to our deepest needs.

Brands have been a source of competitive advantage. The large media dispensation of leading brands itself became a huge barrier to entry, a fortified wall impossible to scale for a challenger brand that needed marketing resources beyond its means to compete. However, in many such companies' customers is still a kind of an afterthought. The relationships between buyer and seller continue to be feudal, not one of equals and has had more than a tinge of subservience about it. The customer may have been labeled the king, as all companies claim, but the producer always kept the crown.

We are now at the cusp of another era, *the Phase Three*, exciting at one level, and frightening at another. Consumers, so far kept insulated by producers, have got together and are chatting as a community, influencing each other, and sharing their experiences. Something we saw in train compartments where complete strangers would pick up a conversation and perhaps be buddies by the time journey ended, is now playing out on the Internet. The hegemony of television sets has a challenger in the form of our computer and mobile screens. In 2013, in the US, consumers have spent more time on digital devices than on television.[4] According to Nielsen's Global Trust in Advertising report, which surveyed more than 28,000 Internet respondents in 56 countries, 92 percent of consumers around the world said they trust earned media, such as recommendations from friends and family, above all other forms of advertising.[5]

The *False-consensus effect* is a concept in social psychology that refers to a cognitive bias wherein a person overestimates the extent to which other people share their behavior and belief. Consumers vociferously voice their opinion, and people tend to rely on the experience of others as a guide to their own behavior. Most categories will testify that by the time the customer now reaches out to them, the customers have enormous information, even opinions and biases of the people who have consumed the product previously. Easy access to data points at the click of a button has the

---

[4] "Mobile continues to steal share of US adults' daily time spent with media," *Emarketer,* April 22 (2014).
[5] "Consumer trust in online social and mobile advertising grows," *Nielsen online,* October 4 (2012).

potential to jeopardize, or leverage, as one sees it, the entire product and brand stories that companies have painstakingly built up.

The role of chief marketing officers stands transformed from the custodian of the brand to custodian of consumers of the brand. How many of us will stay in a hotel we have never stayed before without checking on actual consumer experience at sites like *Tripadvisor?* Or buy an automobile without reading reviews posted by other customers or go to a movie without checking out the feedback from the people who have seen it?

Patricia Seybold, one of the foremost voices in the arena of customer economy, has the following to say:

> Eyeballs aren't the basis of currency in the customer economy; hearts and minds are. You build relationships through experiences. Each experience either cements or undermines consumer trust. Relationships are based on trust. The companies that will thrive in the customer economy understand how to build and maintain customers' trust by carefully managing customers' experience with the brand.[6]

David "Doc" Searls envisions an *Intention Economy* in the future that previews a scenario wherein the tables are turned; it's the buyer who controls the purchase process, not the seller. The buyer notifies the market of the intent to buy, and sellers compete for the buyer's purchase. Companies essentially respond to the intent of the buyer to purchase a product, not merely try for their attention on television and at shopping aisles. "What if all of this was reversed? What if the customers had all the tools? What if every one of us had our own Vendor Relationship Management system, a VRM? What if we owned our own data and collected and mined data about the vendors? What if we could share information about the trustworthiness and reliability of vendors? What if people had the power and companies served us? What if instead of companies soliciting us, we would solicit them?" Imagine announcing: 'I am interested in buying a camera. Here are my requirements. Here is what I will

---

[6] Patricia Seybold, *The Customer Revolution* (New York: Crown Business, 2001).

permit you to do with my list of requirements and with any knowledge you acquire about me. What would you like to offer me?'" While this may sound bizarre, let's think again, this scenario of the buyer in considerable control of the purchase process, and querying the sellers to respond, does transpire already for a range of heavy-duty purchases from machinery to software. *Medypal,* a Bangalore-based healthcare application, does precisely this; it employs "reverse auction" by which patients will have hospitals and doctors bid for their business. The good news is that the reverse holds true as well. A great brand story doesn't cost big dollars of advertising money. Customers themselves will spread the positive message, which can be read by millions of people instantaneously.

THE UNIQUENESS OF INDIAN CUSTOMERS: THE MILLENNIAL GENERATION

The median age in demographics divides the population into two equal parts, that is, there are as many people above it, as there are with ages below the median. China's one child policy has made the country "older" with the median age climbing to 35 years now from the twenties in 1970, and just one child to dote on by six people (two sets of grandparents and one set of parents), some say, has made this new generation feel like "little emperors." India, on the contrary, is young; the median age is just 25 years. About 75 percent of the people in India were born after 1984. The millennial, as they are called, is a new breed, a new generation. Just as grandparents, despite their enormous affection, at times struggle to comprehend the attitudes of the young generation, many companies that haven't moved on with time have a similar combat laid out for them as these budding customers increasingly get to own heavier wallets.

This millennial generation has been born when the Internet was already on, the color televisions were telecasting, the phone lines existed, and fair price shops selling ration were getting far and few. This generation, in comparison to the Gen X, is unlikely to appreciate how hard you have worked to get your customer standards where you have, if these are not fast and good enough. "The millennial has the upper hand, because they are tech savvy, with every gadget imaginable almost becoming an extension of their bodies. They multitask, talk, walk, listen and type, and text. And their priorities are simple: they come first."[7] This group of customers does activities that are visual and social. They don't buy, they look for experiences. They are speed freaks, if your customer orientation is slow paced, chances are you would lose the Gen Y. This demographic cohort of young adults, increasingly constituting the customer base, is bound to change the shape of many industries.

How exactly this generation will transform customer centricity, we still have to see. But companies certainly would do well if they can build their vocabulary and capability keeping in mind some of these emerging themes. These themes are, digital, experience, convenience, speed, social, authentic, and fickle.

CUSTOMER CAPITAL, THE CURRENCY TO MEASURE CUSTOMER CENTRICITY

The issue that interrupts customer centricity in companies is that there is no single acceptable currency to measure it. If you can't measure something, it generally doesn't happen either. Surrogate metrics are then deployed in many companies to suggest that if customers "feel" in a certain positive way, the long-term durability of the business stands assured. No one can deny the power of such an idea. If I feel good about someone and go around praising the person, many more people are likely to like this person. More than that, it's unlikely that I will abandon the person I like. In practice this does change the quality of engagement, as the "providers" of the service at the front end, the coalface as they say, know that they are being measured and the opinion of the customer matters. The very fact of measurement does influence the employee's behavior with their customers. Such a measurement also helps trigger customer conversations in the boardroom.

There is however a slip between the cup and the lip when it comes to putting a dollar value on this just out, modish behavior. A *Harvard Business Review* article has the following to say.

---

[7] "Morley safer, the millennial are coming," CBS News (2008).

...the trouble is that most good intentions remain just that—good intentions. Working with managers from a telecommunications firm and a financial services firm, we polled a set of their customers (9,900 at the telecom firm and 6,700 at the financial services firm) on their referral intentions and then tracked their behavior and the behavior of the prospective customers that the referring customers brought in over time. The number of both companies' customers who said they intended to recommend the firms to other people was high, but the percentage that actually did so was far, far lower. While 68% of the financial services firm's customers expressed their intention to refer the company to other people, only 33% followed through. Fully 81% of the telecom firm's clients thought they'd recommend the company, but merely 30% actually did. What's more, very few of those referrals, in either case, actually generated customers (14% at the financial services firm; 12% at the telecom company). And, of those prospects that did become customers, only 11% of the financial services firm's—and a mere 8% of the telecom company's—became *profitable* new customers.[8]

A manager's mind and life are reasonably hard coded to singularly comprehend the dollar value of their actions. If an index can't be spelt out in dollars and cents, the chances of it being absorbed in the company are low. Managers customarily do not put money where the mouth is unless they believe they can ultimately foretell the cash. The companies I have seen, and the managers around, do like to count the nickel.

We can use metrics that are business appropriate, but we do need a dollar measure of the value of the existing customers. The concept of *Customer Capital* is one such tool to measure the value of the existing customers. The classical definition alludes to the enduring value of the customers, but managers I know measure it near-term as well as lifetime. It is not a new concept and is used extensively by some businesses. Nor will it ever be definitive. The conventional definition of Customer Capital extrapolates current earnings into the future; essentially multiplying current revenue with the experiential life of the customer in a time horizon to

---

[8] V. Kumar, J. Andrew Peterson and Robert P. Leone, "How valuable is word of mouth?" *HBR*, October (2007).

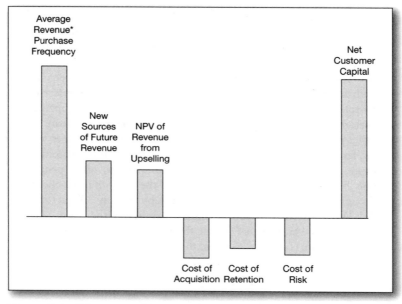

Figure 7.1   Measuring Customer Capital
Source: Author's own.

arrive at the financial value of their customers. Broadly, the definition of customer capital is a sum total of all current and future
likely revenues from a customer, and from this top-line number, it
deducts the cost of servicing and retention. Since this concept is
the future value, the discount rate and risk depreciation are incorporated in the definition. An illustrative chart for measuring customer capital is depicted in Figure 7.1.

The advantages of a number like customer capital are many:

- It is a numeral, expressed in the currency of use, and therefore operational managers find it easy to comprehend.
- Like any other number, one can see the trends. The movement in this number is indicative of what market actions
  create value and what don't.

- The hard reality is that the value of customer is not determined exclusively by actions of the internal employees in a company. The value of our relationship with our customers is as well impacted by competition moves and market changes. This metric is a fine balance of company actions and competition moves.
- Because it is a dynamic number in real life, since it moves up and down, it forces managements to think of solutions. If there is a price war, for instance, price realizations will go down, and managers will need to rummage around for other sources of revenues.
- It is adaptable in its construct. If the "lifetime" seems too long, one can do near-term calculations as well. Indeed multi-time horizons give great perspectives on the business.
- Customer capital, if used intelligently, can begin to change the quality of revenues. It's an important consideration given that there is a consistent struggle to discriminate a dollar of revenue that is good, from the one acquired to deliver short-term results.

In all fairness, the concept of customer capital has been much in debate for some time. It has its detractors. Any metric in a business, which is focused on the value being realized over a long horizon, runs the risk of delayed accountability of the managers and can be abused to paint a "hockey-stick" promise of performance, a reasonably well acknowledged reality in the corporate sector.

A useful approach that combines the traditional way of calculating the customer lifetime value and return on marketing investment is that of *Customer Equity* pioneered by Roland T. Rust, Katherine N. Lemon, and Valarie A. Zeithaml. Customer Equity is the sum of all values over the total customer lifetime of a company. It is thus an aggregation of three sources of value: the *Value Equity*, the *Brand Equity*, and the *Retention Equity*.

A metric is as good as your assumptions and intent. But broadly all parameters lead us to the same path of building customer value.

CONSTITUTING THE CUSTOMER CAPITAL LADDER

The reason this chapter will be populated with international case studies, and not many Indian cases, is by design. Global benchmarks and markets where customers wield influence are important to take note of. A supply deprived economy, enough new pools of the customers forged by economic growth, weaker legislations on customer rights, and a culture quintessentially perpetuated with authoritarian mindsets, is hardly a festering ground for creating a company that seeks to benchmark on customer excellence. This also points toward enormous opportunities that are waiting to be exploited should we heed an oft-quoted advice from none other than Mahatma Gandhi on the worth of customers. "We are not doing him a favor by serving him. He is doing us a favor by giving us an opportunity to do so."

While Customer Capital is a number, the variables that drive it are not singularly numerical. That's no surprise because as you deal with the groups of people, it takes a lot more than arithmetical skills to impact their lives. The buyers of today want you to have more emotion, share more information, be ethical in your conduct, and recognize their points of discomfort; they want to be understood, inspired, and challenged. A quantitative success in business will need softer parameters as the base of a relationship with customers.

Let's turn our attention to seven big steps that collectively contribute to the task of growing Customer Capital, and hence the value of an enterprise, as shown in Figure 7.2.

FROM TRANSACTIONS TO TRUST

The role of brands is to help consumers do simple yet real things in life. That the brand must be trusted and should have a higher role in the lives of mortals is not a new concept. The brands make us aspire, for example, to look good, feel powerful, protect self, care for others, and indulge in small pleasures. Great brands are those that have a role distinctly etched in the life of their customers. Whether you are Gen X or Y, one consistent rule of engagement is trust as the bedrock.

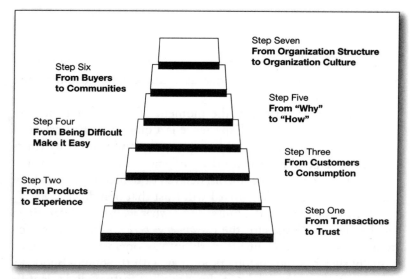

Figure 7.2 The Customer Capital Ladder
Source: Author's own.

Lack of trust takes a clandestine toll. Low-trust brands realize lower price from their customers, and expand higher costs in making their products. Because everyone wants to play safe with such a brand, their credit line is tight, the paper work is bureaucratic, and the customers accept the product only if the price of such a low trust brand is discounted. There is a cost of being a brand that people don't believe in.

The issue is what leads to trust, why customers feel positive and have confidence only in a few companies, and not in all. This has been a subject of intense research. One such evidence of the source of trust has been found in a chemical compound.

Could a single molecule—one chemical substance—lie at the very center of our moral lives? Research that I have done over the past decade suggests that a chemical messenger called *oxytocin* accounts for why some people give freely of themselves and others are cold-hearted louts, why some people cheat and steal and others you can trust with your life, why some husbands are more faithful than others, and why women tend to be nicer and more generous than men....[9]

Trust begets trust, as the research of *Paul Zak* quoted above concludes. If a company will trust its customers, the customers too will trust the company.

The source of trust is in the moment of truth when the customer touches the brand. Experience is a more powerful driver of how we feel about a brand than a promise. If the company trusts me, it is one good experience that will stay with me for long, and if I am quoted process protocols, delayed or denied high quality of engagement, it is unlikely that I will trust that brand.

If the experience is the bull's eye, if what we buy is determined by the empirical exposure, the *Customer experience map* is one such tool to help bring the outside world into an organization. The map visually sketches the customers' journey with the brand. Suddenly consumption gets real. It's not about product features and scientific know-how but its impact on our lives. There are customer stories, encounters, disappointments, and high points, akin to a living organism. We realize the true role our product plays in the life of a customer and the delivery of that experience. Companies that invest in understanding in painstaking detail as to how consumers buy and use their products, also discover what improvements are needed in the delivery of the experience. They know what value has to be put in, and what value to be taken out. Consider an example from an airline. Typically managers in aviation are tasked with metrics like aircraft utilization, load factor, revenue passenger miles, yield, and fuel costs. The pilot sitting in the cockpit navigates a complex instrumentation that covers altitude, speed, temperature, weather, fuel, and time to destination. None of these metrics amazes any customer; much less gets them to trust the brand. What matters to the customers is the entire experience of going from one place to another. The airline *Indigo* aptly captured the essence in a purely operational feature of "being on time" in an industry that regularly talked about their food and the quality of their aircrafts.

[9] Paul J. Zak, "The Trust Molecule," *Wall Street Journal*, April 27 (2012).

It is fair to believe that one would more easily trust someone who has been around for some time. Unfortunately this premise is no longer valid. The concept of trust with the new generation has now become more wholesome, something that has a far reaching impact. It's not any more about *who* you are; it's now about *what* you do, how good you are as an entity, your ethics and morality, and your value system. To quote Tony Hseih, CEO, Zappos.com: "A common trap that many marketers fall into is focusing too much on trying to figure out how to generate a lot of buzz, when really they should be focused on building engagement and trust."[10] Brands that we trust are predictable, reliable, communicate openly, are upfront, practice accountability and continually evolve and grow relationship.

FROM PRODUCTS TO EXPERIENCE

From commodity categories to service brands, customers reward companies that make the effort to go beyond the exacting definition of what business the company is in. The millennial generation buys experiences, and value, not products. Some of our Turbonator companies, not all, too have followed this path of seeking answers to life-determining questions: what do my customers truly want, and what business are we in? Many businesses in India still operate in the "product" space. Large international brands, caught earlier in the commoditization trap though, have been at the forefront of defining uniquely their customer proposition for a while now.

There are four distinct ways the corporate world has responded to this tectonic shift where customers demand more than a product that the companies manufacture, and companies too recognize that this is the route to structural progress in the value of their customer capital. The progressive journey from selling only products to delivering a personal experience is depicted in Figure 7.3.

- *Utilitarian solutions* are the first level intervention for a company trying to enhance the value of the product that it sells.

---

[10] Tony Hseih, *Delivering happiness: A path to profits, passion and purpose*, p. 234. http://www.rehanu.com/books_all/pdf/delivering_happiness.pd (accessed on July 1, 2015).

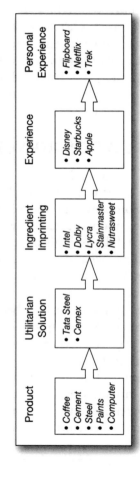

Figure 7.3   Progressive Customer Value Chain
Source: Author's own.

Often the products that companies make, a customer can't use in isolation. They have to assemble many other components in order to get these products into a shape worthy of consumption. Many corporations have pitched them strongly in this space and have created an ecosystem that delivers solutions to customers even though these companies have traditionally manufactured products. *CEMEX,* one of the world's largest building materials supplier, sells ready mix concrete versus cement in gunny bags, *Tata Steel* cuts and bends steel to individual customer specifications rather than sell commoditized retro bars, Paint companies like *Asian Paints* offer to give a painted house, car dealers of *Hyundai* also transact used car resale and insurance, and a bank like *ICICI* offers wealth management services. All these and more are examples of how a manufacturer can transcend the traditional definition of a product. These companies help consumers solve their most compelling problems. The market pole position it gives to the first movers in this space of solutions versus selling of a product is a significant entry barrier for a new competitor. It is relatively easy to replicate product specifications, more difficult to become a solutions company.

- *Ingredient imprinting* is the next level intervention. Customers increasingly peer under the hood to see what exactly they are buying. The product by itself is seen as a mere aggregator of different raw materials that have been put together. When we buy biscuits, for instance, we read data points like sugar and fat content. This trend has coerced many brands to declare their formulations on the pack itself. B2B business has done it always; their clients demand full disclosures. Companies also often resort to leveraging the use of ingredients to convey the sense of value their products have. *Lycra* in clothing, *Stainmaster* in carpets, *NutraSweet* in health beverages, *Dolby* in sound systems, *Android* in mobiles, *Triclean* fuel, *Teflon* and *Intel,* would be great illustrations of ingredients that build customer trust in the products they ultimately buy. An ingredient branding adds a layer of value to the products' overall positioning, and perhaps a level of differentiation versus competition by changing the playing field. What makes the *Intel* story of ingredient branding most prominent is the manner in which they executed the entire ecosystem, not merely branded their product. They have a product and an idea that is so critical to performance of the final product for a customer. Intel's original communication tagline was "Intel. The Computer Inside" before it was shortened. They have cooperative agreements with Original equipment manufacturers and share cost of advertising so long as the Intel Inside logo is carried. It is the creation of an end-to-end ecosystem and consistent messaging that optimizes the value of ingredient branding. Of course, how Intel leverages the mobile and other devices revolution, apart from the PC market, going forward will be an entirely different story, and impact its future.

• *Experience delivery* is the third intervention that companies have deployed to engage with their young customers in an attempt to go higher up the value chain and create a compelling differentiation versus competition. *Disney* and *Starbucks* have done it. *Apple* has defined a new benchmark for every brand to aspire for. *Virgin Money* has bank branches that look more like living rooms. There are no tellers and no queues. There is comfortable seating, Wi-Fi and newspapers to read. A part of enormous wealth created in the new age economy finds its way into either high cost of living or buying into fashion and luxury. Customers increasingly want to do and experience things that define their aspirations and persona.

• *Personalized experience delivery* is the uppermost intervention. Travel companies so used to group tours now offer tailor-made travel to individuals, their family, and friends. There is a tour even for partaking the culinary delights of a region by dining in with local families. A hotel chain asks, records, and remembers preferences of their guests and makes sure their rooms are done up each time exactly to the specifications of their guests. Pod hotels characterized by limited room size but technology gadgets and luxury, the likes of *Yotel*, have begun to spring up. *Flipboard* is our personal magazine, carrying only the kind of news and stories we care about. *Netflix* has personalized the way we watch movies. *Trek* enables cyclists to build a bike from the ground up. *Brooks Brothers* allow men to create their own suits. Consider *Freestyle* soda fountain machines being progressively deployed by *Coca Cola*. It is a self-serve machine that allows users to choose from more than 100 individual flavors. These are some of the millions of business models that truly recognize and encourage value in personalizing consumption.

As you move up the customer value chain, from product to personalized experience delivery, you increasingly lock the customers to your brand and shut off the competition, thereby creating financial headroom to sustain mutually beneficial relationship with your customers.

FROM CUSTOMERS TO CONSUMPTION

India's mission to Mars at $70 million cost less than the Hollywood movie *Gravity*.

To get to Mars, one needs a rocket launcher. Instead of making a new launcher, India deployed an existing launcher to keep the costs down. This launcher was used for our forays to the moon. It wasn't as powerful though. Mars is a good 100 times further away than the moon. We needed to supplement the power of the existing launcher with something that's inexpensive. Indian scientists made use of gravity. It is free. We employed interplanetary slingshot. Earth's gravity was used to gather speed, Sun's gravity was deployed to travel, and we applied gravity of mars to get closer to the destination.

Like gravity, which costs nothing and is a powerful propeller, our existing customers deliver revenues and profits at the lowest marginal cost.

Fidelity in consumption, however, is rare. An estimated 13 percent of unique and active customers in mobiles use multiple connections.[11] In addition, millions of mobile connections were bought and have been inactive, which operators have been pruning now for years. It is alleged that the trigger for *Nokia's* relative demise from astronomical heights in the India market was its inability to timely read that the market was ripe for dual SIM handsets since customers were using service in parts from different operators.

The best measure of trust, therefore, is the depth and profoundness of consumption with the brand. When we consume more of something, and do so frequently, we are committed to the brand we consume. On the contrary, if we are a rare consumer, inconsistent, toying between competitors, we certainly don't have an enduring relationship, much less are we likely to be a loyal advocate of the brand.

The power of aggregating the consumption of your customers can be more than the power of acquiring more consumers, and profitable too.

For consumption, and not consumers, to be the pivot, the traditional construct of the product and its boundaries must be reevaluated. Indeed many companies have deepened their relationship with their installed base of consumers by trying to find what else their customers buy while using their products. Some categories handle it by routine. A telecom operator discounts call tariff to family and friends, or offers free calling to the employees of their large corporate accounts. Manufacturers of chocolates find that their opportunity is in converting the largest diabetic population in the world to consume their chocolates, instead of sweets. More consumption, not more consumers, is a big accelerator to the customer capital.

A consumption life cycle has five stages. Companies, therefore, have five opportunities to realize a larger value than product sales can permit—pre-purchase stage, at the time of purchase, post-purchase, repurchase, and adjacent market, as shown in Figure 7.4.

---

[11] "Multiple SIM card usage set to surge," *Nielson,* March 28 (2012), http://www.nielsen.com/in/en/press-room/2012/multiple-sim-card-usage-set-to-surge.html (accessed on July 1, 2015).

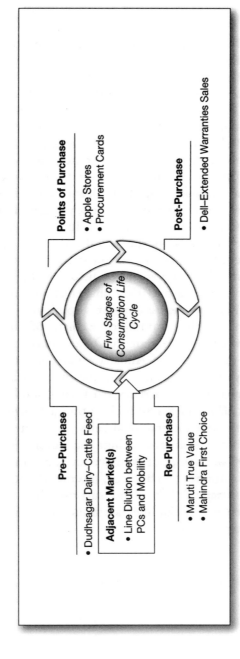

Figure 7.4   Unlocking Value in Consumption
Source: Author's own.

Pre-purchase

In the town of Mehsana, *Dudhsagar dairy*, the largest cooperative for Amul, manufactures cattle feed. They are in the business of milk but recognize that cattle feed has an important role in the health, production, and reproduction of animals. They produce quality feed and supply it at better than market prices. Both the farmers and the cooperative gain with enhanced productivity of the cattle. Similarly, in the computer business, a *value-added reseller (VAR)* is an entity that takes a computer, adds own "value" usually in the form of a specific application for the product (for example, a special computer application), and resells it as a new product. Consider another paradigm. Think you are a brand outside China but want to sell to customers in China, one of the biggest consumer markets in the world. But you stop short because of challenges in customer acquisition, foreign currency payment, and cross-border logistics. Customers in China too want international brands but it's a challenge to buy international merchandise. *Alipay ePass* integrates dominant online payment performance with e-commerce website of the brands, irrespective of the country they are in. On an international website, brands put on an icon of Alibaba e-pay apart from other payment gateways. Customers in China pay in the local currency and *Alipay* manages foreign currency, marketing, and logistics. It is estimated that *Alipay* clears 80 million transactions every day, for both domestic and international sales. To quote the chief executive of their financial arm, "China has never been lacking banks; it has 200 of them, but we have an opportunity to use Internet methods, Internet technology, Internet thinking to disrupt traditional finance."[12] It is no surprise that the young Chinese customers who are online have profoundly endorsed the contemporary way to bank.

---

[12] Quoted by Ant Financial Chief Executive, Lucy Pang, in Businessinsider.com, October (2014).

Point of Purchase

There is nothing exciting about buying computers. Traditionally small stores, in cramped electronic markets, sell this expensive and personalized gizmo. *Apple* changed it all with its retail push at the last mile. Well-lit and airy stores, fanatic attention to detail and processes, competent manpower, all have contributed to the magical purchase experience at the Apple stores. "More people now visit Apple's 326 stores in a single quarter than the 60 million who visited Walt Disney Co.'s four biggest theme parks last year, according to data from Apple and the Themed Entertainment Association."[13] Let us consider another prototype that creates value by triggering consumption during the process of buying. Procurement processes in companies are arduous, bureaucratic, with huge paper trails. *P-Card*, or purchase card or a procurement card, is similar to credit cards, except that these are used in B2B transactions. They have simplified buying in high value transactions. In case a company procures material from another company, they pay for it electronically by way of the P-Card, just as we would pay by a credit card for personal low value transactions. The P-Cards streamline management reporting, eliminate manual processes in generating invoices and a trail of follow ups, and save costs by removing the middlemen, in this case often the banks.

Post-Purchase

Dell India sells extended warranties well after the purchase of their product. A telecom operator continuously up sells to its existing customers a long distance calling card, Internet usage pack, video downloads, and musical ring tones. A direct to home media company pushes to its customers a sports channel, a movie channel, and a regional language channel. A failure to do business after the event of purchase leaves value on the table. Sales teams

---

[13] Yukari Iwatani Kane and Ian Sherr, "Secrets from Apples Genius Bar," *Wall Street Journal,* June 15 (2011), Available online at http://www.wsj.com/articles/SB100014240527023045 63104576364071955678908

are notorious for selling what is the easiest to sell. Generally, the easiest is also something that's the cheapest to sell. Also, it's likely that a new customer would rather experience the brand before committing an entire wallet. Making the sale after a sale adds newer sources of revenue on top of the price realization from the same customer.

Repurchase

Consider these data points.

> A recent report released by the Associated Chamber of Commerce and Industry of India pegged the market for second-hand and recycled products in India at Rs 80,000 crore ($12,814 Mn.), up from Rs 69,000 crore ($1,1027 Mn.) in 2012. The report further estimated that the market would cross Rs 1,15,000 crore ($18,379 Mn.) by 2015.[14]

The repurchase market has recorded a growth of 15 percent per annum. The baby-boomers generation has aspirations of brands, but not always the means to buy. Automobile companies would be the best example of a category that leads repurchase behavior. An estimated 3 million used cars change hands annually. As reported by *The Hindu*, India's used car market is expected to grow up to 2.5 times the size of the new car market, driven by growing acceptance of used cars, rising aspirations and expansion of organized sales channels.[15]

Used car shops like *Maruti True Value, Mahindra First Choice* and *Carnation Auto* take back an old car, and ideally sell a new one of the same brand. This concept plays on the velocity of the replacement cycle for products and also helps expand the market as many customers, who cannot afford an expensive new vehicle, are tempted to buy their favorite brand even if it's a hand me down.

---

[14] Mamta Bharadwaj, "India's shining second hand market," *Al Jazeera – Features,* March 21 (2014).

[15] Yuthika Bhargava, "Used Car Market to overtake New Car Market," *The Hindu,* August 29 (2014).

Adjacent Markets

All cola brands now sell many other beverages including water, energy drinks, and health drinks. A disinfectant company runs a gamut of product extensions from soap to cleaners. Companies that made computers are also selling mobile devices. The allure is undeniable. Growth aspirations often run ahead of potential in the current industry. In addition, sometimes the business we have always been in, as is the case with many products mentioned above, loses resonance with young consumers. This migration can take different shapes and contours, but what works is the fact that consumers in adjacent market are aware of the brand and its capabilities. If the brand has properties that can be stretched, new markets will open up. In all these instances, strict definition of the industry has been demolished. The only definition used is one of the customers.

How far a company can stretch its boundary depends substantively on what it stands for. *Virgin* brand of Richard Branson doesn't suggest clinical product features. They don't say we are the largest or the fastest. As a brand, it is fun, irreverent, adventurous, affordable, and fearless. A brand like Virgin, built on emotional human connect—it's not a surprise—is supremely stretchable. The sprawling business empires that bear the Virgin name include some 200 companies, from music to airlines and a bank.

It is a rare product that doesn't leave the unattended value at the fringes. So focused are we with our in vogue products that we do not see the consumption pipeline in its entirety, or even the generational transformations in the category. Someone currently supplies to that value. And this awareness is the key to unlock new value for the business.

From Being Difficult to Make It Easy

The way you do business is increasingly becoming an important consideration for a customer. Instant gratification, real-time information, authenticity, and flexibility are things that matter to the young.

Ideally, as a customer, if I had a magic wand, I would want the following:

- If I need to reach a *call center*, it should be of *Zappos*, online shoes and clothing store based in Las Vegas. As of December 2012, their longest call recorded was almost 10 and a half hours. Traditional call centers, in a bid to enhance productivity of employees, target average hold time and number of calls handled. The call experience therefore in most call centers is truncated, mechanical, and matter-of-fact. Not *Zappos*, for them it's more about a great customer service. They also have a fantastic script for their employees. It does not exist. *Zappos* generally stays away from policies and circulars, and encourages the representatives to do whatever is right for the customers and the company.

- If I ever need to *return the merchandise* because it's defective, then I would rather shop with *L.L. Bean* and have the peace of mind. "Have questions before; during or after you place your order? We're happy to provide answers. Our 100 percent satisfaction guarantee doesn't end with the sale. That's our promise—one we've been keeping for over 100 years." So says the website of L.L. Bean. Their legendary service guarantees 100 percent satisfaction; it's not unusual they will take back their products, if defective, even 10 years later with no questions or proofs asked for. *Nordstrom* is in the same league. If an item is not working, it doesn't matter when it was purchased, or whether you have receipts, or where you purchased from, Nordstrom will accept it as a return.

- If I need to *reach out on social media,* it perhaps should be to *KLM*. They have a socially connected business that can intelligently and efficiently collect and track all social conversations. They measure brand sentiment on the Web, and proudly display their goal of one-hour response/24-hour resolution time.

- I would rather bank with *USAA*, one of the biggest banks in the US with around $50 billion in deposits and more than 6.3 million accounts. They have been at the forefront of *using technology* and alternate channels. One of the keys to their success is their focus on a narrow and specific audience segment, namely those in military service and their families. It allows customers to deposit cheques by sending pictures of the cheque taken on their smartphones. They are routinely texting account balances to soldiers in the field, and they heavily discount customers' car insurance while they are deployed overseas.

- If I wish to experience the *simplicity* at every touch point, a genuine requirement, I would rather shop at ALDIs, which has fewer items to choose from, everyday low prices, and swift processes. Around the globe, an overwhelming 75 percent of customers said they are likely to recommend brands that are simple, and indeed be willing to pay a price premium as well for such brands.

> This year's Simplicity Index affirms that brands willing to simplify their customer experiences stand to gain more revenue. In the data, we have the percentage increase in price consumers said they would be willing to pay for simpler experiences offered by each brand included in the survey—a tangible illustration of the value of simplicity. Brands are leaving significant money on the table because of complexity."[16]

ALDI, the low cost German supermarket chain emerged as the No. 1 brand of simplicity, closely followed by *Amazon*, *Google*, *Ikea*, and *Pizza Hut*.

- Customer touch points have historically been seen as transaction entities. Let us consider an example of *a touch point that has embraced intelligence* in the way it runs. Personal

---

[16] Howard Belk, "Global Brand Simplicity Index," Siegel+Gale (2013), http://www.siegel-gale.com/the-global-brand-simplicity-index-gbsi/ (accessed on July 1, 2015).

computer problems still zap an average technology phobic customer. Dell India has 24 × 7 call centers. Representatives at the call center are tasked to solve 80 percent of the issues on the call itself. The other 20 percent are problems for which a technician would need to physically inspect the machine. The call center representative would in such cases identify possible problems and the component parts that a technician may need to resolve the malfunction. Thus, multiple PC parts are sent to the customer's place, and the technician thereafter carries out the repair. Excess and unused parts dispatched by design as part of this process then comes back to Dell through a reverse logistics process.

- I would rather endorse brands that *allow me to serve myself.* Rendition of personal details and passwords to unknown agents is not exactly something we like. We book our own airline tickets. We do our hotel bookings. We decide what pictures to upload on Facebook, whom to invite as our friend. We decide what to tweet on and when. We are happy walking through supermarket aisles doing our own shopping. We bank on the Internet, take out cash ourselves from ATMs. The power of customers to serve themselves should not be underestimated. Customers want ease and control of the process; companies want a reduction in transaction costs. Self-service is a win–win.

- I would rather be with a company where *managers are tasked to do what is right for the customer.* So-called processes and protocols can only deliver an average experience. These are just not constituted for customer delight. I have a loyalty card of an airline, just as most of us have. When I went in to redeem the points, the airline made those tickets unavailable. It later dawned that in an airline people are tasked with a metric that looks at cost per mile for redemption. The task of the manager is to redeem maximum points at the lowest cost to the company. There is no metric that puts a metric value on high value, loyal customer who generates good revenue, has a minimum cost to serve, if delighted, can be our brand ambassador, which kicks in more customers. Misplaced KPIs, driven by immediate financial goals, are the biggest culprit, which often keeps customers and producers in a position of distrust.

FROM "WHY" TO "HOW"

Management has always been about managers, their personality types, leadership skills, and ability to deploy judgment and instincts. What if a lot of what managers currently do was to be done by a machine, with more consistency and less errors, and yes at a fraction of the cost being incurred today. Before we dismiss this frightening thought, a scenario like this could be a possibility in our lifetime, or at least a part of it. Gone are the days when traders shouted in the ring for orders in stock markets; today, machines do it quietly in one corner. Algorithms have written music that competes with the best a human mind ever produced, a machine has beaten a much decorated chess champion, our air-crafts do run on autopilot, and cars will soon too.

Such has been the power of science that we have spent well over two centuries trying to understand why things happen the way they do. Why does an apple fall from a tree? Why do space-craft's need propulsion? Why do cats always land up on their feet? Why do I feel dizzy when I spin? Why do leaves change color in the fall? Why don't oceans freeze in the peak of winters?

There are some people who believe that science is outdated, and will now get trumped by math. Getting to know the *why* of things is not as important as finding out *how* to make this happen, or not happen.

Vivek Ranadive is the founder of *Tibco*. In one of the interviews he put forth the case for management decisions inspired by the power of information.

We live in a time where there is amazing amount of data available. Yet we haven't solved the simplest problems. We still have airplane crashes, lost baggage on airlines, security breaches. I think we are entering a new exciting era where math is going to trump science. You don't need to know the why of something. You just need to know the what. You just need to know if A and B happen, C will happen. The data is there. We just have to connect the dots and make it available at the right place at the right time.[17]

You know what your customers are going to do. There is a pattern in collective behavior. You don't need to wait for it to happen. However, while the world runs in real time, the problem is batch processing and innumerable, disparate legacy systems that create the lag, and do not allow the dots to connect. An average customer service shop is reactive and not proactive; they swing into action well after the customer has already churned.

The best source of this intelligence is data of existing customers, their buying habits, their reaction to promotions and new offers, the commonality between consumers who churn, their usage, and their lifetime value. Properly harnessed, this information can help prevent revenue depletion, target promotions more efficiently, and direct retention efforts to consumers who have high lifetime value and are at risk. This will allow you to gravitate away from static performance to more predictive, futuristic performance drivers.

FROM BUYERS TO COMMUNITIES

Individual customers are always more difficult to retain. A community of customers maintains itself and remains loyal. However, companies in their zeal to sell products, at times, forget that there can be a larger force that binds their disparate consumers.

The Harley Davidson owners group is the best example of not only selling a product, but also building a community of consumers, bound together by a common passion. The group has regular jaunts, dinners, and they all ride for charity; indeed they live their collective zeal for biking.

[17] N Mahalakshmi and Rajesh Padmashali, "We are entering a new exciting era where math is going to trump science", *Outlook business interviews*, February 2, 2013.

Existing customers are always more credible than your sales representative will ever be. Companies that have used customer testimonials have discovered an explosive growth in leads, that too at low costs. In the case of software, there are developers who form an online community. They improve on existing software, help remove bugs, give ideas for upgrades, and essentially are an extended research and development arm of the software company.

What is common among our customers? What brings them together to consume what we make? Are they passionate about the value we add? Do we make a difference to their lives? These are some of the big questions to ask as we go around trying to build community of customers.

A community like ecosystem for a brand is built around six vectors.

- There has to be an inspiring idea or *passion* that is the glue.
- The idea must not only be inspiring, it should be *uniquely yours*. It is a promise you are equipped and genetically endowed to best deliver.
- There has to be an active effort aimed at engaging and *value creation* for your committed customers.
- The survival of the community depends on its *usefulness*.
- Any such community must necessarily be *one of equals* for each individual to meaningfully contribute and collaborate. It's like a party you have thrown for a lot of people; everyone must feel invited.
- Finally, if you want value out of this community by way of *referral currency*, then marketing plans need to be built to convert latent advocacy into positive, dollar paying revenue.

FROM ORGANIZATION STRUCTURE TO ORGANIZATION CULTURE

In the good old times of the product economy, employees were taught what to do and how, and so long as they delivered exactly their job descriptions, day in and out, results were executed consistently. But in a consumer era, the controls are no longer confined within your factory. Today, a company is responsible for manufacturing both the product and the experience; you manage the brand and the customers of your brand, the communication and the conduct of the brand. And a more nuanced view of the millennial as employees has begun to emerge that shows that they have a drastically different view of the employment life. They seek challenges and yet want a better work–life balance; they are ambitious and yet like to work in groups; they are individually driven, yet want real time, succinct, twitter-like frequency feedback on performance.

Customer-focused organizations are constitutionally different. These are directed from within. They expand and contract as needed. Hierarchy doesn't matter, and functional silos are disaggregated to serve the end customer. People are bound by one KPI, customer capital, and not individual goals. Difference of opinion and diversity inevitable in any organization actually works to an advantage, as it ensures that the voice of the customer is never missed.

There is evidence of one such organization, albeit in its early days, that's trying to challenge traditional organization structures that divide the company into functional silos, or business parts, or both. *Zappos,* an online retailer, and one of the most inspiring customer service stories of our times, has begun to replace traditional structures with holacracy. Employees have no job titles and there are no managers, power is distributed evenly. People work in groups as part of a circle. An employee can be in many circles as needed, the transparency and contribution though is radically visible. At its core, the philosophy is that there is work to be done, and it's better that the company is organized around work, rather than people.

CONCLUSION

Irrespective of the business one is in, the millennial generation will impact its future contours and development. Also called the boomerang generation, they are tech savvy and connected; they are collaborative, transparent, and want to balance work and life. They seek gratification at the speed of light. And they are authentic. This is hardly the recipe with which the businesses were built in the past. It is an opportune time for farsighted companies to reconstruct their processes around the Gen Y customers.

Commenting on the India progress in the last few decades, Gurcharan Das writes:

> The economic rise of India has been the defining event in my life. It is not only good news for 1.2 billion Indians, but it is also reshaping the world. At a time when Western economies are failing, a large nation is rising in the East based on political and economic liberty, proving once again that open societies, free trade, and multiplying connections to the global economy are pathways to lasting prosperity and national success. India and its people, however, have achieved this prosperity in the face of the nation's appalling governance.[18]

The last two decades have been monumental for India. But as one looks at modern Pudong in Shanghai, one wonders if the economic development in India could be any different. I am sure there is a lot that one can talk about what is amiss in China, and indeed in all parts of the world, but walking along the river in state-of-the art Pudong, I wondered why India, unlike China, can't give its dwellers basic necessities of life-like potable water, reliable electricity, roads that are clean and metaled, quality health care, and elementary dignity. Economic inequality has only aggravated with liberalization in countries like India. If the last two decades are about growth in India, these are also about the richest 1 percent of the population increasing their wealth to 49 percent of the national wealth. The gains in prosperity, literacy, and mortality over the years are real, but also grossly unequal. Rana Dasgupta, who won the 2010 Commonwealth Writers' Prize for the best book, talks about savage realities post-liberalization rather candidly in his latest book on Delhi. In his words, "The transformation was stern,

---

[18] Gurcharan Das, "How to grow during the day," in *Reimaging India,* ed. Mckinsey & Company, 22.

abrupt and fantastically unequal, and it gave rise to strange and bewildering feelings. The city brimmed with ambition and rage. Bizarre crime stole the headlines."[19]

We need means by which we can reach new customers in new ways, open up our markets, and get the disenfranchised populace into our consuming class. We need to leapfrog from the old world, but at lower costs, more equanimity, and greater efficiency. This will not happen with sequential thinking and conventional means. Part of the hope lies in technology, something that we in India are proud of. The next chapter examines the purpose of technology in detail.

---

[19] Rana Dasgupta, *Capital: A Portrait of Twenty-first Century Delhi*, Harper Collins Publishers, 2014.

8 Man *and* Machine, Not Man *or* Machine

From Jaipur, the capital city of Rajasthan, I drove a good three hours to reach the village of Khareda Lakshmipura, in the district of Tonk. The roads are bumpy, the land barren with sand dunes on both sides and all along not much by way of civilization. Khareda Lakshmipura is a tiny hamlet of 50 houses and some 200 villagers. Till not so long ago, people had to use lanterns powered by kerosene to get some kind of light. For charging their mobile phones, and interestingly mobile is their only connect with the mainstream civilization, they had to walk to a nearby town and pay a shopkeeper. Children hardly studied as dusk came in. Indeed all activities shut down by the late afternoon.

A situation like this is not unique to Khareda Lakshmipura; it's an endemic issue across many parts of rural India. The quantum of power generated in the country is woefully short of the needs of the people. And even of the power that is produced, India is estimated to lose a good 25 billion dollars annually by way of theft, pilferage, and non-payment of bills. The construct of the power sector in India currently is no different than the way our telecom was before the mobile revolution—inefficient and inadequate.

Today Khareda Lakshmipura is a proud village in the entire area that has electricity 24 × 7. I could hear radio and see people glued to their television screens, something unimaginable till not so long ago. *Gram Power*, a young company started by 25-year-old Yashpal Khaitan and his fellow student at the University of California where both studied together, has been the instrument of this change in Khareda Lakshmipura. Gram Power provides ultra-affordable and reliable energy to the energy-deficient population. Built on a real time, wireless prepaid system, Gram Power is attempting to imitate the high-impact telecom metamorphosis.

People in Khareda Lakshmipura can now work longer hours, they are able to do small business from home, they earn more, and they spend more. The economy improves, as does the quality of life. Off-grid solutions based on renewable energy sources like the Gram Power deliver a cleaner environment. It promotes health and education. The beginnings of this deep metamorphosis and domino effect of electrification are visible in Khareda Lakshmipura.

THE CONTEXT

Technology interests us for a reason. Technology empowers compression of the conventional concept of the business cycle that most companies have been used to following, first big markets, then smaller, first rich, then not so rich. The belief is that a technology-propelled untrodden value curve at the last mile can alter the trajectory of change in a society from a linear to an exponential curve. Embracing cutting-edge solutions powered by the likes of cloud computing, data analytics, Internet, mobile technology, and geospatial analysis help us leapfrog to the next generation of growth.

Technology, apart from providing "escape velocity" solutions, is also interesting because it is inclusive and democratic in its construct, a key prerequisite for the emerging economies. Even smaller companies and first-generation entrepreneurs can now hope to thrive and succeed. Let's consider cloud computing, for instance. A small-scale company can deploy it as easily and economically as the largest enterprise. There is no upfront cost. When you sign up, you get to use the software without worrying about installing it, maintaining it, downloading updates, or keeping it secure. You also won't need expensive servers or data centers or any other additional IT investment that larger suites of software used to require. You pay a small, predictable fees every month per user for the software you use.

India has a natural affinity to the sciences and mathematics; our people have historically excelled in these disciplines. Now we have the opportunity to use this power to leapfrog our economic growth.

There are, however, limitations to the quantum of "leapfrogging" possible in a country challenged with the basics in infrastructure and education. A dated report of the World Bank on technology diffusion points out this limitation.

Whether technological progress in developing countries will continue to outpace high- income countries will depend on the improvements in this regard. The main impediments to further progress is not access to technologies, but the weakness of domestic skills and competencies, which prevents many developing countries from exploiting these technologies, and rigidities in the regulatory environment that prevent innovative firms from being created and expanding.[1]

The technology has to be appropriate to the context in order to be properly diffused and to make a difference.

The other dilemma is how much should machines be really allowed to run our lives, even more in a billion-people economy, given that these do cause job losses. Carl Benedikt Frey and Michael Osborne, after examining the probability of computerization for 702 occupations, using data on advances in machine learning and mobile robotics, have forecast that in the US, 47 percent of the current jobs are at risk. Everything from telemarketers to routine jobholders runs this risk. To quote Adam Booth:

> Socialism, having done away with class society—i.e. the exploitation of a majority by a minority – would in time do away with the working class altogether by doing away with work itself. Such a future is no longer the mere dream of science fiction, but is a genuine possibility.[2]

Not everyone agrees to this obviously. Detractors of the doomsday scenario have asserted that the "previous technological innovation has always delivered more long-run employment, not less. Industrialization did not end up eliminating the need for human workers. On the contrary, it created employment opportunities sufficient to soak up the 20th century's exploding population."[3]

---

[1] "Global Economic Prospects 2008: Technology diffusion in the developing countries," *The World Bank* (2008).
[2] Adam Booth, Technology, innovation, growth, and capitalism. www.marxist.com/science-and-technology (accessed September 4, 2013).
[3] "The future of jobs: The onrushing wave," *The Economist*, January 18 (2014).

The debate notwithstanding, labor-abundant economies like India are better off when both men and man-made machines work together. Employment is the only institutionalized mechanism that balances growth and social justice. The relative cost of labor in India is still low, which has been a prime trigger for proliferating mechanization in countries in the West. The entire growth of the successful knowledge industry in India is based on the principle of the man and machine. This is not an easy debate but an important one. This does not mean companies live in the Stone Age; it only alludes to a more intelligent balance.

Despite the known power of technology, there is an inevitable time lag between what science knows and what business does. The problem we have is not the lack of technology; it is the proliferation of technology. The contrarian diffusion of the wireless communication technology substantiates the argument; it took less than two decades to proliferate mobile phones even in the remotest corners of the country, while other products still struggle to find mass traction.

From my perspective, there are *six interface points* of technology with the business in the constructs of particularly the last mile. Each of these impels the growth trajectory of a business. Put together, it touches all facets of corporate imperatives—market growth, societal outcomes, better value to customers, process capability, and an ability to resolve complex issues that only a machine is capable of concluding. These six interface points are illustrated in Figure 8.1.

SHIFT THE MARKET'S CENTER OF GRAVITY

Start with markets. For years, the last mile has been fraught with difficulties—from access to efficiency. This fact, among other reasons, has left a large mass of people disadvantaged and disenfranchised, and only a small population participates in the consumption of most goods and services. Add to this, the fact that most of the consumption transpires in a small cluster of urban centers. But a deep metamorphosis is underway. Rural demand is growing, in parts, and urbanization is proliferating at a speed and scale never seen before. Household incomes are rising, and increasing hordes

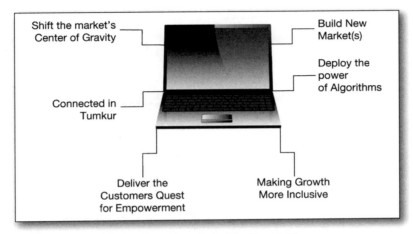

Figure 8.1   Six Technology Levers At The Last Mile
Source: Author's own.

of consumers are considering product categories they had never imagined they would be consuming one day. What it means is that the center of gravity of the market is changing.

The critical task is to leverage the forces of transformation and make sure that we scientifically shape the markets. Inclusive consumption, however, calls for affirmative action by companies.

There are four paths or routes to stimulate the market for our products and services:

- Improve *access*
- Enhance *opportunity*
- *Empower* the populace
- Drive *sustainability*

Each of these paths (shown in Figure 8.2) requires differing levels of effort to increase your consumption base, but each of these also impacts the brand value differently. The *terminal value* is not identical in each case. The deeper the relationship with the market, the more sustainable will be the market advantage, and larger will be the "terminal value" the brand can build.

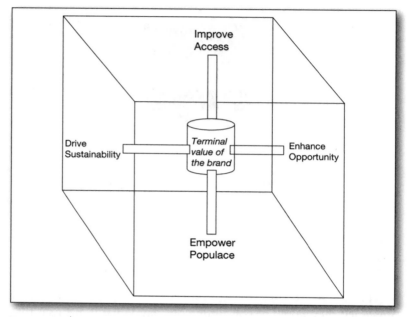

Figure 8.2   Shift The Market's Center of Gravity
Source: Author's own.

IMPROVE ACCESS

It is the elemental needs which most of us take for granted, the likes of clean water, reliable power, inexpensive food, health care, and education, that millions of people seek access to. *Gram Power,* the story told above, tackles the issue of access in electricity.

Gram Power has disaggregated the supply chain of power into atomic parts. Unlike the grid electricity that predominantly uses coal, which is both expensive and harms the environment, Gram Power produces energy using abundant natural resources, thus delivering a cost and an environmental advantage. After power is produced, the task of distribution begins. It has to be supplied regularly to all consumers at the click of a switch. That does not happen seamlessly in traditional grids because there isn't enough electricity for everyone, and also because there are always a few heavy users who consume more than others. Gram Power eliminates this problem of the rich usurping limited resources by democratizing consumption, and no one is allowed to unilaterally consume more to the detriment of others. The Gram Power micro-grid would automatically shut off such connections. Modern Prepaid metering system, unlike postpaid billing cycles, makes customers judicious in their consumption. The customer knows how much their electricity wallet has depleted, and how much longer can their current balance last. Gram Power micro-grids can remotely detect and also eliminate pilferage losses. The net outcome is power at most economical prices, and available 24 hours a day.

Buying a computer in the post, music on the Internet, insurance at the supermarkets, mortgages over the phone, and phones themselves from vending machines are similarly some other innovations in distribution which create competitive advantage as customers are offered newer, faster, cheaper, safer, and easier ways of buying products and services.

ENHANCE OPPORTUNITY

Availability by itself and in itself does not fully unlock the potential. Let us consider a case in the arena of food security. For most poor households, incomes are inconsistent and unpredictable. There are months when the discretionary income is high and people can save. For that you need a bank, but a good half of our population lacks access to formal banking, and therefore even if they want to save for the rainy day, where do they put in the money? Consequently, instead of money being saved for food during a bad patch, their meager wages get squandered on frivolous items of consumption. *Pulse Savings*, a social business, enables unbanked urban slum dwellers to reduce their food insecurity by actively saving small amounts of money, using their mobile phone. There is no physical bank branch to put the money in but customers can buy an electronic wallet from certified grocery vendors, to be redeemed for food coupons when needed. By allowing people to make small deposit/savings when they have a bit of spare change, they are enabling wage earners to feed their families on days where otherwise there would be no money to spare.

Let us consider another case. Farmers are very often illiterate. They are in large numbers. The diversity in the culture and language is onerous. How does one educate them and make them aware of means to better raise the crops they grow? *Digital Green* has delivered results with simple YouTube videos sharing best practices in raising crops and animals. Farmers are likely to listen to another farmer who looks like them, talks like them, and understands the environmental challenges that they face. From pest control to milch animal management, their videos educate the rural populace and give them an opportunity to earn more.

EMPOWER POPULACE

The last mile in each company is a unique ecosystem made up of customers, influencers, and some non-players too. When we sell, we don't sell to a customer, we actually pervade this ecosystem to reach out to our buyers. It is often an iniquitous ecosystem that prevents people from being in a consuming class. As you marginalize this inequality, you allow your customers the freedom to take situation-appropriate decisions. There is a business model in this empowerment that brands like Amul have demonstrated for good six decades. Let us consider the case of *e-Chaupal* of ITC Limited. The farmers in general were at the mercy of local middlemen who exploited the farmers' lack of information about crop prices, market trends, and physical distance from the trading centers. Internet propelled e-Chaupal enables farmers to obtain prevailing information on prices, good farming practices, and to place orders for agricultural inputs like seeds and fertilizers. Transparency of key market data empowers farmers to obtain the best price for their produce. Each ITC Limited kiosk having Internet access is run by a *sanchalak*—a trained farmer. The computer is housed in the sanchalak's house and is linked to the Internet via phone lines or by a satellite connection. At harvest time, ITC offers to buy the crop directly from any farmer at the previous day's closing price; the farmer then transports his crop to an ITC processing center, where the crop is weighed electronically and assessed for quality.

The e-Chaupal model surmounts fundamental issues in our agrarian economy–information asymmetry, weak institutions of commerce, and monopoly rights for trade given to organizations like the Agriculture Produce Market Committee, thus denying a fair play of market forces.

Early days, but increasingly we see not only the corporate and social businesses, but also the state, making efforts to be accountable and responsive. Many state governments today allow people to avail of a variety of services using the Internet, circumventing the bureaucracy. They have realized that a human interface in the delivery of many basic services adds no value, is inefficient by construct, and the inherent unbalanced power equation breeds corruption. *eSeva* of the government of Andhra Pradesh, for instance, permits citizens to pay for water, electricity, and property tax, and more than 45 other services, using kiosks or accessing the portal through the Internet.

Empowerment demolishes set patterns of working, and places trust back in the hands of people whom the system in any case avows to serve.

DRIVE SUSTAINABILITY

It is said that a business has three obligations—profits, people, and planet. The final stage is when a company drives long-term growth and profits by mandating the inclusion of people and larger societal good in their agendas. In general, sustainability means the capacity to endure. Business has a stable relationship with its customers when they put people at the heart of what they do. Companies that understand their customers and use this information in their product architecture and solutions have a sustainable business. *Kiva.org* is an online platform that connects small entrepreneurs to unknown lenders in all parts of the world. All people who wish to borrow are showcased online, with a summary of what enterprise they need the money for. The lender makes the payment, and after a while gets repaid, and the process continues. Kiva works with field partners who are responsible for screening borrowers, posting loan requests, disbursing loans, and repayment. Kiva has a repayment rate of 98.8 percent. Focused on the rural poor in India, *Basix* is also trying to encourage enterprises in the rural areas. They do not call themselves a microfinance company, but a "new generation livelihood promotion initiative."[4] They bring in mainstream capital to enterprising rural communities to help expand poor people's assets.

There is a pattern in all these inspirational business models. These are a mirror to successive governments that have been prophesying and promising an equitable and just society for as long as one can remember, and to the brands that aspire to scale but do not innovate enough to make the scale possible. There is an ease with which these business models blend in contemporary technology at the last mile, in the process transforming simple ideas into powerful movements. These help shift the center of gravity of the markets.

There are universal ingredients in such business models. These are power to the people and hence prepaid systems; ease of availability and hence mobile or Internet or cloud platforms; managed access and hence the involvement of local entrepreneurs; and sustained engagement with local people to usher in changes that are substantive in the magnitude of its impact.

DEPLOY THE POWER OF ALGORITHMS

Automation has been the buzzword in the corporate world for decades now. Companies have put together processes and then got the machines to do the work. Sales forecasting, inventory management, sales force automation, and many more functions are now done by computers. This has cut manpower costs, removed jobs, improved consistency in delivery, and reduced complexity in the ways of working. But this automation stops precisely as the word states; it is merely getting a machine to do what the human being did earlier.

Mere automation is an understated deployment of the power of technology.

---

[4] www.basixindia.com

Business thus far has been a fight for man *or* machine; in this century, companies that succeed recognize that it is an interaction of man *and* machine that will create value. Consider these real-life examples that portray what's really happening in today's times, and portend the future.

A nearly penniless Hungarian came to the US in 1965, and stubbornly defied the conventional model of trading at the Wall Street, to become a billionaire several times over. He is considered as the father of digital trading. In those times, traders used to shout in noisy pits to make an actual trade, and ticker tapes would display stock prices in a continuous loop. A booming voice, ability to hold your nerves, and big bulk made you a successful trader, not your computer skills. The Hungarian, who then hardly spoke any English, had developed smart algorithms to analyze trillions of pieces of data on stocks and options and arrive at fair value for them. Instead of a long, manual, multilayered chain to the markets, he connected his computer directly to the stock exchange cables, receiving inputs ahead of others and trading by executing algorithms he had created.

> Direct-access and algorithmic systems patterned on the Timber Hill (the name of his firm) model have been embraced by the biggest Wall Street firms—including Credit Suisse First Boston, Goldman, Merrill Lynch & Co. and Morgan Stanley—as the best way to scrape out profits in an increasingly efficient, low-margin equity trading business.[5]

This man is Thomas Peterffy who changed the world of stocks and options forever and is responsible for the trading now done by quiet machines inside heavily guarded black boxes.

Consider another precedent. Call centers of companies transcend geographies. They could be located just about anywhere. As calls come in, these are routed to agents on the basis of simple data points—origin/location of the call, the native language of the caller,

---

[5] Suzanne McGee, "A Breed Apart," *Institutional Investor,* New York. Available online at http://www.institutionalinvestor.com/article.aspx?articleID=1025866#.U62QAPnxpSA (accessed on August 05, 2015).

or at best the purpose why the call is being made. While it resolved the ease of the language issue, even routed complicated issues to the more trained agent, this call routing setup still does not guarantee a high resolution rate and a satisfied customer at the other end. The argument doesn't stop here. Many of the call centers regularly upsell to their customers. The script they use is standard. Irrespective of the customer personality types, the same sales approach is unleashed customer by customer, a little akin to a waiter who speedily reads out the menu in a restaurant in an identical fashion and tonality. It is no surprise that conversion rates are universally a poor single digit number in all upsell programs. A research has found that conversion rates improve and resolutions are satisfying when two people who are alike engage with each other. To get a customer and an agent to be alike, we need to know the person they both are, and then find a way to connect them with each other when the customer call comes in. Every human being has a core personality that rarely changes, and people do use standard words and standard ways of speaking. Technology can decipher the personality type of a person on the basis of the way they talk, the words they use, and the manner they speak. Some customers are a matter of fact, they ask for information and would rather not waste time on pleasantries. A few others are highly emotional and when they call up, they expect to be comforted, not merely told the policies. Matching customer personality type to agent personality, it has been scientifically proven, improves resolution percentages and cuts down average call time. *SATMAP* has the technology that optimizes call outcomes by pairing agents with callers based on personality. It captures the relevant data and performs over a billion calculations to identify which personality combination will result in the highest probability of success.

Consider another example of a fantastic deployment of the embedded power in algorithms using computerized learning systems. Filmmaking is one of the riskiest ventures. The success rate in the industry is poor. Most movies do not make money. Is there a way that we can predict what fate awaits the movie before millions of dollars are sunk in? *Epagogix* helps predict the box value of film scripts, even identifying where and how the commercial value of the individual scripts can be improved. "Epagogix analysts read a script and place a value on all of the plot points, everything from love scenes to car chases to quirky sidekicks. And they score them according to a directory, in the way a teacher scores paper."[6] Those scores are fed into the computer algorithm, which then calculates how much the movie will make at the box office, plus or minus about 10 percent. Epagogix will also recommend script changes to make a movie more marketable and profitable, like setting it in a different place.

Such a world, one that is run by complex algorithms, as illustrations given above will testify, comes with ethical and moral dilemmas. How much should machines be allowed to ape and even better the human mind? Ability to process a zillion pieces of data in microseconds does raise issues of mindfulness and responsibility because the machine will surgically execute the algorithm without empathy and emotions, or distinction between the right and not so right. There is evidence as well that technology can cut the wrong way. *Flash Boys: The Wall Street Revolt* by Michael Lewis captures the controversy around high frequency trading. The high frequency traders on the $22 trillion Wall Street used speed and complex algorithms to gain undue advantage. Never conclusively proven, there are charges of front running, market manipulation, and insider trading, to the detriment of small investors.

The power of algorithms is real and substantive. It is a world beyond automation. It is not retrospective analytics on data. It is a predictor of the future. And it is a power that will substantively transform the quality of decisions in an organization.

BUILD NEW MARKET(S)

There is an old adage. Customers don't want a drill. What they really want is a hole in the wall.

Consider *Vinfinet Technologies*, a leading IT firm building technology solutions for agriculture. The company has been founded by an alumnus of the Indian Institute of Technology (IIT) and focuses

---

[6] Stacey Vanek Smith, *What's Behind the Future of Hit Movies? An Algorithm.* Quoted by Nick Meaney, CEO and Founder of *Epagogix*, www.marketplace.org, (last accessed on August 05, 2015).

on innovative solutions in agriculture. Existing manufacturers spend years of considerable effort in improving the efficiency of archival features in their products. Over time with technological parity, there is little to distinguish one company from another in terms of product features. In the past, companies making merchandise for the farming sector were similarly content with just perfecting the products that they manufactured. We therefore have tractors, motors, crushers, and mowers. Vinifinet recognized that its customer, the farmer, has issues not with the machine, but with the way it has to be used. Given erratic power supply, farmers have to get up even in the middle of the night, travel long distance in the dark, just to be able to switch on or off the power button. The farmers run the risk of falling in a ditch or being bitten by a snake or encountering wild animals. *Kisan Raja,* the technology created by Vinifinet, is a mobile based, remote motor controller. Using a mobile phone, the farmer can now control motors from anywhere. The Kisan Raja also raises an alarm if there are large voltage fluctuations that can potentially damage a motor or if anyone tries to steal the motor.

Imagine you are in the business of logistics and you own thousands of trucks. In the past, no one really knew where the truck was once it left point A for point B. Fleet owners could not confirm the delivery date to their clients. They had no control on scheduling or optimization of costs by better route planning. Fleet owners now, including many public sector transportation companies, use vehicle-tracking software that enables real-time connectivity with the vehicle. They can now monitor routes, efficiency, and costs. And they can inform the clients about the exact time the vehicle will reach its destination. *IBM* is the classic first mover in the realm of selling solutions, which realized that companies don't need hardware; they need computing solutions. *GE Turbines* come equipped with software that enables remote monitoring and diagnostics. It allows GE to deliver to its clients uncommon value. They can detect faults in the machine early, thus being able to reduce operational and maintenance costs. Indeed *Industrial Internet* is a term coined by GE and refers to the amalgamation of complex machinery parts with software applications and advanced sensors, thus ushering in an era of intelligent machines.

Paul Rommer had said, way back in 1990, that information goods are immensely copiable, and by the law of economics, over time, the costs must fall to zero or near zero, fundamentally come close to the cost it takes to produce these. Digitalization isn't expensive, and the power it adds to the products is immense.

What do customers do with the products that we sell them? Do they mix and match with something else to make them usable? Do they face any problems while using the products we have manufactured? These questions lead us into the realms of solution selling, and help generate a larger enterprise value.

MAKING GROWTH MORE INCLUSIVE

The developing world's roughly 4.5 billion low-income people already constitute a $5 trillion market, as per the World Bank.

> The market for food and beverages, in the lower consumption segments is significantly larger than the market in the middle and higher segments combined. In most other sectors, people in the lower consumption segments collectively spend roughly as much as those in the higher segment. Only in transport, financial services and ICT do the two higher segments combined outspend the lower segment.[7]

This is symptomatic of the large consumption opportunities across all categories, and the latent potential.

The problem is not the demand. The opportunity is to get the ideas machine to start working furiously, to accelerate the rate of innovation, and create growth opportunities.

A feather-light innovation, the instrument of prodding consumption to the tipping point, is commonly misunderstood as a stripped down version of the existing products and solutions. However, it does not mean inferior technology or low-grade

---

[7] The World Bank, "The developing world's 4.5 billion low-income people already a $5 trillion market", Global Consumption Database for Inclusive Business. Available online at http://datatopics.worldbank.org/consumption/market (last accessed on August 05, 2015).

quality. Feather-light innovation alludes to removing attributes we can do without, or with less, and incorporating new sources of value.

This example is from Kenya, but the contours of the work done should resonate equally as the issues in this case are comparable to the ones in India. Educating children in slums and villages, and millions of them, has been a challenge to the governments. Kids who are a part of the disenfranchised populace can hardly afford quality education, thereby perpetuating the cycle of poverty they are in. There are free government schools, but these are inattentive and overcrowded, thus bringing to question the efficacy of state intervention in primary education.

How do you give education at $5 a month? *Bridges International Academies*, a for profit chain of schools in Kenya, has an inspiring model. Their schools in terms of infrastructure are basic, even primitive. There is no electricity. The roof of each classroom is double-steeped to allow for natural light and ventilation. A pot filled with purified water fulfills the need for hydration. The schools have an elementary lavatory. Parents use a mobile to pay the tuition fee; the schools themselves are cashless. All customary administrative tasks like billing and vendor payments are performed centrally for all schools, using remote computers. Only one manager runs an entire school. There is, however, nothing frugal in the way children are taught. The schools have a structured approach to pedagogy. The content is centrally manufactured for all schools, and teachers are tasked to focus on the delivery of the content that has been centrally manufactured. An e-reader guides the teacher in the classroom as identical content is replicated at the same time for the same class for hundreds of such schools. "The e-reader not only delivers the lesson script to the teachers, but also acts as an electronic time sheet, grade book and supervisor. The tablet tracks what time the teacher arrives, what time she leaves, and how long she spends on every lesson."[8] The Bridges approach is showing results: the company's preliminary testing data indicate that students at the Bridge outperform their peers in neighborhood schools,[9] based on international reading examinations.

---

[8] Jason Beaubien, "Do for-profit schools give poor Kenyans a real choice?" November 12 (2013), www.npr.org (access date August 05, 2015).
[9] *Bridges International Academy* website.

Feather-light innovation aims at preserving the legitimate value, and doing away with inefficiencies that cost money and deprive a large population that can't afford the costs. We know that the health infrastructure in India is urban-biased. Let us consider another case. This imbalance compels people who do not dwell in the major cities, to travel long distances and stay in an unknown place in order to get proper treatment. People sleeping in corridors and on pavements outside major hospitals, a common sight, bears testimony to the insidious imbalance in the country's health system. *Vaatsalya Hospitals* is a no-frills quality medical facility in the tier 2 and 3 towns. These towns generally have only private medical practitioners. There are no hospitals. The Vaatsalya model is geared to removing costs but keeping the value intact. Vaatsalya leases and takes advantage of the lower prevailing rents in semi-urban areas, or they acquire an existing health care facility, instead of purchasing the property. Equipment procurement is kept to the essentials. The hospital does not even own ambulances. Diagnostic facility is outsourced. Their hospitals are typically 60 beds, interiors are spartan, and most rooms aren't air-conditioned. There is no cafeteria. A common kitchen is provided to the families to cook their food. Medical care is otherwise a capital-intensive business, but it is because of this cost reengineering that "today a new Vaatsalya hospital breaks even within a period of 12-18 months and has more than 80 percent capacity utilization in its steady state of operations."[10] The fully qualified doctors, who grew up in such small towns, but had to leave their hometown for job opportunities in other places, are now back home. The net result is quality medical care by accomplished medical practitioners at fraction of the cost and inconvenience patients incur when they are obliged to go to larger towns for treatment.

In any case, given that medical infrastructure is concentrated in urban areas, and the numbers of physicians per thousand people in India is merely 0.6,[11] how does one deliver medical care to the disenfranchised? There is another illustration of how a simple

---

[10] UNDP; *Growing Inclusive Market*; case released in 2011.
[11] The World Bank, 2010, Physicians per thousand people.

technology can help bridge this gap. *Amrita*, a product application from *NewDigm*, is a mobile-based clinical decision-support cum filtration technology that deskills the job of the health-worker and raises their compliance to protocols. The simple to use decision-support requires no memory, little mathematical and analytical skills with vernacular support both in text and audio. It does not need you to have studied medicine. As part of the health visit, the operator feeds in key symptoms, does basic tests advised by the device, and then a diagnosis and treatment are generated. For beyond protocol cases, guided referral is generated to higher points of care. The electronic data generated in the process is used for patient history, follow-up care, monitoring and tracking, and generating reminders and alerts.

The key source in growing inclusive markets is in asking some questions. What is the one value that we must make sure is preserved? What activities can be hard-coded, thereby enabling easier replication and proliferation? What is the real interface between technology and the person at the last mile? In the case of education, the quality of learning was the champion, the pedagogical content and tools could be hard coded; in the case of health care, the practice of medicine is the magnate, and for NewDigm, it was a simple recognition that there is logic behind what doctors do, the inference can be coded in the form of protocols, and with technology this logic can be made available in the remotest villages by a low-skilled worker.

DELIVER THE CUSTOMERS' QUEST FOR EMPOWERMENT

Let's first mull over *Animal Farm*, an allegorical novel by George Orwell. First published in 1945, it is a fascinating read even today.

The story goes something like this. The old boar on the Manor Farm called Major, summons all animals for a meeting, during which he makes the point that humans are parasites and living off the hard work the animals do, and teaches the animal a revolutionary song called the Beast of England. After the death of Major, two young pigs, Snowball and Napoleon, assume command and begin preparations for the rebellion. Being the smartest, they naturally take the leadership role. One night, the animals revolt and drive the owner Mr. Jones away from the farm, renaming it "Animal Farm." They adopt seven commandments they will abide by including one that says, "All animals are equal." The animals thereafter run the farm. But over time power and greed disturbs the credo of equality adopted during the rebellion. The pigs, consumed with absolute power, commence to run the farm a lot like human beings, and the commandment is now changed to "All animals are equal, but some are more equal than others."

This book, while it reflects events leading up to the Russian Revolution and Stalin era, in its true essence, uses satire and parody to caution against the corrosive nature of power.

The tension between freedom and order is an enduring theme, in life, and in business as well. Many companies resist the increasing power of customers. These companies are suddenly finding themselves answerable to a set of people who were thus far passive recipients. The Internet-propelled dissemination of information has diluted as to what was the exclusive domain of sales people. Brands of today are shaped by raw customer stories and thought leadership of companies, and not only paid advertising. Customers have even begun to suggest what the companies must do and what kind of products they must make. They voice their concerns on ethics, health, and environment, anyone can blog or tweet product experiences, and they complain to a worldwide audience if the service they have got is shoddy.

It is the story of *Animal Farm* in the making, of power changing hands from companies to customers, and unless these companies treat customers as their first-class citizens, collaborators and strategic partners, the customers will rebel in their own way and move away to the competition. Indeed the success of WhatsApp, Facebook, and Twitter, which are brands considerably managed by the users themselves, comes with a demonstrable learning, power to the customers is also the power to companies.

The net outcome of collaborations is the fast-emerging world of peer-to-peer as a new business model. This trend threatens the conventional constructs of the company to customers, where the company manufacturers and the customers purchase. Let us consider an example. If you need a loan, where would you go? To a bank, obviously. But how does a bank make money? It makes money by providing miniscule returns to depositors, and charging double-digit interest rates to borrowers. What if I went to someone who has idle cash sitting in bank vaults and earning insignificant interest, and took a loan from this person? I would get the loan at a rate cheaper than the market since no overhead costs are involved and in any case banks have left enough money on the table by the construct of their profitable business. San Francisco-based *Lending Club* is precisely this idea. It is a peer-to-peer-banking site where people lend money to each other. The transactions are all on the Internet; the lender can see the full profile and credit score of the borrower before agreeing to lend the money. The loans are typically small. There are no physical branches or other cost overheads. Each side, therefore, gets better value than otherwise possible in a traditional bank. Even though loans are unsecured, the lender makes enough money to cover potential bad debt, and the borrower gets lower rates of interest.

The online community is growing and is more active.

An offline study conducted by Nielsen on behalf of Google India at car showrooms of leading car makers in the top 8 metros revealed that one in two car buyers had conducted research online before arriving at the dealership. The survey also revealed that of those who had researched their purchase online, over 50 percent changed their choice of car brands after uncovering new information on the web.[12]

If a group of people were talking about you, passing snide remarks, and voicing opinions, what would you do? You have two options. Either you remain quiet; make no more than a one off comment, in which case no further damage will happen but your reputation will not get reformed either. Or you go where these

---

[12] Amit Shanbaug, "50% of buyers research online before final purchase: study," *ET Bureau,* June 6 (2012).

people have congregated, question facts that are incorrect, acknowledge if something is legitimate, promise to set right an error and engage in a dialogue where there is a contrariety of perception. Should you do the latter, you will stand tall and win trust of the same people. Why do companies behave any different online? Why should they not engage with customers where the customers are sharing opinions? Why are product review sites filled with only the voice of tormented shoppers but hardly any response from the companies?

Increasingly, the role of marketers now includes building the experience quotient of their brand by fabricating a community of their customers and advocates; the new tools in the hands of marketers are technology, data, multiple media screens, and digital trails of their brands.

Let us consider an example of one such technology-propelled community. Small business owners or SOHO, as they are popularly called, do not have easy access to the best management practices. They can't always afford the bright legal brains, hardly know much about customer engagement, and have perpetual issues around finance. These people are in hundreds of thousands and spread all over. What they have is a native sense, enterprise, and relationship capabilities. *American Express* has created an online forum for millions of small business owners, a kind of content hub for this community. They educate and enlighten these business owners with contemporary content on a range of issues likely to impact their business. The repositories of articles cover everything from cash flows to social media. Once a year, American Express even celebrates in the US a popular event called Small Business Saturday to support owners of the neighborhood small retail shops and the like. In the process, American Express has integrated its brand intricately with small business owners by delivering a unique value largely on the digital space.

Wal-Mart Supercenters in the US average 187,000 square feet and offer 142,000 items.[13] It can be agonizing for a customer to find where the product they want is stocked. Wal-Mart has an

---

[13] news.walmart.com

application, via GPS, that directs customers to the aisles they wish to go to, and even lets them skip the checkout line and scan and pay for items using their smartphones.

There is a set of questions a company does need to ask itself. How can they build affiliation and advocacy with their customers? How can they take the higher ground of thought leadership in the category and the business the company is in? How can they empower their customers?

CONNECTED IN TUMKUR

Consider you are in a consumer goods business. You use distributors to supply material, 5,000 of them. Each distributor has 10-field sales representatives who, on an average, service millions of outlets in the country. Every salesperson has to have a permanent journey plan, optimized to deliver the best value, which must be adhered to. These representative cut bills, collect money, influence demand, handle objections, motivate trade partners to give them a higher counter share, make sure new products are displayed and pushed, enhance franchise for the company's products by propagating brand stories, and expanding distribution width as also the depth. How would you know precisely what is going on at the last mile at this scale and complexity?

Tumkur is a city in Karnataka, India, that is rapidly growing. Connected in Tumkur is an allegorical expression to suggest the imperative for real-time data and empowered connectivity with the last man at the farthest point.

Lack of process visibility has been historically an endemic issue in the last mile constructs. It happens because the sales machinery over the years has got convoluted. Companies do tend to lose track of their wares once they reach the distribution. There is still a significant amount of data that is perhaps captured on paper but not in a digital form. And, therefore, this data is hardly actionable. At our homes, we rarely throw away something old even if it's of limited use, but keep on adding new gadgets and possessions. Sales systems are guilty of similar behavior that has created a Byzantine of processes. Look at trade margin structure of any company. There are on an average 10 heads of expense or ways to grease the trade machinery. These go by various names like dealer discount, cash discount, regular payment discount, monthly target discount, bulk buy discount, free samples, travel bonanzas, and many more. The dispensation of these discounts is authorized by different sets of people, and by a disparate set of decision rules, thus creating a maze impossible for accountants to be ever able to transparently evaluate. It also ends up creating trade disputes and price disparities between the channels of distribution and trade partners.

Technology is an integral part of any execution. How do you execute if you don't have real-time information? Sales force automation, largely leveraged by smartphone technology, has begun to automate the process that so far was not visible. The entire day of a salesman can be digitized, with near zero latency. Journey plan, billing, cash, and quality of work are all at the click of a button. In the case of a B2B business, the sales funnels are automated, with analytics. The software enables the sales machine to move seamlessly from inside sales to outside sales, from lead researchers to setters and closers. It accelerates the velocity of sales closures, makes sales cycle faster, and it can predict likely revenues and outcomes. As all-in-one dashboards and business analytics pervade the organization, the decision-making gets real and insightful. The Geographical Information System (GIS) tool can give out heat maps to visually point out parts of the market where we are doing well, and where we aren't, the parts where the market potential exists but our share is low.

Jason Elkins coined an interesting phrase. It's called "Vegetarian Marketing." It alludes to obliterating non-value adding activities that do not call for human interaction, thus removing the need to "meet" customers for everything. Payment collection, report generation, accounts reconciliation, pretty much your clients can do it on company servers rather than being explained in person by a sales representative. Empowering your customers and partners to do self-service is a wonderful idea. Companies that challenge the existing models so as to respond to the needs of their customers and business partners end up modernizing their relationships in the market and appropriate generally wider expectations of the society.

The automation of the sales process takes away needless hours spent chasing inane things by the sales representatives, a time they can now use to build quality business. Put together, technology is helping the salespeople sell more, and their managers manage with data.

CONCLUSION

With this, we move to our last competence needed in a billion consumer market.

For that consider ant colonies. These have been a subject of extensive research by Deborah Garden, a biologist from Stanford University, and some others. An ant colony is a classic example of how hundreds and thousands of ants work together to produce a decent output, that too without any supervision or central command. There is a queen ant whose dominant calling is to procreate, and the male ant whose job is to help procreate, and these male ants seldom last beyond one mating season. Worker ants do the work. Commonly even up to half a million ants inhabit a colony. There is division of work. There are ants who forage for food, some just pick this food from the mouth of the colony and carry it inside, a few ants are soldiers who secure the colony, there are many ants who are inside, nest the younger ones, and maintain the queen's brood. The work in the ant colony is executed skillfully, a tall order given that an ant has a brain with only 250,000 neurons (an average human brain has about 100 billion neurons), but because ants work with such wonderful collaboration. Put together, an ant colony has what is called swarm intelligence, or collective power of all ant brains.

> Ants use a variety of cues to navigate, such as sun position, polarized light patterns, visual panoramas, gradient of odors, wind direction, slope, ground texture, step-counting . . . and more. Indeed, the list of cues ants can utilize for navigation is probably greater than for humans.[14]

---

[14] Antoine Wystrach, "We have been looking at ant intelligence the wrong way," *Scientific American*, August 30 (2013, essay is reprinted with permission from *The Conversation*, an online publication covering the latest research.

Herds of animals, which live together in a group, the likes of butterflies, ants, and fish, have cracked the formula of execution the best using swarm intelligence, commitment to the work they are supposed to do, indoctrinated orderliness, an open, participative, classless culture, and trust in each other.

Our next chapter is about the power to make things happen, the execution supremacy, a vital ingredient to success.

9 Swarm Intelligence: The Execution Supremacy

Surat is a port city on the bank of river Tapi in Gujarat, about 250 miles off Mumbai. There are many narratives of the origin of this city, including it being mentioned in the ancient epic of the Mahabharata. It has a trading history that dates back to the fifteenth century, when it was the only west-facing port. Now Surat is best known for its dominance in the business of textiles and diamond cutting.

Anyone who has been to the city in the early 1990s will affirm that despite all its wealth, it was an expensive and a dirty, garbage-strewn city to live in. It has transformed as a city, if not entirely still, but in those days mounds of scrap and roaming live-stock were a familiar sight. Illegal constructions dotted every nook and corner, as did open-air eateries with remnants carelessly thrown on the pavements. Only 37 percent of the city was equipped with sewage. Effluents from the nearby industries were routinely dumped in the river. Almost 40 percent of the people lived in slums that had no drainage. During the rainy season, sewage water would over flow and stagnate around the houses. This was the norm, and accepted.

"Thousands flee Indian city in a deadly plague outbreak," screamed the headlines of the *New York Times* on September 24, 1994. "Surat is perhaps the most decrepit, unlivable, and unmanageable Indian city of its size," wrote the *Telegraph*.[1] The worst, given Surat's track record of cleanliness, or complete lack of it, was waiting to happen, and it did. Pneumonic plague led to widespread deaths and panic in the city. As trains came to the Surat station, it was a ghastly sight.

---

[1] Quoted by Laurie Garrett, *Betrayal of Trust: The Collapse of Global Public Health*, Hyperion, August 15 (2001).

None of the passengers on board got off; they scampered hurriedly to shut all the windows. Hundreds and thousands who could flee the city elbowed their way in. Reportedly half a million people ran away in that one week. Those who could not escape scurried covering their face and nose. Schools and colleges were shut down. People feared that even water was poisoned. Stock of medicines got over. There was complete mayhem for days. India's image took a severe beating, as the entire world's attention got focused on rats and urban filth. Exports were banned, tourism collapsed, our flights were denied easy entry into the foreign sky, those that did take off were fumigated on arrival, and the economy stood severely jolted.

Enter S.R. Rao, as the new Commissioner of the municipality in Surat, and just a few years later, the same city of Surat was voted as India's second cleanest city by INTACH, an independent non-government organization. Clean drinking water became a norm rather than a luxury for the few. Sewage treatment increased sixfold. Morbidity rates declined to 75 percent. Municipal revenues had a whopping increase, as compliance improved.

> The Surat Municipal Corporation (SMC) has one of the best water-treatment plants in the country, while its solid waste-disposal system is arguably the best in the country, meticulously conforming to the Supreme Court guidelines. Compared with 15 gardens in 1995, Surat now has 62 garden. *India Today* (July, 2005)

"The Surat Municipal Corporation has ranked first in the state in terms of recovery of taxes, in octroi collection and in tree plantation," so said *Outlook* in its story in November 1996.

This chronicle of Surat, one of the biggest turnaround fables, forms the backdrop for this chapter. Any business, in a simplistic form, has to answer three questions—where are you right now, where do you want to go, and how do you get there? This chapter addresses the last of these questions.

In the course of writing this book, over the previous eight chapters, transformational themes have emerged.

These are hardly what is often described as "business as usual."

The obvious question is as to how to make it all happen?

We have a choice of two approaches that the topic of execution inspires normally. One is to put together an execution template. I think enough of them already exist, and they are not entirely dissimilar in content. The other avenue is to dig deep into what makes our Turbonator companies, and a few people successful, and to have a framework that captures the essence of the DNA of success. I have chosen to do the latter.

We shall return to this considerable issue, but first we need to understand the context in which the managerial mind has to operate, and the imperatives in the market where execution themes will need to play out.

THE CONTEXT

If you throw two objects from a height, one heavy and the other lighter, which would fall first?

Two objects falling from the same space despite the difference in weight will hit the ground at the same time so long as their shape and surface area is the same. In 1590, Galileo disproved thousands of years of belief in Aristotle that held that heavier things would fall first. The reason both objects fall at the same time is because the force of gravity is stronger on heavier objects in comparison to the lighter object.

The context of the society, and its people, is the big pull of gravity, when it comes to execution. Strategy execution is onerous to build into a company without first comprehending the nuances of culture. Let's put together a few of such perspectives.

Consider the results of research into variances in leadership styles across the globe.

> Emerging market leaders (India, China in particular) have a very strong focus and skillset on operational execution. These individuals focus heavily on hands-on management, operational process, and on managing individual performance. Benelux and Nordic countries, by contrast, tend to have leaders, who focus much more heavily on planning, strategy, communication, and being what we call a "change ambassador." Companies in these countries are older

and they are often very global, creating a need to focus on common vision, values, and long-term thinking. The UK, and US, by contrast, actually have more hybrid leadership models. US leaders tend to be hard drivers (similar to Indian leaders) and have a much more "push-oriented" approach to change management.[2]

Amartya Sen is an economist and a Nobel laureate. In *The Argumentative Indian*, he reminds us of our long history of loquacious argumentation. From the Vedas to epics like the Mahabharata and the Ramayana, from the practice of councils in Mughal courts and Buddhist empires to the prevalence of the folk tales, there is a longstanding tryst with dialogue and discussion. To quote him:

> Prolixity is not alien to us in India. We are able to talk at some length. Krishna Menon's record of the longest speech ever delivered at the United Nations (nine hours non-stop) established half a century ago (when Krishna Menon was leading the Indian delegation), has not been equalled by anyone from anywhere. Other peaks of loquaciousness have been scaled by other Indians. We do like to speak. This is not a new habit. The ancient Sanskrit epics the *Ramayana* and the *Mahabharata*, which are frequently compared with the *Iliad* and *Odyssey*, are colossally longer than the works the modest Homer could manage.[3]

Why do so many companies gifted with high intellect, finally fail to perform? There is always an idealist, who talks of a great future, and does sound inspiring, even if divorced from the world of empirical reality. There is an anarchist, driven by individual agenda, one who makes consensus elusive. All organizations are likely to have a proofreader, someone who gets into enormous details, at peril to the larger picture and the task at hand. There is an omniscient, one who has a view on everything on earth, without necessarily authoritative knowledge. On the board room table would be an eternal pessimist, if everything seems to be going well,

---

[2] Josh Bersin, "How does leadership vary across the globe," *Forbes,* October 31 (2012).
[3] Amartya Sen, *The Argumentative Indian: Writings on Indian History, Culture and Identity,* page 3, (UK: Penguin, 2006).

something for sure is amiss, and has been overlooked. There is inevitably a procrastinator, who is looking for more certainty and consensus, before taking a call. And finally, the trigger happy, a person always on the move, instinct-driven, ready to act and implement even before the ink on the decision has dried. So many management teams are made up of this constellation.

India is a bewildering concoction of idealism and anarchy. "The difficulty the Indian society has always faced in managing large scale organizations is an offshoot of the Brahmanical world view, and its strong emphasis on unconditional anarchic individualism" (Nandy, 1980). Brahmanical idealism compels managers to seek perfection, often ignoring the purpose and end point, and individual anarchism fundamentally makes cooperation and negotiation difficult, since each is on their own, seeking own ideal.

Then there is the context of a billion consumers. There is a bewildering range of consumption, from the rich and conspicuous to the not so affluent and value-biased. Context is the arena for events to transpire. The dynamics of the marketplace and the nature of the mindsets of the people create a unique concoction that has to be shepherded to success.

The Argumentative Indian, the confluence of idealism and anarchy, the hands on, execution savvy, focused, and innovative Indian mind are some of the many motifs we deal with as we set out to unlock what makes things happen in India. The recipe for triumph in India was unfortunately not cooked in the global markets, certainly not in its entirety.

THE SIX DIMENSIONAL SWARM INTELLIGENCE FRAMEWORK OF TURBONATORS

Success in the emerging markets calls for abilities that are beyond the obvious pillars of the concept of execution, at least in the spirit in which these are enacted.

Swarm intelligence refers to the collective intelligent behavior of individuals. Gerardo Beni and Jing Wang introduced the expression in the context of cellular robotic systems.

Let's go back to the story of the ants that we had commenced in our previous chapter. Almost every specie that ever existed on the Earth is either extinct or has transformed substantively. Not ants. They have survived for millions of years and are estimated to constitute 15 to 25 percent of the earth's animal biomass. The total weight of ants is guessed at equal to that of all humans on the planet.

Ants usually live in nests or colonies. There are hundreds and thousands of them. The colony has to be maintained and protected. Food has to be made available. The new colony has to be sired once the current one reaches the capacity. All this is executed flawlessly without any central authority. No one is the boss in an ant colony.

Long trails of thousands of ants that we see are the older ants that leave the colony to forage. On their way back, they drop a scent called pheromone that is unique. This creates the path to food. If the food is plentiful, as the Stanford research concluded, the foraging ants will return faster to the colony, which gives a cue to the other ants to join in the task, else the work of collecting the food will go on at a certain minimum rate.

The power to make things happen is not in the individual ants; it's in the ant colony.

Swarm intelligence refers to the simple actions of individuals leading up to collective behavior that can solve complex issues, often even without supervision. Indeed our own brains work perfectly fine without a central command, despite a hundred billion neurons that have to function in a reasonably coordinated manner.

Imagine you are S.R. Rao, you have landed in Surat, just after the outbreak of the plague, in the mid of complete anarchy, and tasked to set the situation right. What is the range of questions that will confront you? Indeed these are not very different as you go around executing the reincarnation in your companies. Some of the contemplation would be around these lines.

- What should I do near term, medium term and long term?
- What are our core strengths as a team that we can leverage?
- What are our assets that can deliver value?

- What is it that we should stop doing?
- What should we keep on investing in despite initial hurdles?
- What is that new and innovative something that can make the difference?
- How to simplify, focus, and do a few versus all?
- How do I get people to drive the agenda?
- How to make the organization inspired, trusted, and positive?
- How to strengthen accountability in the organization while being fair?
- How do we track, monitor, and control the impact of what we are doing?
- How do I communicate the essence of speed and purpose to all?

The structure of success is not so obvious in India. What we are looking for are the intangibles that drive a few companies to success. These intangibles are purposeful and experiential, impactful and sustainable, tactical, and strategic.

There are six forces (as depicted in Figure 9.1) at work that define success in India, put together in a framework best defined as *Six Dimensional Swarm Intelligence Framework of Turbonators.* By definition, the concept has both the magnitude and the direction.

WALK THE TALK: AC TO DC

S.R. Rao took on the assignment as the head of municipal services in Surat, a few months after the plague. The task was indeed exacting in a city where the average citizen, singularly obsessed with becoming rich as fast as possible, possessed little civic pride. A large part of the population was made up of migrant laborers who in any case felt no particular empathy with their temporarily adopted dominion. Fifteen thousand municipal workers of the town also saw no cause worth exerting for. The first thing that S.R. Rao did, as soon as he took charge, was his slogan "from AC to DC," that is a call to his officers to move from their air conditioned offices to the execution of daily chores.

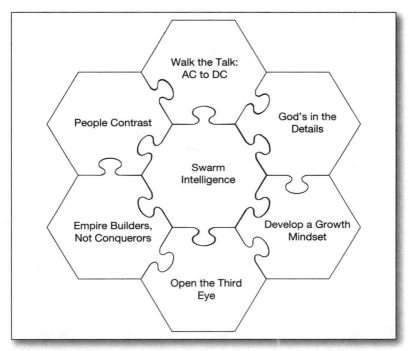

Figure 9.1   The Six-Dimensional Swarm Intelligence Framework of Turbonators
Source: Author's own.

Strategy, values, and culture code across organizations run a serious risk of dilution through proliferation. It's like the Chinese whisper, what the last man hears is far removed from the original content and intent. Public agreement and private disagreement are a common malaise in a culture where people are taught to defer to hierarchy. Managers agree with the leadership to be on the right side of the law. This is our Brahminical idealism. But troops pick up informal cues, not official messages. With leadership at the coalface, this gap between agreement and conviction stands narrowed.

"You came empty handed, you will leave empty handed. What is yours today, belonged to someone else yesterday, and will belong to someone else the day after tomorrow." This quote from the

Bhagvad Gita forms the backdrop of many temples in India. Some people misunderstand the significance of the above quote. They carry it all the way even to their work, almost sleep-walking their entire work life.

Any change, before it hits markets and customers, has to first transform people in the organization. As they say, everyone must see the same elephant. A sense of urgency, distinct from the sense of panic, needs to pervade. Surat roads did not clean up before municipal workers brought in a change in themselves. Thus far municipal workers had seen their job as merely a necessary inconvenience to earn their livelihood. They were confronted with a work expectation completely alien to their preparedness and conduct until now.

There is an important life lesson; know the end game before you set out on the journey. People need to know that the work they do is meaningful and makes a difference. This is the discriminating contrast between going through the motions of work and actually deploying your capabilities for a larger good. Christobal Colon, a Spaniard and a psychologist, worked in a hospital for the insane. The patients were assigned useless tasks to keep them occupied. The rationale was as follows; these people are insane, it doesn't matter what they do, so long as they are kept busy and confined. What they made, from ashtrays to bookmarks, was junked. Colon, on the contrary, believed that while people are insane, they couldn't be unintelligent. They need a sense of pride in what they do. They must do meaningful jobs and create things that the market will endorse. Over the years, he gave shape to his non-conformist views. He went on to start a dairy farm, *La Fageda*. Almost half the workforce at the farm has people with some form of mental handicap, who now do regular, purposeful jobs. A for-profit venture, it has annual revenues of Euro 11 million, and competes in the same market space as Danone and Nestle.

Inspiration often remains confined within the four walls of an organization. The battle cry is loud, the intent is noble, and the dreams are big, yet the impact on consumers and trade partners is minimal. Contrary to the belief that great inspiration is enough to change the world, it is a fragile spark. The purpose needs to marry execution, for an inspiration to function. What unlocks the value of a dream is the ability to bring its last mile alive.

AC to DC curtails degrees of freedom for errant workforce, if any. A whole lot of the last mile infirmity arises from this disinclination in the people to focus on tasks. In a classic argument between Arjuna and Krishna, so wonderfully captured in the Mahabharata, Arjuna ponders and procrastinates over the consequences of his action in the battle and fears for the dead, while Krishna exhorts that the only responsible act for the self is to perform one's duty. Without taking sides of either, as indeed there are strong arguments for both, the truth is many smart workers take up positions that defy logic. Work discipline is a noticeable differentiator between the Turbonator companies and incumbents.

How to transform an organization from AC to DC, and how does it allow the companies to build execution in their strategy? The answer lies in an unrelated category. Imagine fitness trackers, from sports watch to wristband, that record your heartbeat, burnt calories, and blood pressure. Just the knowledge of how much activity you do makes you walk a little more, take the flight of stairs instead of a lift, and stroll your dog an extra lap. Whether your health goals are moderate or transformative, short term or long term, these devices and the data points help you footmark your goals. As you work the best last miles systems in Turbonator companies, quite similar to these fitness trackers, the daily chores stand identified, subdivided into activities, automated on different mobile applications, tracked, measured, and analyzed. *Bharti Airtel* has a system of Critically Watched Numbers (CWNs) that every day publishes performance on metrics that are critical to success and efficiency. Not only do these metrics tell what has happened, but also they reasonably predict the near-term future as well, and thus catalyze managers to act decisively.

To the people on the ground, when they saw S.R. Rao and municipal officers out on the roads at 7 in the morning, supervising sweepers, it was complete consternation, disbelief, even anger. "I had to accept the resignations of several officers. And I am still not convinced that we totally weeded out all corruption,"[4] so said this, now retired, officer of the Indian Administrative Services.

God is in the Details

LIMRA is a worldwide research, consulting, and professional development organization that helps more than 850 insurance and financial services companies in 73 countries increase their marketing and distribution effectiveness. They had few years ago published a report card on the life insurance industry. Based on research, they concluded that life insurance agents need to call *15* qualified prospects, to make *six* presentations, which eventually lead to *one* sale. The staggering 93 percent failure rate is symptomatic of the various facets that deeply impact and will confront any change agenda.

15-6-1 points to tenacity needed in today's business to succeed. It also amplifies the society's attitudes towards something as fundamental as protection and preservation. And while this research is focused on the financial services, all categories, in varying degrees, have this issue of perseverance and of making things they sell be seen as meaningful by their customers.

Only 40 percent of the households in India are financially inclusive.[5] This has had disastrous consequences with many inadequately regulated non-banking institutions that have mopped up large sums of money from the poor and ignorant in the hinterlands, often even forgetting to return it to them. Many banks, without having to name any specific one, including a long list of multinationals, every few years, excited by the scale of the India opportunity, get to the task of building a "retail" portfolio. But barring a few, most have been unable to execute the last mile. They could not craft out a unique proposition for consumers. Poor control on how and to whom funds get disbursed, swells nonperforming assets, and has forced them to abandon their retail foray. Since this saga has been repeated so often, one is inclined to believe that consistency of purpose is missing.

---

[4] Shekhar Ghosh, "Cleaning up the Plague City," *Outlook,* November 27 (1996).
[5] Speech delivered by P. Vijaya Bhaskar, Financial *Inclusion in India: An Assessment*, Crisil inclusix index for 2011, quote in RBI, December 10 (2013).

Let's return to the insurance industry and see how they cope with *15-6-1*. Their solution is uncomplicated. The insurance product is a piece of paper; all competitors have an almost identical product. Their biggest asset is people. Their task is to make their people successful. The agents in an insurance industry, however, are an outsourced workforce. They are independent. Their numbers run into hundreds and thousands in any company. The work that most people do, however, can be apportioned into meaningful buckets. A typical acquisition sales process, for instance, goes through stages. Prospecting potential clients fix an interview to meet a client, make a presentation of the solution after understanding customer needs, give clients a text and graphic presentation of how the product will perform, and to close the sale by getting customers to pay. Best in class insurance companies would measure for individual agents, week on week, performance in a numeral, in each of these five buckets, and use this data to improve the productivity of their workforce.

Over time, trends in data bring forth issues that adversely impact the performance of an individual agent. The trajectory of the data over a period of time tends to sharpen the issue and efforts needed to enhance productivity. Some agents don't have enough market, others can't close sales, and a few don't know how to pitch the right product that fits customer needs. A trainer, along with the manager, would work hands on with an individual agent to resolve precise obstacles to their success. Unlike most corporate training plans, which in general have one shoe fit all content and format of the training, in this case the purpose of training is to right skill each individual. The agents are coached and measured to make sure that the learning has a purpose and a measurable destination.

The best proof of intelligence is the ability to simplify the complex. "If you can't explain it to six year olds, you won't understand it yourself," so said Albert Einstein. Tasks will always look Herculean till these are ruptured into their smaller component parts.

Let us examine the case of revenue management, for instance. Sales people are asked this number innumerable time in the day by their supervisors. "How is the business" must be the most prevalent discussion? Such fleeting, commonplace conversations in the corporate corridors are at a level so high up that these at times need authenticity. Let's scrutinize the business of telecom as an illustration. The revenue in telecom is, at a simplistic level, Average Revenue per User (ARPU) multiplied by the numbers of subscribers. The number has its components—traffic, value-added services, data, churn, and new acquisition. Each of these components has further subdivisions. Traffic can be international calling or national long distance or local calling. Value-added services can be ringtones or cricket or religion. There is something like 30 to 40 levers that drive revenues. Every lever is unique, value accretive, and responds to sensible market moves. A few subscribers receive international calls but make none. It's best to make an offer of an international calling pack to these customers. Some have not activated ringtones. Send them a sample free for a few days. A few have taken a pack they don't really use. Why make them waste their money? The organization structure too, in this case, is fabricated around the revenue vectors. It is the smallest components that aggregate to deliver the large picture. God indeed is in the smallest details.

Perseverance called for in getting the India equation right, will need an ability to break the complex whole into smaller, uncomplicated, and straightforward parts. The Surat story is now 16 years old. What they accomplished cannot be described as impossible. But to replicate a visibly successful formula must be tenacious since no other city in India either felt the urge or the determination to replicate the Surat formula.

DEVELOP A "GROWTH" MINDSET

For long we were told that Intelligence Quotient (IQ) is a fair predictor of success in life. It is something one is endowed with. It grows only so much and then stays fixed. Simply put, your destiny stands defined pretty early in life as the development of the brain significantly peaks around the ages of 7, 12, and 15.

Carol Dweck is a world-renowned psychologist. Her work in the area of intelligence and motivation, and achievement and success has a startling conclusion. It's not our abilities and talent as measured by different intelligence tests that lead to success; it is also determined by our approach to life events.

As part of the research

> Dweck and her colleagues offered four-year-olds a choice: They could either redo an easy jigsaw puzzle, or try a harder one. Even these young children conformed to the characteristics of one of the two mindsets—those with "fixed" mentality stayed on the safe side, choosing the easier puzzles that would affirm their existing ability, articulating to the researchers their belief that smart kids don't make mistakes; those with the "growth" mindset thought it an odd choice to begin with, perplexed why anyone would want to do the same puzzle over and over if they aren't learning anything new. In other words, the fixed-mindset kids wanted to make sure they succeeded in order to seem smart, whereas the growth-mindset ones wanted to stretch themselves, for their definition of success was about *becoming* smarter.[6]

People with the fixed mindset come with the notion of genetic endowments. They will only want to keep repeating the tasks which they do well, will not wish to challenge themselves, they will replicate the proven success formula, and if they hit a difficulty, in the words of Carol Dweck "that's it."[7] But people with a growth mindset achieve better results than those who feel that intelligence is finite and unalterable.

Come to think of it, companies too either have a fixed mindset or a growth mindset. What delivers outcome in the emerging markets is the "growth" mindset.

In all fairness to the incumbent companies, they also have matured in the last two decades. They are doing more sales than ever and generate more cash. Even in the last five years horizon of 2008 to 2013, the incumbents have grown their revenues by 60 percent. But the difference is that they are only doing better of what they did best in 1992. The Turbonator companies, however,

---

[6] Maria Popova, "Fixed vs. Growth: The two basic mindsets that shape our lives." www.brainpickings.org

[7] Carol Dweck's interview at Khan Academy.

have more than doubled their sales, and are increasingly drifting far and away from their incumbent counterparts.

Just look into the profit architecture of a company today versus how they made their money in the past, not the quantum of cash, but the components of profits; a good two-thirds of the money many a company earns today is not a legacy left behind by forefathers, it is new wealth, created by new means, and generally by a new generation of people. *Wipro* is at one extreme end. Originally called Western India Vegetable Products Limited, they made the extraordinary transition from selling vegetable oils to being a Global IT service company, and in the process, with annual returns in excess of 35 percent per annum, it's the greatest wealth creator at the stock exchange over a two decades horizon from 1992.

It is easier said than done. Companies with red on their balance sheets cannot be comforted by the possibility that they can do something entirely different down the road. What, then, is the path to a "growth" mindset? How does a "growth" mindset process really work? Perhaps the answer lies in looking at not the obstacles, but in identifying what is best described as positive deviance.

The general approach to problem solving is to decipher root causes, and then methodically solve the issues. Often this approach does not resolve the problem beyond some short-term quick fixes. The *Positive Deviance Initiative* is an international organization whose credo is to look for "positives" among "deviants" as a means to get answers to problems that need sustainable solutions. In their path-breaking work on malnutrition in Vietnam villages, for illustration, they did not go about finding what was wrong with nutrition in Vietnam; instead they focused on children who in the same environment were relatively healthy. "They were 'positive' because they were doing things right, and 'deviants' because they engaged in behaviors that most others did not."[8] What they found is that these kids were being fed fresh water fish, and were eating multiple times a day. This became the basis for the turnaround of the malnutrition issue. All kids were asked to eat fish available for free and eat more meals, with enormous success in regulating the malnutrition.

---

[8] www.positivedeviance.org/case studies

Bandhan Financial Services has best carried this credo to work. No formal bank is willing to lend to small borrowers in rural India. These large banks worry about repayment risks, issues in documentation, and the cost to serve the rural poor. *Bandhan Financial Services* figured out those giving loans to community, and to women in particular, worked well, despite no collaterals securitizing it. The social pressure to return money for the good of the community, and the women's' desire to create a business and livelihood for the family, is the positive deviance in the constituency of consumers who would be an untouchable in a formal banking system. Thousands of their local employees, working in deep hinterlands, have helped them build a loan portfolio of more than $1 billion, an incredible journey that began just 13 years ago with a capital of just about two lakh rupees.

Persistence, effort, challenges, learning, inspiration, struggle, and a clear vision of the future are the currency that constitutes the "growth" mindset. When there is broad opportunity, as is the case in India, companies need to be faster and innovative, comfortable in dealing with ambiguity, and shorter but multiple business cycles.

OPEN THE THIRD EYE

It's impossible to be precise, but Hinduism has reportedly three million deities. Scholars argue that such large numbers comprise forms and reincarnations of God. Proponents of the faith hold Lord Shiva in high reverence. The most iconographic representation of Lord Shiva is three eyes, with the third one ensconced dramatically in the middle of the forehead. Myths abound on the purpose of this third eye. At one end of the spectrum is the belief that it connotes destructive prowess. But the more generally accepted notion is that it is purportedly representative of wisdom and intuition, and of an evolved life beyond worldly desires.

As I go around with the companies I consult for, and ask the managers what keeps them awake, it's almost inevitably the push for numbers, and the tasks of the present moment. The currency of conversation people have with their managers is largely the following—this is what you forecast at the beginning of the year, and let's see how good we are at holding on to the promise.

All competitors have equivalent information about the existing market. The thing that sets Turbonators really apart is *Third Eye*. They see the future market and the emerging profit architecture ahead of many others. The Turbonator companies are obsessed with the task to grow the market and the category, even if it favors their competitors as well. There is not a single company in the list of Turbonators that has not actively grown the category. They compete in the current space but do not lose sight of market expansion. They work at a disproportionate share of the future. It is no surprise that the Turbonator companies that had an operating profit margin of 9.3 percent in 1998 scaled up to 16.5 percent in 2013, and incumbent companies, while they have grown, are still at a single digit-operating margin.

The issue is why does it happen that some companies have a third eye and others don't. The reasons can be many, but let's explore two niggling causes. *One* common factor is far too much of a focus on quarter numbers, in isolation to the long-term development of the asset. Anything new, or incremental, is a distraction from the pursuit of pressing revenue goals. It's the clichéd battle between the urgent and the important, with the inevitable triumph of the "urgent." As one digs deeper, the reason for the obsession with the numbers is not symptomatic of a desire to achieve numbers; it is predominantly driven by the inability of a company to control headwinds in the market. Lack of processes, meager discipline, and inadequate technology combine to put onerous pressure on execution. People end up fighting fire; business partners wait to see who will blink first. Where is the time in such companies to build the market and create something untrodden in a structured manner?

The *second* element that keeps third eye away is the budgeting process in companies. The budget process gives a financial dimension to the strategy. It helps create relevant milestones en route to this strategy, becomes a center of gravity of the work for all employees, and is a benchmark to discriminate between success and failure. Sales people are held accountable for these numbers, month on month. The process is hugely rigorous and time-consuming. *The Hacket group* discovered that, on an average, companies spend a whopping 95 of 365 days making a budget.

The problem with the budget process is that it often gets restricted to the number crunching of the existing business. The dimensions it covers do not bring forth the opportunities that a company should pursue. The practice of budget formation has become a test of who can play the funeral song the best when the numbers are being discussed, who can negotiate better, and whose political skills stand first-string.

The communication of goals thus arrived is an event by itself. I attended one such sales meeting. The leader announced tasks for the year, and then asked the audience in a spirited voice, "Will we do it." A somewhat tepid yes was heard. The leader shouted again. A louder yes followed. More animated, gesticulating, saying I can't hear, the leader repeated the question. A very loud yes was heard. This is what is called testosterone leadership. Needless to say, in this particular case, the goals were never really delivered.

C.K. Prahlad once said, "It is essential for top management to set out an aspiration that creates, by design, a chasm between ambition and resources." The reason the profit share of Turbonators grew faster than revenue, if you look at our research findings over a two decades horizon post-liberalization is because they reached the future first and caught the secular trend of upending markets.

I did find companies in India that do not subscribe to the theory that the task at the last mile is to merely hunt numbers, as if it's an end by itself, and the only end. They have a more holistic view of business. Their belief is that the job of the sales force is to build a quality ecosystem for their products to sell. There are no endless annual operating plans, no quarterly reviews, no rush to buy business in the last week, no discounts, and no differential pricing. It's important to reach internal targets, but that's not so meaningful unless it transforms revenue and profit shares, and builds enduring equity for the brand.

One such company was established in 1935. It's a stock that has delivered an annual return of almost 30 percent in the last two decades, next only to Wipro as the biggest wealth creator, and has a market cap of $8.5 billion. It is a $1.2 billion company, has a 5-year revenue growth CAGR of 20 percent and profit growth

CAGR of 28 percent, substantively ahead of the market. Yet this company thus far has worked with no sales targets for the Frontline. They aren't shooting in the dark, but their belief is that the sales teams must focus on inputs, educate and inform the intermediaries, in their case the medical practitioners, and output will get delivered. The company is Cipla pharmaceuticals.

People don't move without a sense of purpose in these businesses. Their performance speaks for itself. This is not a philosophical case for dispensing with annual financial plans, which in any case are needed for optimizing all the component parts in a company, but revenue targets alone can't motivate enough and do not create an inspired sales system. Some other successful companies run an independent and unconnected strategy processes focused on market development, and delink that with the process of budgets. A firm grip on emerging opportunities is the key differentiator in markets that are still expanding, sprouting new customers, and yet to germinate many categories.

Empire Builders, Not Conquerors

Gas balloons are lighter than air and use buoyancy force to fly. Kites on the other hand are heavier than air and make use of the principles of aerodynamics. Running a business in India is like flying a kite; you won't gain much by buoyancy in this market, but you would need to balance the forces of the lift and drag. The opportunities in a billion consumer market like India are large, but the profits are also back-ended, sometimes far away into the terminal value of the business. There are "people" as far as you can see in the country, but the number of "consumers" shrinks no sooner the price is displayed. The markets call for focus but distractions thrive.

> Emerging markets lack a stable of mature markets and the consistency that such markets offer. Consequently, the opportunity for entrepreneurship in emerging markets is pervasive. While Western entrepreneurs operate at the fringes of the economy, emerging

market entrepreneurs operate closer to the core—the needs and opportunities are more widespread.[9]

The execution in a scenario like this necessarily has to be a step-by-step progression of the business idea, a slow testing of the concept, and an ability to scale it up with speed when convinced of the potential.

There is a Chinese proverb that says "Be not afraid of growing slowly, be afraid of only standing still." Look around at the successful companies. They have grown in chunks. They have never tried to execute more than they can manage. At every stage, they have tested the water and been around for a while, before climbing the next peak. Empire builders, not conquerors, seem to be winning.

There are four distinct phases of growth across industries post market reforms.

Act 1: Temporal euphoria—In this phase, the growth engines started. The companies continued to compete, but no one really had an upper hand. Indeed the incumbent companies grew at a rate faster than the Turbonator companies in the first bucket of five years till 1998 (95% growth in revenues versus 73%). The market grew from a rather low starting base. Because of reasonable buoyancy in demand, unleashed by economic growth and choice for customers, the profit structure of the industry improved. It appears the incumbent companies had assets on the ground that they leveraged well in the first five years, while the Turbonator companies looked at broader opportunities in the future and went about assembling people, skills, and capital capability to exploit this opportunity at a subsequent time. All the companies had a handful of "hero" brands that had been around for some time, and formed the basis of their business growth.

Act 2: Land grab—This is the phase, roughly a period starting from 1998, when the incumbents lost the battle. The Turbonator

---

[9] David Lingelbach, Lynda de la Vina, and Paul Asel, *What's distinctive about entrepreneurship in developing countries,* Working Paper No.1, University of Texas at Saint Antonio college of Business Center for Global Entrepreneurship.

companies, having prepared well during the first phase, went for land grab; new geographies, marched into new towns, new product segments, mergers, and acquisitions. The currency of business began to change from the old to the new. Shift in social values and behavior, many new customers in the spending class, contemporary technology, and uncontaminated monetization models for the businesses characterize the second act. Customer Service for the first time began to emerge as an independent entity in the companies, and poor purveyors of service, largely the public sector, lost their monopoly advantage. The net result was almost doubling of the revenues of the Turbonator companies, and a sluggish revenue growth for the incumbent companies, just a third of what the Turbonator companies did.

Act 3: Grow the industry—The Turbonator ambitions were hitting now a roadblock. There weren't enough customers. The categories had to be expanded. This is the phase when the Turbonator companies allowed the operating margins to dip in pursuit of a larger share of a larger market. Indeed a lot of advertising in this phase changed its tonality from competitive comparisons to category enhancement. The telecom advertisement where a phone rings and the man in the car furiously begins to hunt for the phone, only to realize that it is a rickshaw puller whose mobile is ringing, is symbolic of attempts to enlarge the base of the customers. This was also the time when companies started to grow beyond their core into adjacent markets; the appliance companies were expanding into new categories like electrical and switchgear, for instance, the hardcore soaps and detergent companies started to build new brands into the space of "Beauty and Grooming."

Act 4: Shape the industry—By this time, the Turbonator companies were really in the driver's seat. Fortunes on the stock market had been made. Now confident, the companies in this phase pursued both growth and profits. They sired new categories and new sources of growth, but at better margins. The industry architecture began to emerge; the profit model, growth canvas, value chains, and powerful enabling structures. Across industries, there are signs of consolidation of market shares with fewer competitors. Turbonators are shaping the architecture of the industry deeply, and indeed if incumbents do not counter the growing influence and stranglehold of the Turbonator companies, they will stand permanently marginalized. The culmination of this phase may end up leaving only a handful of companies in each category. These 4 phases are as depicted in Figure 9.2.

The skill to carefully calibrate growth cycles isn't that easy. It entails

- Learning from the lead indicators more than the lagging indicators.
- Having a clear mind map of where the organization is headed.
- Ability to choose apt themes in different business cycles.

There is a science and a pattern to build business. Companies that chose the right theme at the opportune time are called Turbonators today.

PEOPLE CONTRAST

It is people who execute the strategy. Most managers do say that this is the breakdown point in organizations. Based on the work we have done, when it comes to organizational ethos, there are four fundamental reasons that account for the disparity between the strategy and its execution.

The first roadblock is *Myopia*. Companies focus far too hard on the output, but not enough on the inputs that make the output possible, even lesser on the outcome and impact of the goals they pursue. Exclusive focus on internal goals and targets also endangers the quality of revenues being earned by perpetuating tactical compromises in pursuit of near term goals, and in the process compromising the long-term winnability of a company.

The second blockade is one of *Inadequate Diffusion*. Everyone in the company does not have the same agenda. It is the issue of public agreement and private disagreement cited earlier. People have varying views on what should be the strategy and priorities in a company. The concept of diffusion does not mean alignment of all; it simply means that people who impact strategy execution

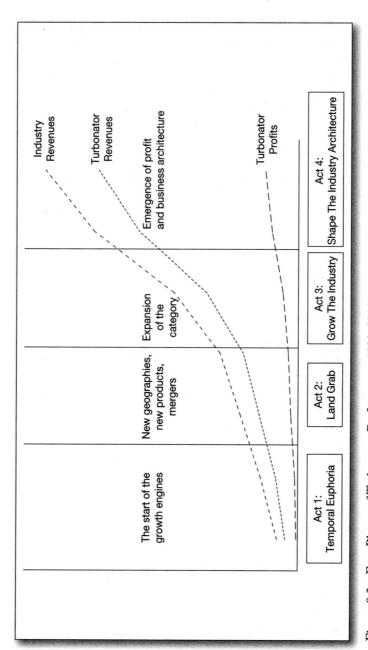

Figure 9.2 Four Phases of Turbonator Performance: 1993–2013
Source: Author's own.

must be engaged with the process. Everyone does not make happen the strategy equally. It, therefore, implies focused diffusion to the key stakeholders in the acceptance of the strategy rather than brutish proliferation.

The third blockade is one of *Variability*. The performance standards of managers in a company are in such a wide band that execution equally is divergent. For company-wide execution to work, the managers have to perform in a narrow band.

The fourth blockade is the lack of *Discipline*. A bit surprising, but if we go back to the Indian context of individual anarchism and Brahamanical idealism that was presented earlier, it is not entirely unanticipated. Even if people know what has to be done, and why, adherence to the brief is unsteady and sluggish.

In the story of the ants lies the agenda for leadership. Engage with people to perfuse the direction of the company. Manage by the power of positive cues to develop a collective behavior that is self-maintaining. Get the do-ability quotient steady by defining "how" with the same rigor as "what," and create frameworks from hiring processes to skill development to move all people into a narrow corridor of performance. In simple words, the task of a leader is to generate "Swarm Intelligence" akin to tiny ants that collectively work with unprecedented efficiency.

Business outcomes need to be underpinned with people strategy. I will talk of four practices (shown in Figure 9.3) that are the success ingredient of our Turbonator companies. These help build the collective power and wisdom of the larger workforce.

The first such practice is *The Talent Inequality*. Turbonator companies hire for success. Put simplistically, their managers are superior to the competition. They simply have more intellectual depth. The entry point in the company is guarded zealously. The very concept of recruitment is one where personal biases thrive. These companies have minimized the intrusion of personal biases by converting their recruitment process into a science. They have decoded the DNA of their best performers. They know what kind of experience, attitude, and behavioral traits work the best for them; the companies seek to replicate it. This does not mean senseless cloning, it only implies that every company has its own

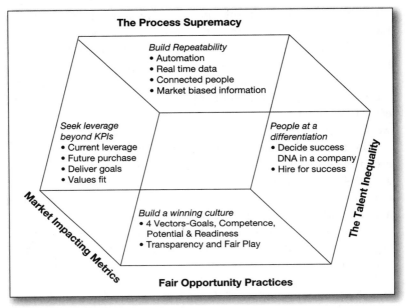

Figure 9.3   People Contrast Framework of Turbonators
Source: Author's own.

secret recipe, unique to their social and commercial setting, and a flock of a kind can deliver the best output. Unfocused, rambling, random, unstructured interviews bring no value to the process of hiring talent. Multiple interviews with multiple people, specific and sharply focused on accomplishments, supplemented with other forms of information, help both the candidate and the companies make a better choice. And for the potential recruits, the big attraction is high-octane, high-freedom, empowered environment provided by such organizations.

The second practice that builds Swarm Intelligence is *Market Impacting Metrics* of the Turbonator companies. It sounds strange as one articulates it, but one look at the metrics that companies track, and hold people accountable for, and you know the kind of company this is. At the atomic core of performance processes in a company today is the concept of key performance indicator (KPI).

It's what an individual manager is held accountable for during the year. Accomplishment of collective KPIs must necessarily mean that the company goals stand delivered. But truth be told, it's the most deviant molecule in an organization. Verbose language of job descriptions, when converted into a set of metrics, gets lost in translation. The result is that the substance and content of the job become like a bonsai planter, manufactured for dwarf output. These companies deploy market impacting metrics, and not merely KPIs. The market-impacting metric has six attributes, and all managers are tasked along these vectors. A market-impacting metric:

- Maintains current competitive leverage depending on the source of your competitive advantage (e.g. lower costs, higher velocity of cash, better supply chain, and ability to sell product range);
- Measures tangible impact on markets and customers (e.g. Revenue Market Share);
- Measures impact on future purchase using lead indicators (e.g. Customer satisfaction and client feedback);
- Delivers performance (goals for the year, revenues, costs, profits, free cash flow, Return on invested capital [ROIC] market share, brand value acceleration, and employee engagement);
- Measures the evolution agenda (new process, new products, new sources of growth, and new channels); and
- Fits the final *Filter-Values* fitment.

The third practice is *Fair Opportunity Process*. It involves a calibration of people and their contribution, the company and its ecosystem, to create a winning culture. Like ants in the nest, it entails matching jobs and people skills, and appropriate cues to communicate with every person the right and the most efficient path. For the employees, it means giving them a fair opportunity to succeed.

The process that brings opportunities to life for the people is the performance management process. The arena of performance management that forms the basis for opportunity processes is neither conclusive nor entirely without dissent. But successful companies that I have seen have tried to put a discipline around it. These companies look at performance from four vectors, not just the solitary lens of delivery of targets.

- The four vectors are performance against *Goals, Competencies, Potential,* and *Readiness* for the next job.
- Each vector drives a unique part of compensation and career growth.
- There is no forced ranking on goals; people are paid as per their contracted contribution to the company. On other vectors, most companies do deploy forced rankings.
- Discussions are calibrated over the year, not once a year, thereby humanizing the contact between the people and their managers.
- Transparency and fair play impart credibility to the process.

The fourth and the final pillar of Swarm intelligence is *Process Supremacy.* Ants repeat simple tasks without any apparent signs of a breakdown. Painstakingly, with discipline, core activities are performed. The reality in many companies, that are for now consigned to be an "incumbent," is infirm processes, broken workflows, and friction with business partners and within employees.

Here is an insight into what Turbonator companies do exceptionally well. They have automated all routine processes. All people share the same data points. The field sales team works on smartphones and relevant information is pushed daily to them. The business partners are on an identical technology platform, and their interface with the company is automated for customary activities. Metrics are extensively deployed, and incisive dashboards perpetuate their offices. Among the daily metrics, for instance, at *Tata Steel* distribution points are the price points of the competition. These companies have a heightened awareness of market developments, and assiduously the competition is benchmarked. They have a defined value system, and no one is above it. The processes used by the Turbonator companies are, therefore, transparent, fair, and simple. They do not adopt machines to merely automate or report. These are extensively utilized to drive descriptive, predictive, and prescriptive analytics.

CONCLUSION

The promise of India is real. Economic growth is creating exciting new opportunities. Like the country we are, India's billion consumer market is dynamic, evolving, fragmented, and value savvy. Notwithstanding the demographic dividend, and a fundamentally young population, it is not a market that can be changed into contours as we wish to see. It will develop, but slowly. Making things happen in this market is often the most impactful difference between the successful companies, and the also ran.

With this we move to our last chapter. The last miles used to unlock a large market opportunity can never be anchored forever, even less in a market full of emerging customers, unstable governance, and rapidly proliferating competition. To be a Turbonator company in the future, and in volatile times, calls for competencies that can withstand the test of time. The next chapter sets out the agenda for sustainability and renewal of the last mile.

10 Epilogue

I

THE SUSTAINABILITY ROADMAP

The roadmap for winning a billion consumers is not a task that has to be done once, and will last forever. In markets, hardly any position is perennial. No sooner does one company build a strategic advantage, the competition will begin the task of decoding, and dismantling what you have built, and who knows, perhaps come with something even better. The fact that new issues will arise should not detract us from doing what is right as of now. The only thing it means, therefore, is that it's an exercise to be repeated at all inflexion points in the business; when the competition makes an industry move, when new market segments open up, and when routes to the market or technology undergo a structural shift.

For now I would ask myself reasonably elementary questions. What is the structural and competitive advantage we have over our rivals in the market at the last mile? How much of our category has diffused the customer base, primarily how many potential consumers still do not buy our products? Where is this unrealized demand, and how can we excavate it? Is our revenue machine simply a machine, or is it a turbonated structure? Is my value chain the most optimal, and does it carry only efficiencies? Can I make a difference in the way customers get to experience the product? Do I sell just a product, or have I amalgamated software, technology, utility, and experience, something that makes me go up the value curve? Do I know the dollar value of my existing customers, and do I track its movement over time? Is my customer facing processes steeped in the past or aligned with the fickle and the less patient millennial generation? Given that how you sell is more important than what you sell, do we push customers' thinking and bring cutting-edge insights to the clients? Do we use technology to leapfrog, and skip old generation business models? Do we have the organizational capability to execute our strategy?

No agenda is complete until it has a sustainability road map built into it. Renewal is a compulsion. Having done an inquisition today, the task is to build the strategic and differentiating dimensions of the last mile. And having built them, we will need to institutionalize the entire process so that we will continue to grow our business and be meaningful to our customers in the future as well.

II

THE WORLD OF TODAY

The US Army had coined a term VUCA, referring to Volatility, Uncertainty, Complexity, and Ambiguity in the world of today. Even before the ink dries on a strategic plan, the environment has likely turned quite different from what one had anticipated. It is even more onerous to predict the future and build the business around it. In India perhaps even more, everything is kind of "up in the air"; markets and demands are yet to be entirely accessed, infrastructure and skillsets are still to mature, and the industry structure is yet to settle down into a predictable pattern. But we cannot cease to work today because of an unknown tomorrow.

There are a few things that are likely to stand still even when the sand shifts all around. While we build the last mile today, for today, we must not lose sight of the long-term market we are likely to eventually get to. These megatrends are not the only issues that matter, it is just a recipe for us to shape our collective future. These are unlikely to predict something with precision a decade from now, but can truly guide our near-term actions, which in any case, is the right approach in the VUCA world. While the leaders of today have to have an eye on the future, and be generally trending in the right direction, they also need microscopic precision to execute agendas of the day.

III

THE GAME CHANGERS

Some game changers are discernible in the market. Of these, the four big ones deserve special mention.

The *millennial generation* is real. The consumers will increasingly turn younger. Thus far, the consumers could be newish for some brands but the person paying for the merchandise wasn't so young. When wallet also moves to the millennial generation, as it would inevitably, the real power of Gen Y will be visible across product categories. The tonality and dispensation of service to this new breed of customers will be entirely different from the one thus far doled out to the populace that grew up in an era of shortages and state controls on supplies. This is an inflexion point in the business. And for companies an opportunity to be meaningful, authentic, and social.

The *economic growth* of India is also real. Our Turbonator companies have grown by a multiple of 15 in the last two decades. The scale and size of the India opportunity are overpowering. Rising population, urbanization, and increasing middle class are the macro-factors that will propel growth. But this growth will be uneven. There is a developed India that will increase its appetite for luxury goods; the developing India that will enter the consuming class; and the invisible, underdeveloped India whose potential will need to be unlocked. This uneven customer base is unlikely to find homogeneity in the near future.

Urban areas will strongly influence the India of the twenty-first century. With growth, people move from villages to cities. This phenomenon is rather uncontainable. India is a reluctant urbanite, but "every minute during the next 20 years, 30 Indians will leave rural India to settle in urban areas."[1] Urbanization, the concentration of the population in urban areas, and the rapid growth of mega-cities will deeply transform the landscape of India.

Digitization is a reality. New technology is often a paradigm shift and disruptive. More Indians today have access to mobiles

---

[1] Amitabh Kant, "The future of India's growth process lies in cities," *Daily Mail*, December 20 (2013).

than to clean and private toilets. Internet proliferation and social commerce on the net is a given. How to build a digital market is the next big challenge. The Internet is an opportunity for most businesses that currently struggle with the access and information asymmetry of their buyers.

IV

THE AGENDA FOR THE NEXT PHASE OF GROWTH

Two decades have passed since the state controls were dismantled, and the market was freed in India. These 20 years of competition have created the predictable churn; we now have some Turbonator companies, and many others of their competitors stand bruised on the way.

We are again at the cusp of the next phase of growth. In the first phase, the advantaged companies that were ahead of the game were the ones more efficient, with superior management skills, and a larger faith in the future of demand. The next phase is unlikely to be a replica of this success DNA. The future is likely to belong to companies with Innovation and Execution DNA; companies that can innovate their products, markets, customer interface, and value chains, and build the capability to translate thought into a value. The agenda, going forward, is likely to be more transformational and metamorphic, rather than static competence in isolation.

Six large propositions dominate this thinking on the near-term future. If one has to imagine the essential construct of the Turbonator companies of the future, with the millennial generation, large scale, urbanization, and a digital world as a backdrop, these six are likely to be critical requisite competencies.

Higher Purpose

To find a higher purpose in a consumer's life is the first imperative for a business. The rendition of the purpose is not the product you sell, but the solutions you provide, the opportunities you create, and the empowerment you bestow.

Conceptually, these are different companies than the ones that were established to manufacture and sell goods in an era of enormous demand and stifled supplies.

"It is not the strongest or the most intelligent who survive, but those who can best manage change," in the words of Charles Darwin, inspired by the principle of natural selection, postulating that those who are eliminated in the struggle for survival have to be necessarily not fit. It is a theory that is equally appropriate for the businesses. The sole purpose of business in the past was to grow and create value (read wealth) for its stakeholders. These are indeed important objectives, but these now need to be supplemented with another consideration, the purpose of the business needs to be grounded in meaning. Business must make a difference in the consumer's life for it to resonate deeply.

Innovators, Trendsetters, and Groundbreakers

Indians are born re-engineers, frugal technology experts, and product multiplication champions. But we aren't really disruptive. In our education and traditional hierarchical institutions, conformance, and not severance, is the genetic code.

India as a country dropped 10 places to be ranked 76th in the 2014 Global Innovation Index. The examples quoted in this book of the firms trying to innovate, and there are many of them, are still work in progress. The scale has to be larger for the first breed of *Innovators* that we see around, from Gram Power to Sarvajal, and many more, for a society wide impact to be felt.

New age technology offers an opportunity to disrupt and redesign the very concept of a product we may have lived with for long. *The Bill Gates Foundation*, for instance, is about to reinvent the toilet; the specifications given are that these toilets must not need either water or electricity, and convert the waste into useful resources. Fifteen million low-weight and premature babies are born each year around the world, 350 of them die every day. *Embrace Innovations* has empowered the disadvantaged by developing easy-to-use portable infant warmers that work with little or no power.

The choices are many when it comes to a new idea, a device, or a process. There is convergence between mobility, social media, and computing; and given this, it is difficult to imagine that our product portfolio of tomorrow will not be structurally and dramatically different from what we consume today.

Dexterity and Swiftness

Shorter business cycles and longer waves will be the new average.

The net impact of the world we live in is not so much about the product or the service we sell. It strikes at the root of the business model the companies have had for long. The rise of the Internet commerce, for instance, has been thunderous, but it has caught most manufacturers by surprise. The reactions from companies are aimed at stopping one channel of distribution or starting another, while what the Internet has done is to strike at the very base of what the companies have always done. From *Amazon* to *Alibaba*, in varying degrees, there can be noticed a sequence and a pattern in their proliferation. Electronic commerce started with one category first, then multiple categories and inaccessible geographies were accessed, the products were discounted to encourage trial, thereafter virtual stores, next they sell services of all kinds, there is no end to the waves of change that is being unleashed. Indeed *Amazon* has a Latin motto: "Step by step. Ferociously."

The ability to think like an architect and construct and reconstruct the business models over a short duration will be the key to secure the future which itself is coming in waves of deep transformation rather than as a whole.

CORE VALUES: FRUGALITY, CUSTOMER CONNECT, BIAS FOR SPEED

Business is about finding an opportunity that is not easily visible to most people. The knowledge industry grew because someone saw the opportunity in arbitrage and skill availability. The e-bay took off when someone recognized the potential in a virtual flea market.

Inefficiency in the existing markets has sired many new businesses. The sources of the origin of a good business are many. But to remain good, over different phases of the market, is a skill distinctly different from incumbency, even luck. The three values that can hold steady for the next phase of the turbonation are being value biased, customer biased, and action biased. Irrespective of the price point of the product, frugality at its core, such that it minimizes transmission losses, is likely to be very much a champion theme in the next phase of growth. As the younger generation takes command, both as employees and customers, and India rapidly moves into the median age of 25 years, customer centricity and speed to market will become the necessary preconditions to perform.

High Bar for Talent

More than the brawn, it's the brains, the intellectual capital that will determine the future. India' youth bulge is the demographic dividend, but this value has hardly been harnessed. It is estimated that one in three graduates has no job. It is not a surprise that highly educated people man low-level jobs. This is the largest opportunity for companies to build business with *people at its core*. We became the world's favored destination for Business Process Outsourcing (BPO) by amalgamating adequate supply of quality manpower with our skills in disciplines like analytics, finance, and accounting. The globe today chooses India as a hub for verticals like healthcare, shipping, research, and many others. The concept of people is not a face off with automation. Technology development must necessarily consider both man and machine, improve productivity, and enhance the quality of jobs people are doing.

Give and Take

The pursuit of material growth has left the planet severely depleted. In all fairness, the Earth doesn't really have the means and the capacity to carry as many people as it does, more so in nations such as India. We hold 2.4 percent of the world's land mass but carry 17 percent of the global population. Sustainability and inclusive development, a fine balance of reciprocity between the company and the society, is the difficult agenda for us.

Give and Take is a book by Adam Grant that seeks to change our fundamental ideas about how to succeed. To quote him: "For generations we have focused on the individual drivers of success: passion, hard work, talent and luck. But in today's dramatically reconfigured world, success is increasingly dependent on how we interact with others." E-Chaupal of ITC, Aravind Eye Care and Narayana Hrudayalaya are perfect examples of a refreshed value chain addressing issues that have been endemic to the concerned markets, and of, in the process, finding the optimal balance of reciprocity. While in the first phase, some of the companies could grow without accessing the fringe economy, in the next phase, being meaningful to a larger populace will be a sensible business imperative.

With these six agenda elements, aimed at sustainability and renewal, you and I come to the end of our journey by way of this book. Over time, there is little to differentiate on product features. The tilt depends on what happens in the market and with the customers. If what you do at the last mile is unique, differentiated, proliferates demand, exudes value, and builds customer experience, you are headed to be a Turbonator company of the future.

Henry David Thoreau had said, "Things do not change; we change." Here is wishing you the change you want to see in yourself.

Index

About the Author

Atul Joshi is an accomplished business leader. In his 27 years of professional career, he has been in leadership roles with Asian Paints, Max India, Bharti Airtel, and other Indian and multinational companies. He is the Founder and CEO of *The Last Mile*—a consulting practice with an impressive list of brands—and describes his mission as bringing the decisive last mile supremacy to business strategy.